PLAYGROUNDS
TO THE PROS

LEGENDS OF PEORIA BASKETBALL

JEFF KARZEN

3 FIELDS BOOKS
An imprint of the University of Illinois Press

3 Fields Books is an imprint of
the University of Illinois Press.

© 2023 by the Board of Trustees
of the University of Illinois
All rights reserved
Manufactured in the United States of America
P 5 4 3 2 1
∞ This book is printed on acid-free paper.

Library of Congress Cataloging-in-Publication Data
Names: Karzen, Jeff, 1979– author.
Title: Playgrounds to the pros: legends of Peoria basketball /
    Jeff Karzen.
Description: Urbana: 3 Fields Books An imprint
    of University of Illinois Press, [2023] | Includes
    bibliographical references and index.
Identifiers: LCCN 2022027180 (print) | LCCN 2022027181
    (ebook) | ISBN 9780252086939 (paperback) | ISBN
    9780252053894 (ebook)
Subjects: LCSH: Basketball players—Illinois—Peoria—
    Biography. | Basketball—Ilinois—Peoria—History. |
    College sports—Ilinois—Peoria. | Basketball—Social
    aspects—Ilinois—Peoria. | University of Illinois at
    Chicago—History. | National Basketball Association. |
    Peoria (Ill.)—History.
Classification: LCC GV884.A1 K37 2023 (print) | LCC
    GV884.A1 (ebook) | DDC 796.323092/2 [B]—dc23
LC record available at https://lccn.loc.gov/2022027180
LC ebook record available at https://lccn.loc.gov/2022027181

PLAYGROUNDS TO THE PROS

*For Olivia and Claire. Watching you girls grow up
is the greatest joy of my life.*

Contents

Preface

It was May of 2019, and my dad was in the hospital recovering from his second hip replacement surgery in the past six months. Dad was tired and sore but was feeling okay. He had company in his room most of the day: my mom and one of dad's oldest friends, Sandy, who drove in from Peoria to be with his old University of Illinois fraternity brother.

After hanging out in dad's room for a while, the three of us who weren't hospital patients that day went out to dinner. Sandy and I fell into our usual sports conversations about baseball, the Illini and . . . Peoria basketball. You see, Sandy is Sandy Farkash, the former Peoria Manual principal during the Rams' incredible 1990s heyday. And it was during this evening that a bell went off in my head: I think my next book should be about Peoria basketball.

Because of Sandy, who is quoted in this book, I have long kept an eye on Peoria hoops. Dad and I made a few trips down to Peoria when I was a kid to watch high-profile games, including when Manual played Chicago King and its two seven-footers, Rashard Griffith and Thomas Hamilton, at Peoria's Civic Center. As a basketball junkie, I loved hearing stories about Howard Nathan, Sergio McClain, Marcus Griffin, Frank Williams, A.J. Guyton, Shaun Livingston, and more. But in this city where basketball is so important, I knew there had to be great stories and interesting people to profile in ways that had never been done before. Most of you already know about the big names, and if not, that's what Wikipedia is for.

I wanted to dig deeper. And learn the stories that hadn't been reported. Once I started digging, I became hooked. The richness of Peoria basketball, the significance it held during the glory years, and the personalities involved were fascinating. I couldn't stop thinking about it and who to interview next. Along the way, I learned about redlining and social dynamics that shaped the city. There are parts of the book that discuss race and poverty and violence; I didn't necessarily expect that from the start, but it became an undeniably important aspect that intersected with basketball.

With the passage of time, I think subjects felt freer to tell their truths about certain topics. There's also a measure of understanding and maturity when you have the chance to look back on events without the emotions of being in the moment. All of this was a huge boon, and as we all struggled through COVID-19 quarantine together, interviewees were easier to track down than normal. Because hell, everyone was home.

After several trips to Peoria, it started feeling like a second home of sorts as I would run into familiar faces and learned how to get around town. This feeling was reaffirmed at a Manual-Central basketball game when I ran into former Rams athlete Courtland Tubbs, who said, "You might as well just get a house down here." We shared a laugh, and although I was not a local, it was reassuring to be considered part of this new community.

There's a great sense of relief in finishing this book, but I also miss the day-to-day grind. I had a ball.

PLAYGROUNDS
TO THE PROS

1

Anatomy of a Basketball Town

Tom Wilson piled his six-foot-seven frame into his mother's white Pontiac Bonneville in a garage on Mission Road on Peoria's north side of town.

"Get in the back seat and get down," his mother Glenda Evans told him.

Wilson was doing the unthinkable, and Peoria was in a frenzy. It was January 1987 and Wilson, a promising sixteen-year-old African American sophomore basketball player at Peoria Central High School, was transferring to bitter rival Peoria Manual High School. North side to south side. Lions to Rams. Maroon and black to orange and black. Not only that, but merely days earlier Wilson had played for Central in a losing effort against undefeated and top-ranked Manual. Less than a week later, he was switching sides.

That's why on this January morning a Peoria Public Schools District 150 vehicle was sitting outside the Wilson home on Mission Road. Word of the transfer had leaked in the Peoria *Journal-Star,* and it was decidedly not sitting well in the Central community. In order to attend Manual, Wilson had to establish residency within the south side school's attendance boundaries. Evans and her husband, Fred, owned a rental property at 1320 West Aiken Avenue, less than two miles from Manual. They had to prove that Wilson lived there in order for his transfer, and immediate basketball eligibility, to be allowed.

The district car followed Wilson and Evans across town as Wilson hoped to attend his first day of school at Manual. As they approached the rental house on Aiken Avenue, which the family was truly moving into, the district vehicle pulled up in front of the house. Evans drove to the back, parked in the garage, and Wilson snuck in through the back door. Moments later, he sauntered outside through the front door, Evans came around front to get him, and the ruse was complete.

"So, I guess the school district confirmed that I changed residency because they saw me come out of the house," Wilson said. "I couldn't believe they went to that extreme but they did."

Wilson was now a Manual Ram. And, wow, what a series of events it had been.

Wilson was actually a south side kid born into a family of Manual graduates. When he was in the fifth grade, his family moved north and into Peoria Central's attendance area. Standing six-foot-six by the eighth grade, he was a known commodity in Peoria's intense basketball scene and considered attending private Bergan High School (now Peoria Notre Dame) before settling on Central and respected head coach Chuck Buescher.

After averaging around 10 points per game as a freshman on Central's varsity, Wilson was excited about his future there. Wilson says things turned sideways during the spring of his freshman year, when he attended a rally at Manual for the Rams, who had just finished third in the Class AA state tournament. Wilson says he was just there supporting his friends who attended Manual—no big deal in his eyes. But word got back to Buescher at Central and it caused friction.

"Maybe a couple days after that event Buescher asked me to go to his office," Wilson said. "One of the first things he says to me is, 'How much does it cost to take the bus to Manual?' And I didn't know why he was asking me that. I was like, 'I think it's like 50 or 60 cents, something like that.' And he actually took 50 or 60 cents out of his pocket and threw it at me and said, 'Here, take the bus down to Manual.' That's where things started going south."

The former coach doesn't deny it. "I may have," Buescher says.

Wilson says the relationship with his coach soured further during his sophomore year. In January, the two big rivals played the first of three games against each other that season. The Central-Manual games had gotten so popular that the high school gymnasiums were no longer large enough to support the city's massive fan interest. In what would become a yearly tradition, the game was moved to Robertson Memorial Field House on the campus of Bradley University. The Field House was a terrific old-school gym built inside two surplus World War II airplane hangars in 1949 with a 3-foot raised floor and a seating capacity of 7,800. When packed for the rivalry games, it provided an unbelievable atmosphere for high school hoops.

Wilson came off the bench for Central in a 60–43 Manual victory as the Rams remained unbeaten.

"It was that game that I realized this was going to be my last game (at Central)," Wilson said. "In my mind, and my parents' minds, and people who were closest to me, I think everyone had enough. Things had soured over the first half of that year, there was talk from my family and my uncles and everything of me leaving Central. And the reason I stayed as long as I did is because I didn't want to leave Central. I wanted to stay there and play. But after the Manual game, my parents and my uncles sat me down and were like, 'No more of this. This is not doing you right. You need to go somewhere where you'll fit in and you can blossom.'"

A few days after the Friday game, a headline in the *Journal-Star* read, "Central's 6–7 Tom Wilson transferring to Manual?" At the time, Manual was 18–0 with aspirations of its first state title since 1930. Central was no slouch either, ranked 16th in the state and carrying a 13–3 record. A couple days later, the newspaper's headline read, "Wilson to Manual—today, maybe?" That's when Wilson was ducking down in the back seat of his mother's car and sneaking through the house to fool the district representative. A day later, the *Journal-Star* put some finality to the matter with, "Wilson could play for Manual tonight." The article said, "Tom Wilson, the 6-foot-7 sophomore considered the flower of Central's rosy basketball future, went to school Thursday at Manual and could see action tonight when the top-ranked Rams play at Bergan. Asked what were the chances of Wilson playing tonight, Manual coach Dick Van Scyoc said, 'They should be pretty good. But then, I haven't even had a chance to see him (in practice) yet.'" Van Scyoc went on to say Wilson would likely play in both the sophomore and varsity games that night.

Wilson played a game for Central one week, and then played for hated rival Manual the very next week. In a month, the two schools were scheduled to play at the Field House again, and that's when things truly got out of hand. Sports passion is one thing, but . . .

"Leading into that Central game I started receiving death threats," Wilson said. "Our (south side rental) house was vandalized several times. We had eggs thrown at our house, we had paint thrown at our house. People would call, they would make threats, call and yell obscenities. It was very political. I did what you're not supposed to do back then. Manual and Central were bitter rivals, and you just don't go from Central to Manual or Manual to Central. That was like a no-no. It was like a forbidden rule that you don't do that."

Located on Griswold Street on the south side of Peoria, the current Peoria Manual opened in 1963. Over the years, it has seen a who's who of college basketball coaches come through its doors to recruit players. (Photo by John Grap)

Rumors circulated that Manual set up Wilson's stepfather, Fred Evans, with a new job as he had been laid off by Pabst Brewing Company a few years prior and was now working odd painting jobs; gossip also surfaced of Van Scyoc and Manual's staff recruiting Wilson to join forces on his team. Wilson flatly denies all this. His parents did their best to protect him from the controversy's unpleasant effects, but it was a difficult time for everyone around him.

"My mom would get the call and she would hang up very quickly," Wilson says of the threats. "All I remember is, 'You're dead' and things of that nature. My parents took me away from a lot of it so I wasn't privy to a lot of it. Coach Van used to come to my house at six o'clock every morning and they would talk about it. Because I had to work out with him every morning (before school). I remember my mom crying after a phone call, that's the thing that kind of broke my heart. And my dad snatching the phone out of her hand and yelling, 'Don't call here anymore!' It just was a hard time for

Peoria Central, also called Peoria High, is the second oldest high school west of the Allegheny Mountains. Established in 1856, Peoria Central students moved to this location on N. North Street along Interstate 74 in 1916. (Photo by John Grap)

my family, and my stepdad because there were all the accusations of him being given a job and all this other stuff."

On February 27, 1987, round 2 between Manual and Central was slated for Friday night at the Field House. It had been 35 days since the rivals' first game and Wilson would now be playing against his former school, a surreal movie-like scenario of playing a game on each side of a rivalry in (almost) the same month, let alone the same season. The day of the game, Wilson was taken out of class by Big John Watt, Manual's head of security. In a closed office, Watt, Manual principal Eric Johnson, and a Peoria police officer told Wilson that they had received death threats about him playing in that night's game. They confirmed that it was to be taken seriously, and Wilson shouldn't go home after school.

The policeman put Wilson in his squad car and drove him to the house of Zephery Allen, Wilson's uncle who had been instrumental in executing his transfer. While the rest of Manual's team gathered at the house of star guard Lynn Collins, who lived within walking distance of the Field House, Wilson was told to bunker down at Allen's house until 6 p.m., when the team met at the arena.

"They did not want me to go home, they did not want me to go to Lynn's," Wilson said. "A squad car stayed outside of my uncle's house and from about 2:30 to 6 p.m. I had to be at my uncle's house with him, and I had to stay there until it was time for me to go to the Field House. And when I went to the Field House, we were escorted by the squad car that was out front and I couldn't even go through the front door like everybody else, I had to go through the back of the arena. There were still people out there, and I remember them hurling cans as they saw me trying to go through the back door."

The sold-out crowd was a mix of boos and cheers when Wilson checked into the game, this time wearing a black Manual No. 52 jersey. The Rams won and stayed undefeated all year until losing a last-second overtime game to Quincy in the Class AA quarterfinals in Champaign.

Wilson went on to play two years at Bradley, then transferred and played his last two collegiate seasons at Southern Illinois University-Edwardsville. He now lives in the New York City area, where he is the director of global sourcing and procurement services for AIG, an international finance and insurance corporation. Nearly 35 years have passed since his high school transfer caused a brouhaha, but Wilson says Peoria basketball is never far from his mind.

"I would only make one change if I had to do this all over again," he says. "If I had my way and I knew what I know now, I would have gone to Manual (all four years). People love Peoria basketball. You were passionate about your school, and you weren't going to let someone disrespect your school. You wanted your school to come out on top. [Nearly] Forty years later you can still hear the passion in my voice. But that's Peoria basketball. That's who we were, that's who we are. It doesn't matter if it was 5 years ago or 40 years ago, you still have that love and that passion for your school and for Peoria basketball. And that's what makes us different. Really, basketball is all we had."

Located in the central part of the state, Peoria, Illinois, was established in 1691 by French explorer Henri de Tonti. The town is named after the Peoria nation, one of five Indigenous nations in the Illinois confederacy that inhabited the region long before European settlers. A major port on the Illinois River, Peoria is a trading and shipping center for a large agricultural area that produces corn, soybeans, and livestock.

In 1910, an uncle-nephew tandem named Benjamin and Pliny Holt opened a manufacturing plant in East Peoria. They started with 12 employees, but the company soon became a giant in the industry. Caterpillar Inc, a Fortune 100 company that makes heavy machinery, trucks, engines, gas turbines and much more, was headquartered in Peoria for more than 90 years before moving its executives to suburban Chicago in 2017. At its height, Caterpillar employed more than 100,000 people around the world, including thousands in Peoria.

The city is also associated with the phrase "Will it play in Peoria?" an old vaudeville line that refers to how an issue will be received in mainstream America.

Boasting a population of 113,150 in the 2020 census, Peoria is the eighth most populous city in Illinois and the largest city on the Illinois River. It is a diverse, if mostly segregated, place with a racial makeup in 2020 of 59.4 percent White and 26.8 percent African American. There have been a few famous moments here and there, from an Abraham Lincoln speech in 1854 to the fungus originally used to produce penicillin being found in a moldy cantaloupe at a Peoria grocery store in 1942 to being the site of Michael Jordan's first professional appearance for the Chicago Bulls during an exhibition game in 1984.

Legendary comedian Richard Pryor was from Peoria. So, too, were feminist writer and activist Betty Friedan, singer Dan Fogelberg, and Bishop Fulton Sheen. It also is the birthplace of Hall of Fame baseball player Jim Thome.

Pryor's legacy, in particular, is interesting. He is easily the most famous Peorian of all time, yet like the city itself, his legacy is complicated and muddled with some uncomfortable truths. It has been well-documented that Pryor grew up living in a brothel owned by his grandmother. And while he left town and became a superstar, he also made headlines for drug problems and domestic violence.

In an outstanding compilation of essays titled, "Black in the Middle: An Anthology of the Black Midwest," book editor and Peoria native Terrion L. Williamson wrote about her hometown, Pryor, and racial disparities. Williamson, an African American scholar and University of Minnesota professor, talked about being raised in the economically depleted, resource-deprived south side of Peoria.

"Then and now, the south side is largely seen as Peoria's site of consummate failure, the places from which one must flee in order to be understood as

successful or 'upwardly mobile,'" Williamson wrote. *"Then and now, the south side is talked about as a neighborhood almost wholly given over to criminality and vice, where one's life might be snuffed out at any given moment."*

In keeping with the theme of Pryor's tangled legacy, Williamson wrote that outsiders almost can't imagine positive things happening on the south side, or the "black side of town," as she referred to it. But that line of thinking lacks nuance. Of course, there are success stories and impressive people living on the south side.

"Perhaps for those who know nothing of what it means to live on the black side of town, it is difficult if not impossible to imagine that people like Peoria's black south siders—who aren't just thugs and gangsters but are also (like my mom) bookkeepers and (like my best friend) nurses and (like my stepdad) business owners and everything else in between—know something worth knowing," she wrote. *"And what they know is that while their lives ain't no parts of easy, they are fundamentally irreducible to their worst days or their hardest moments. What they know is that black social life is life that is lived in spite of."*

For many young Black men on Peoria's south side, basketball offered a refuge from the day-to-day struggles. Whether the ball was bouncing on outdoor asphalt or inside a gymnasium, basketball was a safe haven and an opportunity to feel part of a community. Among friends and peers on the court, the young athletes strove for a better life beyond the boundaries of their hard scrabble surroundings.

It was in this environment that Tom Wilson was moving from Peoria's north side to south side. The basketball decision was one thing, but Wilson and his family were voluntarily moving to the part of town that "outsiders" looked down their noses at. To the part of town that lacked resources, funding, and more. And yes, to the Black side of town.

Were there racial overtones regarding rumors and accusations of Wilson's stepfather being handed a job? Absolutely. Was that simply part of life in Peoria (and many other places) in that era? Yes. Still, it must be stated that Peoria's segregated landscape served as an intriguing backdrop when Wilson opted for his move from Central to Manual.

Racial disparities aside, for a large segment of this city, basketball is what makes residents of all colors proudly puff out their chests. Peorians get a little pep in their step when talking about the game James Naismith invented in 1891. And with good reason.

After years of feeling disrespected by Chicago and its larger-than-life basketball scene, Peoria basketball finally got its due in the 1990s. Whether it's entirely true is debatable, but the Peoria hoops community felt it had been ignored by its much larger neighbor to the northeast for decades. A little less than three hours away, Chicago is the country's third-largest media market, and it covered the heck out of its high school basketball. Well-known prep sports writers at the *Chicago Tribune* and *Chicago Sun-Times* (papers with large circulations at the time) helped fill multiple pages per week during the high school season with feature stories, game coverage, rankings, recruiting updates, and more. Central Illinois had boasted excellent prep basketball for a long time, but until the '90s there wasn't much championship hardware to hammer home its standing. So, with Chicago's intimidating media presence repeatedly fawning over its stars, teams, and coaches, Peoria basketball had a chip on its shoulder. It probably had a bit of a Napoleon complex as well. Look at us, dang it! We've had great teams down here, too!

When Manual star guard Howard Nathan won the city's first Mr. Basketball in 1991, he helped move the needle for Peoria to the forefront of basketball conversations in the state. A few years later when Manual roared onto the scene by becoming the first school in state history to win four straight state basketball titles, well, frankly Peoria officially overtook Chicago as king of high school basketball in the Land of Lincoln. Then in 2002, Peoria's basketball reputation rose a step further. Highly regarded *Sports Illustrated* basketball writer Alexander Wolff traveled the world for his book, "Big Game, Small World," a travelogue in which he chronicled the sport in 16 different countries, including Poland, Switzerland, Bosnia, Ireland, Israel, and Angola. He also visited 10 states to document hoops domestically and made a trek to central Illinois for a chapter on Peoria.

In Peoria, Wolff focused on the crossover dribble, a move where a player is dribbling with one hand and quickly shifts his or her body and the ball to the other hand in an effort to dart past a defensive player toward the rim. Peoria, ever a guard's town, was rife with speedy ball handlers who were constantly working on their crossover dribble. Wolff spent time in Champaign with Manual stars Sergio McClain and Frank Williams, both of whom played at the University of Illinois at the time. Williams, in particular, was a wizard with the ball in his hands. As luck would have it, the author was also introduced to a seventh grader at Peoria's Concordia Lutheran School named Shaun Livingston, described in the book as someone "whom the most voyeuristic recruiting magazines already ranked as the best prospect of his age in the country, though Shaun was still only 5–9 and 110 pounds." It was in this book, too, that Wolff called Peoria the "cradle of the crossover," a nifty line that natives still recall with pride some 20 years later.

"Maybe one of the reasons Peoria has been so great is that they have the crossover and they have all of the more mundane basketball arts going for them," Wolff said. "These guys are actually creating a product; their signature move is like a product. They made a rap of Frank Williams and he's doing the Madison Avenue people one better. He actually lives in Peoria. He's like birthing this product in Peoria and doing the test marketing right there, he doesn't have to use an office suite on Madison Avenue and say, 'Let's go into Peoria for a focus group.' You know Frankie Williams had it right there. So that was fun to play with too. As soon as I had a critical mass of basketball stuff to deal with that gave me an excuse to go to Illinois, I was going to head there."

From the late 1980s through the early 2000s, Peoria could stand toe-to-toe with any hoops town in America. New York City, Philadelphia, Chicago, Washington D.C., Houston, and Los Angeles are among the huge cities that routinely churn out incredible basketball talent. But make no mistake—for this moment in time, Peoria flippin' Illinois was every bit of a basketball peer, or superior, to those hoop meccas. For a period of 16 years, beginning with Peoria Central's 1989 heartbreaking triple overtime state title game loss to East St. Louis Lincoln and ending with Central's second of back-to-back titles in 2004, a River City school played in nine of 16 Class AA state championship games, winning six. There was a year in the mid-1990s when the *Journal-Star* had to figure out which future Big Ten player to leave off the newspaper's All-Area team. Defense, discipline, toughness, tremendous coaching, and a love of the game that motivated players to seek competition around the city all summer long were the hallmarks of this hardscrabble town's basketball greatness.

The city's top hoopers all knew each other and played against each other during the summer at Carver Center, Proctor Center, and at various high school open gyms. There was open gym at Manual at 3 p.m., Central at 6 p.m., and playgrounds before and after. Other places may have embraced a wide-open offensive style and high-flying dunks, but in Peoria, coaches hammered home the importance of defense and preventing your opponent from scoring. You want to play on Friday nights for Manual, Central, or Richwoods? Then get in a defensive stance and move your feet laterally or you've got no chance of seeing the court.

Generations of Peoria basketball players grew up playing outside at various courts in the summertime, including Carver Center. Players and coaches alike attribute the high school teams' successes to playing morning-to-night at places like Carver against the best competition in town. (Photo by John Grap)

"I think Peoria basketball was really good because of the streets," said A.J. Guyton, a 1996 Peoria Central graduate who became a first-team All-American at Indiana University. "Carver Center, Proctor Center, all the places that we met up to play. Bradley's Haussler Hall. Our edge was toughness. We were never the biggest team on the floor. Ninety percent of the players were guards, with one tall dude running around. We got that edge by being out here in the streets getting after each other all day, every summer. And people think you exaggerate when you say every day. I played every day. All day long. As soon as you got up, you ate some cereal, you said what time is the game? They say 11, you're there from 11 a.m. to 8 p.m."

It is difficult to quantify toughness and discipline. But you know it when you see it. Basketball observers saw that mental and physical toughness and hardened edge *a lot* in Peoria.

"Defense and discipline," said Buescher, the Peoria Central coach. "Peoria guarded. With 30 seconds to go, I don't want to be 1 (point) down. I'd rather be 1 up and they have the ball. I just believed in our defense."

"The reason I think smaller, less talented (Peoria) teams were able to beat national powerhouses over the years consistently was the ability to play full court, man-to-man defense," said Greg Stewart, who covered high school basketball for 15 years at the Peoria *Journal-Star*. "Picking a guy up right off the inbounds and then dogging him all the way up. At a certain point in the game when they started to press full court, I don't care who was bringing the ball up, they were going to turn it over. In a 32-minute game, being able to control clock and lengthen possessions and guard people, Peoria just outworked people on the defensive end, and that's why they beat a lot of more talented teams over the years."

Brian Randle, a 2003 Peoria Notre Dame graduate who played at Illinois and professionally overseas for 10 years, lived in Chicago for a time during his off seasons as a pro. He says the pickup games and Nike Pro-Am events in the Windy City were ruthless, where one bad day could ruin your reputation and sully all the positive performances you exhibited in the past. But for Randle, this environment was nothing new.

"If I play Central, if I play Manual, if I play Richwoods, if I play Woodruff, I had to step out there and whether I won or lost, I at least had to make sure that I didn't leave that game letting anybody think that I was vulnerable," said Randle, now a Phoenix Suns assistant coach. "I think everybody who played ball was like, 'You're never going to find me in a vulnerable position.' That was the mentality of Peoria. No vulnerability, ever."

"Somewhere along the line basketball became upper case letters in Peoria," said former Richwoods coach Bobby Darling. "People in Decatur when I went there (to coach) said why is basketball so good in Peoria? I said there's basketball and there's BASKETBALL. It's just hard to explain how intense and how relevant it became back in the late 1970s and then forward. It just became a great cycle of kids with athletic ability that wanted to be basketball players. So, they wanted to (become players) and they had great coaching. And it just kind of continued on."

Ah yes, the coaching. Rare is the conversation about Peoria basketball that doesn't find its way around to the role tremendous coaching played. From Dick Van Scyoc to Chuck Buescher to Wayne McClain to Wayne Hammerton to Ed Brooks to Chuck Westendorf and beyond. Peoria's high school basketball coaches knew the game. They also knew how to teach the game and it helps when you're surrounded by talented kids hungry to play. And that coaching extended well beyond the traditional November through March season. There were open gyms, camps, off-season conditioning, and sometimes an eleventh-hour discussion with a player's mother that changes a kid's life.

In the mid-1980s, in a world before high-level AAU basketball or the onset of national prep schools, there were a couple key camps each summer for prospects to be seen by college coaches. One of those was the B/C All-Stars Camp in Rensselaer, Indiana, about 140 miles east of Peoria. Led by soon-to-be juniors David Booth and Lynn Collins, Manual was loaded with talent, and thus its entire team was invited to the prestigious B/C Camp. This was *the* camp in the Midwest back then, and it boasted alumni such as Julius Erving, Earvin "Magic" Johnson, Larry Bird, Isiah Thomas, Charles Barkley, Hakeem Olajuwon, and more. The Manual team was set to take a few cars to the weekend event, but there was one problem: Booth was grounded. In the home of Rudy and Yvonne Booth, there was a strict rule—if you had a D on your report card, you were grounded until the next report card. David, who was normally a good student, got a D during the spring semester of his sophomore year and therefore was grounded until the fall. No basketball camp for him.

Van Scyoc knew how important the camp was for his players' college futures. He had also taken a keen interest in Booth since he enrolled at Manual and helped develop him into an emerging star. That's why the coach knocked on the Booths' front door on Folkers Avenue that Saturday morning to have a talk with Yvonne before the team hit the road to Rensselaer.

"When you say going to a camp, my mom was thinking a YMCA summer camp with the lake and stay in the cabin, I think that's what she thought it was," Booth said. "She didn't understand that it was a basketball camp, like colleges are going to be there. She told me I couldn't go and I knew I wasn't going. Coach Van comes over, I remember him knocking on the door, and he stood there and was explaining to my mom, this is an opportunity for colleges to see him. I stayed in the back room while he was talking to her in the living room."

Much to Booth's surprise, Van Scyoc's power of persuasion won the day.

"She was like, 'Just get your stuff and go!' So, I packed up really quick, my shorts and everything, got on the road and went," Booth said. "And then our team, I think they split us up on different teams, but I ended up playing pretty good. So, I came back from that camp, and I ended up being the 32nd-ranked player in the United States. I didn't even know there was rankings back then."

Thanks to his showing at the camp, Booth became one of the most coveted basketball prospects in the Midwest, and he became a priority recruit for programs in the Big Ten and beyond. When he was in his late 90s, Van Scyoc sat comfortably in the living room of his home on West Manor Parkway across the street from Madison Golf Course, the same house he lived in since 1966 when he moved to Peoria from nearby Washington, Illinois. The old coach still had incredible recall regarding his long career, including when he intervened on Booth's behalf back in the 1980s.

"I told her how important this was," Van Scyoc said of his talk with Yvonne Booth. "David's college scholarship depended on maybe attending this camp. He had to go. She said, 'OK, I'll let him go this time.'"

Van Scyoc is rightly considered the godfather of modern Peoria basketball coaches. Countless coaches worked with Coach Van before taking over programs of their own, and he's credited with bringing ideas like open gym and year-round workouts to the area. A fierce competitor, Van Scyoc cared deeply about winning, but players knew he had their best interests at heart off the court, as well. Wins and losses will always be important; real life is more important.

In August 2022, Van Scyoc passed away at the age of 98.

In 1987, Morton native Jim Mattson was a recent University of Illinois graduate working at the ABC television affiliate in Peoria. During his first high school basketball season on the air, Mattson was assigned to cover Manual in the early-season Pontiac Tournament. The young reporter ended up getting an education much richer than standard highlights and soundbites.

David Booth is one of the best players to emerge from Peoria. A star at Manual in the 1980s, Booth went on to become the second all-time leading scorer in DePaul history and now is an NBA executive. He is pictured here at Proctor Center, another of Peoria's storied outdoor courts. (Photo by Jeff Karzen)

"I remember one of Manual's starters wasn't there in the first half," Mattson said. "That's weird. Then in the second half he shows up and they put him in the starting lineup. We'd never do that at Morton. We'd suspend that kid. And after the game I said to Coach Van, 'Why is that kid going in the game? What happened?' He said, 'oh he slept late.' I said, 'and you still played him in the second half.' Coach Van finished the interview and he pulled me aside and told me (the player) doesn't have a dad, he's got a mom who's never home. He doesn't have an alarm clock. Wayne (McClain) went down there and knocked on the door and Wayne drove him to Pontiac. And he said what's it going to do if I take away basketball from that kid? What kind of life is he going to have? I was floored."

For the last 10-plus years, Mike Ellis has run one of the most successful basketball programs in the state while leading Evanston Township High School to multiple appearances downstate. But before he coached in the Chicago area, Ellis cut his teeth as an assistant and head coach at Peoria

Richwoods, beginning in 1993 as a 24-year-old volunteer assistant under Wayne Hammerton. It also happened to be the senior year for Mike Robinson Jr., Peoria basketball's all-time leading scorer who matriculated to Purdue. Ellis, an Ohio native who went to college in Iowa, quickly learned what Peoria hoops was all about.

"The phrase 'tough love,' you could probably hang that sign on the city limits of Peoria," Ellis said. "But it's successful. The way Peoria basketball was played is going to win you a lot of games, teach you how to be successful in basketball and in life. Peoria basketball is on another level. People don't understand. I think it's tradition, but it's recent tradition. Some people talk about the tradition of their programs . . . in Illinois you talk about the Centralias and the Quincys and you talk about that tradition, but you have to go back a long way. But when you talk about Peoria tradition, it's so rich in a brief amount of time. I think that's a credit to the coaches in that community. Everybody wanted what was best for their players, they wanted what was best for their programs. And if you look back, there were a lot of influential people that made a difference in a lot of young men's lives."

2

The Prince of Peoria

The last steps that basketball hero and former NBA player Howard Nathan would ever take were from the Landmark Bowling Alley to his 1972 Oldsmobile Cutlass. Late at night on July 30, 2006, Howard drove near the intersection of University and MacQueen toward downtown with his younger brother Charles and friend Willie Irby. Ignoring MacQueen Avenue's stop sign, a drunk 49-year-old Miguel Ceja smashed his van into Nathan's Cutlass and sent arguably the greatest basketball player in Peoria history and his two companions flying through the summer night.

Nathan's car eventually landed upside down and slammed into a brick front porch at 2313 N. University St. All the tires had flown off. Car battery too. Willie was ejected from the backseat of the car. Stuck inside the mangled car but conscious, Charles looked at his brother and asked, "Bro, you ok?"

"Yeah, I'm good," Howard assured him.

The night was pitch black as the Nathan brothers tried to remove themselves from under the destroyed vehicle. Charles, who began the ride in the passenger seat, had no room to squirm out on his side. Looking over at his brother, he spotted a smidge of space to get out from the heaping pile of twisted metal, smoke, debris, dirt, and confusion. Charles tried pushing his brother out from under the car. "My legs are stuck," Howard said.

Unable to get out, the Nathan boys rested and waited for the paramedics and fire department to arrive. After a few minutes, they started to smell gas from the shattered car.

"I made phone calls to my parents and my sisters letting them know what's going on and pretty much saying our last goodbyes, because I thought the car was going to explode," Charles recalls.

When the fire department arrived at the gruesome scene, they used the jaws of life to remove Howard, then 34, and Charles, 29. The three men were rushed to OSF Saint Francis Medical Center. Willie and Charles had sustained broken ribs but managed to escape without further damage. The news appeared much worse for Howard. He had a broken neck and was paralyzed from the waist down.

Doctors may have told Howard Nathan he was never going to walk again, but you wouldn't have known it from his demeanor in that hospital. Sure, Nathan had a halo around his head as a result of the broken neck. But he was still Junior, the name his family called him. Still Nate the Great. Still the most confident man in the room at all times. And oh yes, that trademark swag and upbeat demeanor was ever-present.

Derrick Booth, perhaps Howard's closest friend, remembers arriving at the hospital during the early hours of that Sunday morning immediately after the crash to an already packed scene of Nathan's family and friends.

"This is incredible to think about because this is without social media," Booth said. "This is not a Facebook post and everybody just arrives. This was the phone chain."

After some time, a waiting room packed with Nathan's loved ones was informed that he would be taken out of one room and moved to a different area of the hospital. The group nervously and anxiously crowded into the hallway to see a glimpse of their wounded star. Seizing the moment the way he used to during big situations on the basketball court, Nathan started yelling, "I'm walking out of this hospital! I'm walking out of this hospital!"

Booth compared it to Muhammad Ali just before a fight.

"They're wheeling him down the hall, and he knows this crowd is behind him," Booth said. "He can't see anybody. And he's yelling from a stretcher, 'I'm gonna walk again! I'm cool! I'm cool!' And no doubt in my mind that he believed it."

Tom Kleinschmidt, one of Nathan's best friends since their high school AAU days, tried to prep himself for the hospital visit. On the three-hour drive south down Interstate 55 from Chicago to Peoria, Kleinschmidt, who was a year removed from an overseas professional basketball career, attempted to envision what it was going to be like seeing his incredibly athletic buddy bedridden.

"I had this speech practiced, and I was going to say all these words of wisdom when I saw him, and I choked when I walked in," Kleinschmidt said.

"I just asked, 'How are you doing?' He looked at me and said, 'I'm straight. I'm gonna be fine.' I'm crying and he's comforting me. He's on his stomach looking at me and he's comforting me. I choked."

Some of Nathan's friends truly didn't believe the diagnosis. Junior won't walk again? Nah, that's crazy talk. Such was the aura of Howard Nathan Jr. in his beloved hometown. Walking on water might be a stretch, but it's not ridiculous to say Nathan glided on air in the eyes of Peorians. The thought of him unable to crossover a defender on the court ever again? Unfathomable. Not *our Howard*, Peoria reasoned.

• • •

Room 3517 at OSF St. Francis became a revolving door of friends and family as everyone flocked to check on Nathan. Howard was the third of Howard Sr. and Sue Nathan's seven children. Less than nine years separated the oldest of Howard's five sisters, Angennette, from Charles, the family's youngest child. The family is extremely close, and when one of them is ailing, you can be sure the rest are nearby.

About a week after Howard's accident, an unfamiliar White woman approached the room and said, "I'm trying to find the family of Howard Nathan."

You're in the right place, the Nathans—who are African American—answered. Visibly nervous, the woman explained that she was the wife of Ceja, the drunk driver who slammed into Howard, Charles, and Irby. Now she was standing a couple feet away from Howard, who was tethered to a hospital bed, unable to move his legs.

The woman explained that her husband couldn't make it, but they just wanted to say they were so sorry for what he'd done. She said people told her the Nathans were angry and that she should watch her back. The Nathans were stunned. Here they were grieving a traumatic accident and now this? "I said no, that's not us," said Angennette. "Whoever told you that . . . they don't know us."

Amazingly, Howard held no resentment for Ceja. He was convinced he would walk again. He once told his sister he was glad this happened to him and not someone else, because he was strong enough to deal with it.

"Seriously, that's who he was," Charles said. "He forgave people. He didn't hold grudges. He brought people together. If people were feuding, he tried to figure out a way to get these people together to resolve this matter. That's who Howard was."

About a week after his wife's visit, Howard's grandfather, Charlie Nathan, Howard Sr., and Sue drove to Ceja's Peoria house to let him know he was safe and nobody would harm him.

"Howard (Junior) didn't blame the man," Sue said. "He told me, 'Mama, I don't want to see him go to jail or anything happen to him. He said once upon a time in my life, I was a drunk driver.' So, he didn't want nothing to happen to the man. He forgave him. So, if he forgave him, what could we do but tell him we forgave him?"

Angennette has another theory on why her parents took that extraordinary step of visiting a man who had recklessly paralyzed one of their children and injured another.

"My parents had to go and straighten out our last name and who we are as a family," she said. "We don't want anybody to think we're bad people. My dad had to go and take care of that business. As long as my parents had their son and he didn't die from that car crash, we were OK."

• • •

Peoria is the kind of basketball town where top players are identified at an early age. Middle school games are events. Years later, fans can easily recall which player went to which middle school. So, when a kid is scoring 40 or 50 points per game—in 24-minute games with no 3-pointers—at Blaine-Sumner Middle School on the south end, word gets around quickly. That's what Howard Nathan Jr. was doing in the 1980s, becoming a household name in basketball circles by the fifth grade. His name was a familiar one for another reason, too. Howard Sr. had been an excellent player for Peoria Manual back in the early days of legendary Coach Dick Van Scyoc's run. Howard Sr. was good enough to play in college, but before that could materialize, Sue became pregnant with Angennette, and Howard Sr. gave up his basketball dreams to stay in town, work, and provide for his young family.

More than two decades later, people were buzzing about the younger Howard Nathan in gyms and playgrounds across Peoria, wondering just how good this powerfully built young guard could be.

"I told people he got his basketball skills from his dad and he got his quickness from me," Sue said. "When he was born, I went to the hospital at 11 o'clock and at 11:49 he was born. So, he was fast."

In the fall of 1987, Howard Jr. enrolled at Manual. The Rams had been 31–0 and ranked No. 1 in Class AA the previous year before losing a heartbreaking overtime game to Quincy in the state quarterfinals to end their state championship hopes. Led by star forward David Booth, Derrick's older brother, and point guard Lynn Collins, the Rams were a verified powerhouse. This was typically no place for a freshman to carve out a role on varsity. Then again, the new kid was no typical freshman.

"He didn't even touch a freshman uniform, he didn't touch a sophomore uniform, he didn't touch a J.V. uniform," Derrick Booth said of Nathan. "He strictly played varsity. And the games that he didn't start, he was the first one off the bench. He was that good."

"So good, so fast, so confident," said Chris Reynolds, a Peoria Central point guard who later played four years at Indiana. "He had the 'it.' Because he was so good, so fast, and so confident and there really wasn't any flaw in his game."

In 2018, with his age north of 90 but his mind still remarkably sharp, Coach Van and his daughter published a book titled *Manual Labor*. A World War II veteran, Van Scyoc tells some terrific stories about a bygone era most people today can hardly believe existed beyond the pages of a history book. He also recounts interesting basketball stories and incorporated excerpts from many players over the years, including Howard Nathan Jr. Speaking about entering the fray as a freshman, Nathan says in the book, *"It wasn't always smooth sailing and Coach and I would develop a father-son, love-hate relationship; me being a hard-nosed, cocky, wide-eyed teenager and Coach being the ultimate disciplinarian. I should have been more prepared for the discipline because my dad was also a strong disciplinarian. I had the same love and respect for Coach as I did for my dad. I knew he wanted the best for me, and so did Dad. They both told me that where I was going, my friends wouldn't necessarily be able to go. If I wanted to use my talent and allow it to open avenues of possibilities, I needed to understand that it was for me and me alone. That is hard for a kid to understand."*

The Rams took third place in the state in 1987–88, Nathan's freshman year. That team was led by seniors Booth, who would star at DePaul, and Collins, who went to Odessa (Texas) Junior College, playing alongside the great Larry Johnson, before matriculating at Arizona State. The two seniors capped their fabulous high school careers with a 29–5 record.

The next two years, Nathan's sophomore and junior seasons, the Rams went a combined 50–10. During Manual practices, assistant coach Wayne McClain would force the team to make 10 straight free throws at the end of practice to mimic game situations when big free throws must be converted to close out wins. Five kids needed to make two free throws apiece before the team could head to the locker room. One miss and everyone had to run painful suicide sprints up and down the court. It became an unspoken rule that Nathan would take the final two shots.

"He wanted it on his shoulders," Derrick Booth said. "But he always made them. It got to the point where if it got to Howard, it was game over. We were holding our breath with the first four people. That was our culture, if Howard has it and Howard says we're cool, we're cool. We could read Howard and if Howard was confident, we're cool. And Howard did it day after day in the gym."

On gamedays, Nathan had a strict routine. After school, he would head home and pop Michael Jordan's "Come Fly with Me" video into his VCR machine. After watching the 42-minute short documentary film, he and Booth would walk over to Kelly Allen & Kelly barbershop on Richard Pryor Place, down the street from Carver Center, where barber Pepper Allen would touch up Nathan's flat top. From there, the players headed back to Manual as the team gathered at 5 p.m. in advance of the night's game.

Nathan idolized Jordan and watching "Come Fly with Me" got his mind right for playing ball. Unsurprisingly, he also had Air Jordans on his feet when he took the court. Looking and feeling good was important to the strong, compact Manual star.

Manual's coaching staff ran a tough program and players were not coddled. This applied to the star or the last player on the bench. Show up on time, tuck your shirt in, respect your elders, etc. It was the 1980s, and the modern politically correct practices and norms were still years from being enacted.

One of Manual's standard defensive drills in practice was a sliding drill aimed at improving players' footwork and making sure they kept their bodies in front of offensive opponents. Wayne McClain stood across from players on one side holding a basketball, and fellow assistant Chuck Westendorf was parallel to McClain also holding a ball. When a player took his turn during the drill, he had to slide his feet while keeping his eyes on whichever ball was being held up by a coach. Coach Van was always nearby, looming large, with his clipboard in hand. To make sure players stayed focused regardless of what was happening around them, Coach Van would ask his assistants, "Who wants a milkshake tonight?" McClain or Westendorf would say, "I want one," and it might cause a hungry player to turn his head away from the ball. When that happened, a coach would fire the basketball at the distracted player.

"One night, Howard Nathan was the first one, and he starts sliding watching the ball and he turned his head, and I am 10–15 feet away and I threw it," Westendorf said. "And he turned right when the ball was right here (face). Boom! Knocked him backwards. I hit the All-American and knocked him right on his butt."

Van Scyoc remembered the practice incident as well.

"It ticked him off and he walked off the floor and went and sat down on the bleachers," Van Scyoc said of Nathan. "I was watching everything and waited for about 30 seconds, and I walked over to him and I said, 'Howard, you've got 10 seconds to either get your butt back on the floor, or there's the door.' My tonsils were up here in my throat hoping he would go back on the floor, because he just as easily could have said, 'The hell with you, coach,' and gone out the door. For some reason, I had ahold of him and he went back on the floor and we continued practicing."

Nathan, who wore No. 34, was gaining a reputation outside his hometown. The summer before his senior year, he received an invitation to the prestigious Nike Camp at Princeton University in New Jersey. This was a long way from the south end or a familiar Peoria high school gym. America's best in the high school class of 1991 would be there, and it was go time for Nathan and the rest.

"It was intimidating for me personally because you sat in class and it was on an Ivy League campus so that was intimidating," Kleinschmidt remembers. "And then you roll the balls out and see who's there and it's 'Wow.' At the Nike Camp you're playing for a ranking and playing with ego. And guys don't like each other even though they don't know each other, just because they have a different (ranking) in front of their name. So, it was high level stress for kids."

Nathan excelled. Playing against the best point guards in the country, he didn't give an inch. That toughness, confidence, and bulldog mentality traveled, and it didn't matter who the competition was. One of the other point guards at Princeton fighting for a top ranking was a little left-hander from the West Coast by the name of Damon Stoudamire. The player later dubbed Mighty Mouse went on to have a great career at Arizona before being selected by the Vancouver Grizzlies with the seventh pick in the 1995 NBA Draft. Stoudamire ended up playing 13 seasons in the NBA, scoring almost 12,000 points and earning around $100 million. However, before all that, he was just a kid from Portland trying to keep pace with a dude from Peoria.

Howard Nathan is generally considered the best basketball player ever from Peoria. The 1991 Mr. Basketball winner lived a life of extreme highs and lows, including reaching the NBA and living the last 13 years of his life in a wheelchair. His death in 2019 was devastating to many in town. This mural of him was painted by Megan Troglio, a graduate of Columbia College in Chicago, on the wall of MSL Barber Lounge on South Western Avenue. (Photo by John Grap)

"To me, Howard was the best point guard in our class, class of 1991," said Stoudamire, now an assistant coach for the Boston Celtics. "I was trying to catch Howard. I was looking up at Howard. I told him this years later, that without him even knowing, I studied him a lot. I studied a lot of the guards in my class that were ranked higher than me because I knew in order for me to get where I wanted to get, the bar had to be set high, and they already had a platform and I had to step my game up. Besides being a great basketball player, he was a winner. I don't think people really realized that. Peoria (Manual) was really good. He came from a great program, a great tradition. I think people would be lying if they said Howard wasn't the bar. He was the bar."

When asked what made Nathan special, Stoudamire says, "I've got to believe what made him so good is just Peoria. It's an underdog spot. I think he took a lot of pride being from Peoria and how he learned the game. Playing in the streets, playing with older guys, he had a lot of good teachers. That's a heckuva hotbed for some hoops. I would have to believe at a young age once things start taking off, that confidence came. Howard wasn't a talker, but his game and his aura on the floor let you know that he was really fucking good. He had a command of the game that guys just didn't have at that time."

The class of 1991 featured names like Chris Webber, Glenn Robinson, Juwan Howard, Cherokee Parks, Donald Williams, Travis Best, Jalen Rose, and Stoudamire. By the time Nathan left New Jersey and headed back to central Illinois, he had cemented himself as a top 15 player in his class and a 5-star prospect. His buddy Kleinschmidt, who prepped at Gordon Tech in Chicago, was traversing in the same lofty ranking territory. Soon, the two Illinoisans would have a college decision to make.

• • •

The home where Howard Sr. and Sue Nathan raised their seven kids on Proctor Street in south Peoria was a destination for some of the country's most high-profile college basketball coaches in the winter of 1990–91. Arkansas coach Nolan Richardson, coming off a Final Four and Elite Eight appearances the previous two seasons, stopped by. So, too, did Arizona's Lute Olson. In this pre-Internet world and before recruiting websites kept fans breathlessly in the loop of day-to-day comings and goings of prospects and their intentions, Nathan navigated the college process with very little fanfare.

"You wouldn't know," said his friend Derrick Booth. "I bet you nobody else on the (Manual) team realized he was leaving practice to go talk to Nolan Richardson or Lute Olson. And that's when Arkansas was playing in (Final Fours). This was the pinnacle of Arkansas' tradition. But no, he didn't take that outside the gym. He didn't even take it in the gym to be honest with you. Nobody else knew. I knew because we probably weren't going to McDonald's that night, he was like, 'Nah, I got a visit tonight.' It wasn't something like everybody in the school talked about or knew about."

Perhaps he downplayed his recruitment because at home basketball star Howard Nathan was just Junior. There were rules and chores, and he was one of seven kids in a three-bedroom home, boys in one room and girls in the other. The crowded house was no place for preferential treatment.

"Mom and dad didn't play," brother Charles said. "In school, I think a lot of ballplayers get away with some things, but I know there were people who held him accountable. People told my parents and he got disciplined at home, I know that. There were times where he would get in trouble at school, and they would take care of that at school and then he would get in trouble at home."

As their senior years unfolded, Nathan and Kleinschmidt had developed a close rapport. The unlikely duo, a White kid from Chicago's Catholic League and a Black kid from public school Peoria, bonded over their competitive fire and love of basketball. Both could play on the playgrounds all day and then ask where the games were that night. They played on an incredible AAU team together, The Support Group, based in Chicago and coached by local businessman Bennie Henry. Their team included the Three Amigos from Proviso East—Michael Finley, Sherell Ford, and Donnie Boyce—along with Chicago star Juwan Howard and Glenn Robinson from nearby Gary, Indiana. Kleinschmidt would take trips down to Peoria for all-day hoops sessions, and Nathan would drive north and do the same. They would stay at the other's parents' houses and each was accepted with open arms.

High school prospects are allowed five official visits during their senior year of high school, per NCAA rules. The official visits are paid for by the university, including travel expenses, and can last up to 48 hours. Nathan and Kleinschmidt had a couple of mutual schools on their final lists, namely Arizona and DePaul. Olson convinced the talented pair to hop on a plane southwest to the desert and come check out the basketball powerhouse in Tucson, Arizona. "It was too far," Kleinschmidt said. "We both got off the plane like, 'Man, I don't know.' It was culture shock. We got off with Starter coats on and it was 80 degrees. We're not gonna make it here."

Nathan was strongly considering Arkansas, though. Kleinschmidt, for his part, visited Kentucky and had also developed an extremely close relationship with a young assistant coach at Michigan State named Tom Izzo. Then there was DePaul. Back in the 1980s and early '90s, the Blue Demons had a recruiting advantage that was tough to compete with: WGN television. ESPN was televising college basketball back then, but that was basically it, save for a couple games on network TV during the weekends. There was no ESPN2, ESPNU or FS1, and channels like the Big Ten Network were decades from inception. But at DePaul, well, DePaul had WGN. The superstation that was available nationally and had turned millions of Americans into Chicago Cubs fans also had Blue Demons basketball in its portfolio. Legendary DePaul coach Ray Meyer retired in 1984 after a staggering 42 years and 724 victories. He handed the clipboard to son Joey Meyer, and DePaul was humming along pretty well with the second-generation Meyer.

Joey Meyer made five consecutive NCAA Tournaments to start his tenure, and he also had a Peoria ace up his sleeve when it came to recruiting Nathan—David Booth.

"Howard was always over at our house because he was really close with my brother," said David Booth, who went from Manual to become DePaul's second all-time leading scorer. "I think Howard loves home, loves Peoria, and the idea of him coming home whenever he wanted to, couple hours away, was something that really intrigued him. I think with DePaul, back then we all went to DePaul because it was on WGN all the time. We understood that to make it to the NBA you had to get exposure, and I think Howard saw that, too. With me going to DePaul, he knew kind of what it was about because he had come to visit me. So, I didn't have to work on him."

Athletes coasting by academically and being given longer leashes than average students has been happening since the beginning of time. At least it seems that way in American schools with the star treatment athletes have been afforded. So, Howard Nathan was not the first nor the last to take advantage of his status and not exactly work terribly hard in the classroom. This can come with a cost, though. By his senior year at Manual, Nathan's academic levers had been parked in neutral for three years. And with a scholarship waiting at DePaul, he suddenly had grades to improve and benchmarks to clear if he wanted to be eligible to play collegiately as a freshman.

"Definitely Howard did not extend himself in the classroom until his senior year," Derrick Booth said. "And then it was like emergency, red alert. I definitely remember Howard his senior year sweating and hustling from class to class because there were some benchmarks he had to meet to qualify for DePaul. There were certain classes he knew, certain grades he had to get . . . and while a lot of us were enjoying our senior year, I do remember Howard hustling and sweating and doing more studying than he had ever done. Really understanding what every test meant, what every grade meant. And he locked in, which showed that he was definitely capable of doing it. It wasn't a matter of ability, it was focus."

Much to the relief of Nathan and the coaching staff at DePaul, Nathan met all the academic requirements, and he was cleared to enroll at the Lincoln Park campus in Chicago in the fall of 1991. But this would not be Nathan's last bout with classroom worries. Far from it. And next time, the consequences would be dire.

• • •

Basketball-wise, things were looking great for Nathan and the Rams as they barreled through the competition in search of the school's first state championship since 1930. Van Scyoc, by then in his 43rd year of coaching, including 17 seasons at Washington and Armington, had racked up tremendous seasons but was still yearning for that first state title. With Nathan at the controls and a solid supporting cast in 1990–91, it appeared to be a terrific opportunity for Coach Van to break through.

The problem for Manual and everyone else was the unforgiving two-class system in Illinois high school basketball. From the first boys' basketball state tournament in 1908, which Peoria High School won, until 1970–71, only one school in Illinois would be crowned state basketball champion each year. Then from 1972 through 2007, the tournament expanded to two classes. Small schools competed in 1A, big schools in 2A. (This changed in 2007–08, when much to the disappointment of old-time fans devoted to tradition, the IHSA expanded from two classes to four. At that time, there were 752 schools in the state competing in basketball).

For Manual to win a Class AA title, it had to reach the finish line ahead of Chicago's basketball juggernauts—at that time Chicago King was a national power—and schools like East St. Louis, Carbondale, and Rock Island just to name a few. Before even getting to one of the Chicago schools, Manual had to get past the best that central and downstate Illinois had to offer, be it Quincy, Springfield Lanphier, or another Peoria school. The gauntlet was brutal. And it's a single elimination tournament without a shot clock. If you're trailing by more than five or six points in the second half, an opposing coach might try to burn the clock out without ever shooting the basketball.

But Manual was good, and it had Nathan, a five-foot-ten, 170-pound sturdy load of basketball talent, smarts, and burning desire to win. Nathan looked like he spent half the day in a weight room, but alas that was not the case. He was just genetically gifted with a chiseled physique. Nathan, however, was a fan of good, old-fashioned push-ups.

"He would buy these little gadgets, little poles that go in the ground with handles, to do different types of push-ups," Derrick Booth said. "He would take those to the court with him and between games he would knock out a set. He was into push-ups, it was interesting."

Hours upon hours of sweat equity readied Manual for a state tournament run. Practicing in their well-lit gym, built in 1963 with a seating capacity of 3,360, the Rams often felt like games were easier than practices because of the coaching staff's demanding style.

From left to right, Tony Freeman, Howard Nathan, and Derrick Booth look on during the 1991 Class AA state semifinals as Manual defeated Chicago Marshall to advance to the state title game. (Photo provided by Derrick Booth)

With a whopping 10 players on the roster who eventually played some level of college basketball, Manual advanced downstate (final 8) with a 77–50 victory over Danville. In the quarterfinals at the University of Illinois' Assembly Hall on Friday night, the Rams downed Rock Island, 89–60, behind Nathan's 25 points. A Saturday morning tilt against Chicago Marshall, led by Arthur Agee of *Hoop Dreams* movie fame, was next. Final score: Manual 68, Marshall 55 as Nathan's 28 points powered the Rams into the state title game. (Several moments from this game were actually featured in *Hoop Dreams*, and the narrator leads into the game talking about a Peoria Manual team led by All-American Howard Nathan.)

The stage was set for Saturday night: Manual versus Proviso East, a school just west of Chicago in the town of Maywood that boasted an incredible three-headed monster of Sherell Ford, Michael Finley, and Donnie Boyce who all played AAU ball with Nathan and Kleinschmidt on The Support Group. Manual took a 31–2 record into the final, while Proviso East entered 31–1. A Class AA heavyweight showdown, indeed. (According to the IHSA, Proviso East, with about 2,100 students, was nearly double the enrollment of Manual at the time.)

The game was close throughout, but Proviso East's size, particularly the six-seven Ford, gave the Rams fits. Three games in 24 hours was probably a factor too, but both teams were dealt the same hand there. With Manual trailing 40–36 in the third quarter and Nathan making only two field goals so far, television announcer Kenny McReynolds said, "It's not the same Howard Nathan we saw earlier today or the Howard Nathan we saw last night." A 3-pointer by Nathan with about 90 seconds left cut Manual's deficit to 60–55 and prompted McReynolds to remark, "We talked about Howard Nathan having a bad game and all of a sudden he comes to life." In the end, it wouldn't be enough. Proviso East won 68–61 behind 23 points and 12 rebounds from Ford, who would later become a 1995 NBA first-round draft pick by the Seattle SuperSonics.

Nathan was named to the IHSA's All-Tournament team after finishing with 91 points in his last four games, tops in the state. Manual finished 31–3 and took home the second-place trophy. The sun came up the next morning, but the great Howard Nathan had played his last game in an orange-and-black Manual uniform and Coach Van was still searching for that elusive state championship.

• • •

Nathan's storied Manual career was over, but two major high school accolades still remained. A couple weeks after the season ended, Booth was over at the Nathan house. The close friends were casually hanging out in the Nathans' living room when Booth looked over and saw a large, shiny trophy with a basketball on top. "When did you get this?" Booth asked incredulously, motioning at the 1991 Mr. Basketball trophy. "Oh, that was yesterday," Nathan replied nonchalantly. "We had to go to Chicago yesterday for that." Booth just laughs at the memory now. "I was like, 'Man, you didn't even tell me! Congratulations, man!'"

Indeed, the previous day Nathan became Peoria's first winner of the Illinois Mr. Basketball award, presented by the *Chicago Tribune* in conjunction with the Illinois Basketball Coaches Association. Nathan edged out his buddy Kleinschmidt by a slim margin of 822 to 804 votes to secure the award. As a senior, Nathan averaged nearly 20 points, 5 rebounds and 4.5 assists per game. In the *Tribune* article announcing the award, sportswriter Paul Sullivan penned, *"Nathan was named to the first all-tournament team and did just about everything you possibly could do with a basketball except make it talk. And, after some of his tournament dazzlers, some observers weren't so sure that he couldn't get a word or two out of the ball if he wanted."*

In the article, Coach Van says that Nathan's outstanding run in the state tournament was the main reason his point guard was able to edge Kleinschmidt in the voting. *"People kept asking me about him all during the tournament,"* Van Scyoc told Sullivan. *"I've seen that type of play every time out for four years. In practice, too. I guess it's just second nature for me watching him play like that."*

One game remained before Nathan would graduate and head north to DePaul. It was a biggie—he had been selected to the McDonald's All-American game to be played in early April at the Springfield Civic Center in Springfield, Massachusetts, home of the Basketball Hall of Fame. The all-star game, which debuted in 1978, had become the crown jewel of high school basketball games. Televised live on CBS, the game aimed to feature the top 20 senior basketball players in America. Nathan was on the West team along with two other players from Illinois—Kleinschmidt and Chicago Vocational's Juwan Howard. Joining them on the West squad were Chris Webber, the country's top-ranked player, Jalen Rose, Glenn Robinson, and Cherokee Parks, a highly ranked center from California who was headed to Duke.

In a high-scoring game—these all-star games are typically defense-optional dunk fests—Peoria's finest dished the ball to future No. 1 NBA pick Webber for the game-winning dunk in the closing seconds as the West team downed the East, 108–106, in front of more than 8,200 fans at the Civic Center. Webber finished with 28 points and 12 rebounds and was named co-MVP along with Temple-bound guard Rick Brunson.

Shortly after the game ended, the phone rang at the Booth house. It was Nathan.

"I don't even know how he called me," Derrick Booth said. "I don't think cell phones were too big back then. But he called me from the sidelines of that game because he broke his ankle the last play of the game. And you don't realize it from watching on TV. The last play, he passed to Chris Webber for the winning layup. He breaks his ankle. They win the game and celebrate, and then he calls about 30 minutes later. I'm like 'Good game, man!' He says

'D, you ain't gonna believe what just happened. I broke my ankle.' I was like 'What?! I was just watching.'"

Friends remember Nathan showing up at prom wearing his McDonald's game sweatpants and a walking boot as he nursed the broken ankle in the spring of 1991. The Howard Nathan era at Peoria Manual was officially over, and what a run it was. Peoria's first ever Mr. Basketball winner rested his ankle that spring and summer, and soon was ready to roll at DePaul in the fall. An interesting freshman season with the Blue Demons lay ahead.

In the 1991–92 season, DePaul was part of the Great Midwest Conference with five other schools: Cincinnati, Memphis, Marquette, Alabama-Birmingham, and Saint Louis. The league may have been small, but it was talent-laden. Names like Anfernee Hardaway, Nick Van Exel, Herb Jones, Corey Blount, Jim McIlvaine, and DePaul's David Booth and Stephen Howard gave the GMC impressive star power for a six-team conference. At De-Paul, seniors Booth and Howard provided the Demons with one of the top 1–2 tandems in the country. Booth finished third in the league in scoring at 17.4 points per game, while Howard was fifth in scoring (17.1 points) and the league's leading rebounder with 8.7 boards a game.

Competition like that would be tough for any freshman, but Nathan made an impact. After four years of high school varsity experience, facing off with top competition at the Nike Camp and McDonald's All-American game, he was ready.

In late February 1992, DePaul visited Cincinnati for a big GMC contest. Nearly 30 years later, former DePaul coach Joey Meyer can still remember it vividly.

"The thing that I remember most about (Nathan) is that he could dominate a game without scoring a basket," Meyer said. "And there's very few players who can do that. We beat Cincinnati at Cincinnati, and they had two losses that year (in conference) and went to the Final Four—two of four losses were against DePaul. And at Cincinnati, he didn't score many points. But steals, defense, passing the ball, he just can dominate a game. He was just so quick and so strong that he made things happen. He was so unselfish and he also knocked down two big free throws. But besides that, he was just so strong and unselfish . . . he made winning plays."

DePaul beat Bob Huggins' Bearcats that day, 71–69, to improve to 17–6 on the season. In the *Chicago Tribune* the next day, the headline read *"DePaul's epic rally a Nathan production."* Legendary sportswriter Bill Jauss wrote, *"DePaul freshman Howard Nathan played the kind of game Thursday night that most basketball players only dream about . . . Nathan's final steal so in-furiated Bearcats coach Bob Huggins that he rushed the officials at the final buzzer and had to be pulled away by assistants."*

A win over No. 16 Florida State followed, running the Blue Demons' win streak to seven games as they headed toward an NCAA Tournament berth. Nathan's play validated his five-star label and rewarded the effort DePaul took to recruit him. In the regular season finale at DePaul's Rosemont Horizon, the Demons hosted Notre Dame and its trio of stars, LaPhonso Ellis, Daimon Sweet, and Elmer Bennett. Each averaged more than 16 points per game, and Bennett in particular had been on a late-season tear. Notre Dame led most of the game on this day, and a Bennett jumper gave the Irish a 64–60 lead with about 1:30 left. DePaul's Stephen Howard hit a 3-pointer with a little more than a minute left, cutting Notre Dame's lead to 1. Bennett brought the ball up the court as a packed Rosemont Horizon readied for a tense final minute.

In an instant, Nathan stole the ball cleanly from Bennett and raced down-court for an uncontested layup to give DePaul a 1-point lead as the crowd roared. On WGN television, announcer Dan Roan said, "Howard Nathan . . . Mr. Pick Pocket. He just pick-pocketed DePaul into the lead with 58 seconds to go!" After a commercial break, the camera focuses in on a sign in the crowd that reads "We got Nathan!" and Roan adds, "DePaul fans, you got that right. Howard Nathan doing an Oliver Twist on Elmer Bennett out front." On the next possession, a questionable foul is called on Nathan in the backcourt, his fifth, causing Roan to say, "I'll tell you right now, there's no one on that bench who can step into that kid's shoes." Alternating between moments of brilliance and questionable decision-making, Nathan fouled out with 11 points and had to watch the final minute of the game from DePaul's bench.

A crazy finish ensued. With the score tied and under 10 seconds remain-ing, Notre Dame guard Brooks Boyer drove hard to the basket and had his shot blocked, along with a ton of body contact. No foul was called, Notre Dame coach John MacLeod went nuts and got whistled for a technical foul with 2.2 seconds on the clock and a tie game. DePaul's Stephen Howard made one of two technical foul free throws and the Demons escaped with a 66–65 win. So much happened on this long-ago day in Rosemont, but Nathan's steal off Bennett is still recalled by teammates.

"He comes back to the huddle and I said, 'Man, you were supposed to foul,'" Kleinschmidt said. "He said, 'Man, I've been setting him up all game.'

Now this is a freshman (Nathan), and Elmer Bennett was on like every highlight of SportsCenter for like a month. He was on a mad run. And Howard was real calm, not arrogant, 'TK, I've been setting him up all game.' I was just like this guy is out of his mind. But that was Junior."

DePaul went 8–2 in the conference, tied for first with Cincinnati, which ended up reaching the Final Four. The Demons were given a 5-seed in the NCAA Tournament's West Region but bowed out in the first round to 12-seeded New Mexico State. DePaul finished 20–9 and Nathan had an excellent freshman season under his belt. He averaged 7.7 points a game, and 10 per game in conference. He was fifth in the league in assists per game with 4.2 and third in steals at 1.8 a game (Penny Hardaway was first).

The future looked exceedingly bright for both Nathan and DePaul. But those academic concerns that Nathan had flirted with in the past? They were about to return, and the effects would be felt from Lincoln Park all the way back to Peoria.

• • •

Charles Nathan still remembers the scene. It was the spring of 1992 and he walked home from school like any other day. But when he arrived, he saw his father, Howard Sr., home from another shift at Caterpillar, sitting glumly inside his truck. Charles knew something was amiss.

"I asked what was wrong and he said that my brother had flunked out of college," Charles said. "At that time, we were dependent on him as a family; he knew he could play and knew he was going to be the next NBA superstar. And we were thinking in a couple years, we're gonna be rich! Then he got kicked out. My parents were devastated at first but they quickly adjusted and kept it moving."

Indeed, Howard Nathan would not be returning to DePaul. After a promising year on the court where he established himself against some of the best competition in the country, Nathan's lack of effort in the classroom proved costly. There were stories of DePaul's coaches walking Nathan to class, only to see him escape the university building out the back door. And remember that athlete privilege bit? Yeah, that may have played a part as well.

"Any freshman (star) who goes away to college, you've got that name," Charles said. "You just felt like things should be given to you. He didn't think he had to work as hard as he should have. He just wanted people to give him things at that time. Maybe he felt like he didn't need to go to class and the teacher would give him a grade just because of who he was. And it didn't happen that way."

During Nathan's freshman year at DePaul, his Peoria Manual friend David Booth was a high-scoring senior. Booth, who tallied more than 1,900 career points, thought he was headed to the NBA at the time. Like most seniors, especially ones with a shot to play ball professionally, Booth was coasting academically and putting his mental focus on getting ready for the next level. He was meeting with agents, working out and doing the bare minimum to handle his coursework. But his running mate on and off the court was only a freshman.

"He wasn't going to class either," Booth said of Nathan. "I look back on that like, 'When were your classes?' He just wasn't going. I wasn't chastising him for it—I wish I had. He was doing what I was doing, but I was done. I was a senior so my class load had gotten light. But he was just a freshman, and he wasn't going at all."

Booth's then-girlfriend, now wife, lived a couple blocks from campus in a one-bedroom Lincoln Park apartment where Booth spent most nights. There was often a third person sleeping there too: the dynamic point guard from Peoria. The two basketball players frequently would go out at night and Nathan would sleep on the couch in the apartment. When Booth woke up the next morning, Nathan was still there. Not exactly a recipe for academic success.

Nathan's coach, Joey Meyer, was entering his eighth year as head coach at DePaul when Nathan flunked out. All these years later, Meyer is still wistful when he thinks back on Nathan's lone season at DePaul and what could have been.

"Howard wasn't committed to it, as much as we preached and as much as his parents worked with him," Meyer said. "He was just immature at that time and didn't want to go to class. Didn't want to study. We kept telling him at DePaul you have to go to class or you won't make it. And I think, you know how young guys are, 'I'm a star. I'm the best, they're going to take care of me' kind of thing. He just wasn't dedicated in the classroom and it cost him his career at DePaul."

Coaches lose players all the time, whether it's transfers, academics, getting arrested, homesickness—the reasons go on and on. It is also why college basketball coaches never stop recruiting—you don't know when there will be another scholarship to fill. But when you lose a budding star, at the ultra-important position of point guard, no less, it stings. Especially when that player has three years of eligibility left and you suspect he'll use at least two of them.

Meyer loved Nathan—the toughness, the basketball IQ, the confidence, and willingness to do whatever it took to win a basketball game. So, when he only got 29 games with him, you bet it hurt. Meyer is not bitter about what transpired with Nathan, but he admits it had a major impact on the DePaul program and even his career.

"That's an understatement," Meyer said about the devastating repercussions of Nathan's absence. "I really believe that at that time, it was a very big blow to the program and to my career. I think we would have had a heckuva run if you put Howard Nathan at point guard for four years. I don't think there's any doubt we are an NCAA Tournament team every year. It was very disappointing, but he just wasn't ready to go to class."

After just one year of playing together collegiately, Tom Kleinschmidt had to forge on without his running mate. The two were roommates that one year, although Nathan may have spent as much time at the off-campus apartment with Booth and his girlfriend as he did at his assigned dorm room. The pair were tight, though, and it was a tough pill to swallow for Kleinschmidt. A terrific player in his own right, the six-foot-five former Gordon Tech star says Nathan was his psychologist that year.

"I was this McDonald's All-American and I was (barely playing)," Kleinschmidt said. "He was playing more than I was, but he just helped me with my confidence. I transferred 15 times (in my mind); I wanted to quit. I was transferring every week. I was immature."

Peoria was never far from Nathan's mind. Everyone in his circle knew that. It's absolutely a big reason why a kid being courted by Arkansas and Arizona ended up a tidy three-hour drive from home. He also had a spontaneous side, and if you were with him you never knew where the night might end up. Oftentimes, it was back in the 309 area code.

"It would be 11:30 p.m. on a Tuesday and he'd be like, 'Want to go home? Want to go to Peoria?'" Kleinschmidt said. "I'm like no, but he could talk me into anything. I'd be sitting in the car on I-55 at 1:30 in the morning thinking, 'What am I doing? We have practice tomorrow.' He'd talk you into anything. He was the best. Long road trips, late nights. He was very impulsive. He missed home to be quite honest. Even though he wasn't that far, he missed home. He loved Peoria."

After flunking out of DePaul, Nathan was at a crossroads. He was dying to get back on the basketball court, but transferring to another Division 1 school would have meant sitting out a year on the court, per NCAA rules. Arkansas, the Southeastern Conference powerhouse that Nathan nearly chose out of high school, was said to have placed him at Northwest Arkansas Community College with the idea of improving his grades for a year and then joining the Razorbacks. Northwest Arkansas didn't even have a basketball team, and Nolan Richardson and his staff wanted to "hide" Nathan for a while so other colleges wouldn't recruit him.

Without competitive basketball, Nathan lasted just one semester at the junior college in Bentonville, Arkansas. He was on the move again. That's when Mike Vining, the head coach at Northeast Louisiana (now Louisiana-Monroe) received a phone call from Peoria. The Indians played in the Southland Conference and were an excellent low-major program in the midst of four consecutive trips to the NCAA Tournament. Jim Youngman, a high school coach in the Peoria area, knew of Nathan's situation and was an acquaintance of Vining's. Youngman apprised the college coach of the situation and passed along Sue and Howard Sr.'s phone number.

At that point, Vining had never heard of Nathan.

"When he asked me about him and told me he was available, I quickly found out about him," Vining said, laughing. "He wasn't someone we could have signed out of high school."

Vining contacted Howard Sr. before speaking to Junior to determine if the player and school might be a match. Nathan then came down to Monroe for a visit. The ballplayer was thirsty for another shot in Division 1 and felt comfortable in Monroe on his visit. He had found his next home.

Nathan enrolled at NE Louisiana in the second semester of the 1992–93 school year. He could practice right away but would not be eligible to play games until the second semester of 1993–94. The team he joined in practice in January 1993 was a good one. The Indians were a veteran club that beat No. 9-ranked Arkansas en route to finishing 26–5 overall and 17–1 in the Southland.

The roster full of southern country boys heard a McDonald's All-American from up north was joining their squad, and they weren't quite sure what to make of it. It took less than one practice for Nathan to dazzle them, and nearly three decades later those who were there still remember the play.

"The first day we practiced against Howard, guys were going at him hard," said Isaac Brown, a senior guard on that team and later Wichita State's head coach. "And I'll never forget, we pressed that year, I'm picking him up full court, he took that thing between his legs, behind his back, turned around and threw a half-court pass behind his head to the other end of the court for the guy to get a dunk. Right after that, everybody gained his respect, and they knew he was the real deal."

What did the coach think when that happened?

"Well, you just smile and say we finally got one," Vining chuckled. "You've lost a bunch but now we've finally got one. That (play) made an impression. It was unbelievable."

Though Nathan couldn't play in games right away, he immediately acclimated to campus. With an enrollment of less than 10,000 students that are overwhelmingly from the South, Nathan managed to fit right in thanks to his outgoing, friendly disposition.

"It was like he was from Louisiana," Vining said. "Everybody loved him, and he was probably the most popular player on the team. Both on the team and with fellow students. They hung around him, they liked to be around him."

Brown echoes the sentiment. A fellow transfer, Brown came to NE Louisiana from Texas A&M, although he never played in a college game with Nathan. Brown's eligibility was up after Nathan's sit-out year, but he stayed in Monroe to complete an internship for his graduation requirements and attended games the next season when Nathan was suiting up.

"He was a great basketball player but I think guys liked him more off the court," Brown said. "Howard was a well-dressed guy. Us being country boys, he had a lot of style. His haircut, the clothes he wore. Just one of them guys who brought positive energy. Howard would always pick out somebody on campus that nobody else ever hung out with, everybody probably thought they was too good for this person, and he befriended him and made that person the most popular person on campus."

A native of Pascagoula, Mississippi, a town of about 25,000 on the Gulf Coast, Brown says he didn't pay much attention to clothing in college. As such, he wore his NE Louisiana sweats every day in Monroe. Literally every day.

"But every time we got ready to go somewhere like to a movie, or a volleyball game or a party on campus, (Nathan) would always say, 'Brown, go down to the closet and get you an outfit,'" Brown remembered. "He was one of those guys who always had gear and always had your back. He had a car in college, which a lot of guys didn't have. If you needed to go to the store, he'd be like, 'Go get the keys, just put gas in it.' Just a caring, giving guy."

After missing a few games as part of NCAA rules that require a transfer to sit out two semesters, Nathan's NE Louisiana debut came on December 17, 1993, against Troy in a tournament at Wright State in Dayton, Ohio. In his first live action in about 18 months—since DePaul's 1992 NCAA Tournament loss to New Mexico State—Nathan poured in 35 points and 12 assists as the Indians rolled to a 110–92 victory.

The Southland had seen stars before, but it was a significantly lower level of hoops than a major conference like the Big Ten or Big East, or even the Great Midwest Conference. Joe Dumars, who starred for the Detroit Pistons in the 1980s and '90s, is the greatest player to emerge from the Southland. Long before he was elected to the Basketball Hall of Fame, Dumars played at McNeese State in Lake Charles, Louisiana. Additionally, NE Louisiana's Calvin Natt was the eighth pick in the NBA Draft in 1979 and averaged more than 17 points per game over an 11-year NBA career.

Facing schools like Nicholls State, Texas-Arlington, and Sam Houston State, Nathan and NE Louisiana were lighting up the scoreboard and gaining steam down the stretch in 1994. Playing along two high-level scorers in Larry Carr and LSU transfer Paul Marshall, Nathan was racking up assists in bunches as the Indians routinely scored more than 80 points. They rattled off 11 straight wins for a conference title, finishing 15–3 in the league.

At the time, the regular season conference champion hosted the all-important conference tournament. (Typically for leagues like the Southland, the only path to an NCAA Tournament bid is securing the automatic bid by winning the conference tournament.)

"He made great plays look normal," Vining said of Nathan. "Somebody would cut backdoor to the basket, you wouldn't think he even saw him and then (the teammate) has the ball. It was just unbelievable in a close game, everything is just kind of going along where they get one, we get one. And all of a sudden, he makes some unbelievable play. It may be on offense, it may be on defense, he'll come up with a steal and make a great pass. It just happened and it always involved him."

The Southland tournament would be played at Fant-Ewing Coliseum in Monroe, and Nathan and Co. needed three wins in three days at home for an NCAA berth. After downing Stephen F. Austin by 19 points in the quarterfinal, NE Louisiana faced North Texas, a squad it had beaten twice that season. But with Nathan nursing a sore ankle that required treatment, North Texas got 34 points from star Jesse Ratliff and knocked off the top-seeded Indians 77–74 in front of 3,409 fans at Fant-Ewing. NE Louisiana's season was over at 19–9.

At the time, Vining didn't know that Nathan's 23rd game in NE Louisiana maroon and gold would be his last. Nathan averaged 14 points and was sixth in the country at 7.8 assists per game. California sophomore stud Jason Kidd led the country that year with 9.1 assists a game.

Unfortunately, as he had at DePaul, Nathan basically stopped going to class after the basketball season ended. He wasn't going to be eligible for the following season and decided it was time to make his push for the NBA. Although he only played 23 games for Vining, Nathan left an indelible mark on the coach who won over 400 games in a very successful career.

"He was a natural born leader," Vining said. "People just followed him. I don't know that it was anything he did, you couldn't describe it, you couldn't put your finger on it, but they just followed him. And so my job was to get him leading in the right direction."

Despite two strong seasons at two different schools, he went undrafted.

"If you change eras, I think he would have had more (chances)," Stoudamire said. "We tend to give guys that go to those Northeast Louisiana and those mid-major type schools more respect now. I don't think back then it was really like that."

The basketball junkie from Peoria wasn't done, though. Dating back to his high school playing days, Nathan had a pedigree that NBA organizations were aware of. They knew about his talent, confidence, and determination. The Atlanta Hawks and famed Coach Lenny Wilkens took a chance on Nathan in the 1995–96 season after an impressive showing in Chicago's summer league. It was a weird time in the NBA, as the league was coming off its first lockout in history and two-plus months where trades, free agent signings, and contract extensions were not permitted.

"I got drafted by the Toronto Raptors and we end up playing the Atlanta Hawks like the third or fourth game of the preseason, and lo and behold I look down there, shit there he is right there," Stoudamire said. "I was like, 'Oh shit.' He still played the same way. He was still Howard."

Nathan made his regular-season NBA debut with the Atlanta Hawks against the Orlando Magic on November 4, 1995. He scored three points in a blowout win. But in a perfect example of how incredibly hard it is to make it—and stick—in the NBA, Nathan played only four more games in the league. Fittingly, the Hawks went 5–0 in games he played, and Nathan finished his cup of coffee with 13 career NBA points.

Each NBA team is allowed 15 players on its roster at a time. With 30 teams in the league, that's a total of 450 active NBA players. That's it. The turnover each year is not substantial at all. This is all to say you have to be unbelievably good to make the NBA and to hang around a while. There are hundreds of awesome players, and the line is so incredibly thin to make the league or not.

"I'm not a speculator," Stoudamire said. "But it's like one thing can hurt you from making it. You just never know. For Howard, whatever that might have been, unfortunately he just never got the shot that maybe he should have got."

Looking back, just about everyone who came into contact with Nathan and knew what kind of player he was says the pivot point in his career was leaving DePaul. With the Blue Demons, he was playing every game on national television and facing top competition. Neither of those things were true after he left. There is a measure of acceptance that Nathan would have been a ten-year NBA player if he played three or four seasons at DePaul.

"I think he would have been the second-best point guard I ever coached, so you can tell I'm pretty high on what a basketball player he was," Meyer said, alluding to Rod Strickland, a first-round pick from DePaul in 1988 who played 17 years in the NBA. "I would have been pretty surprised if he didn't make it (if he stayed four years). The classroom just wasn't his cup of tea. It was a battle, let me tell ya. Mom and dad were in the middle of it, they were great. They supported us and really tried to help but he just wasn't ready for it."

Stoudamire added: "Back at that time, DePaul was DePaul. He was playing with his high school teammate David Booth, they had Tommy Kleinschmidt, they had good teams. They had a really good team and he had a really good freshman year, and then I just don't know what happened. It seems like some type of stigma was put on his name and just like he never recovered from that."

• • •

It's uncomfortable talking about the star who didn't make it. Well, let's step back a moment first. Howard Nathan did make it. Despite an unorthodox path that took him in and out of colleges, he reached basketball's highest mountain. The young man from Proctor Street played in the NBA. In a study released by the NCAA in 2019, it stated 1.2 percent of men's college basketball players reach the NBA. Howard Nathan Jr. did that. He's part of the 1.2 percent. And yet, it doesn't feel fully like a success story, does it? When a kid is tabbed for stardom from an early age and hits all the benchmarks along the way, varsity as a high school freshman, Mr. Basketball, five-star recruit, McDonald's All-American, etc., we start expecting the world.

You can't talk about Howard Nathan without riffing about the confidence. David Booth recalls a time when the outdoor courts were packed at Carver Center with some of the best players in town on a typical summer day. Nathan was there, of course, as was a kid he'd frequently gone up against from Peoria Richwoods. Like most of his opponents, Nathan got the best of him in high school, and the two were frequently engaged in trash talk on the court. On this day, Nathan said to him, "Let's play one-on-one for $100 right now." The Richwoods kid wanted no part of it. So Nathan upped the ante. "I'll tell you what," he continued, "We'll play for $100 and play to 21. I'm gonna give you 20 points and the ball first, for $100."

Naturally, those nearby became incredulous. The Richwoods kid still wouldn't budge.

"Howard is my friend but I'm like you better play him, man," David Booth remembers saying. "All you have to do is make one shot. Right now you're winning 20–0 . . . and he wouldn't do it."

Classic Junior.

Nathan played his last professional basketball in 1999 with the Rockford Lightning of the Continental Basketball Association. He appeared in just two games on a roster that included Earl Boykins, the five-foot-five dynamo who ended up playing 667 games in the NBA, and Chicago basketball legend Ronnie Fields from Farragut High School.

After that, Nathan was back in his beloved Peoria clinging to his NBA dreams. The next call never came. According to a *Chicago Tribune* article in December 2006, Nathan had a rap sheet with five convictions between 1996 and 2002, with one resulting in jail time—a 90-day sentence in 1999 for misdemeanor resisting and obstructing a peace officer. During that time, Nathan married Danielle Smith, a former Manual point guard herself.

The list of athletes who struggle to find their way after organized games end is a long one. Nathan badly wanted to get back to the NBA, where he knew he belonged yet had played only 15 minutes. Back in familiar surroundings in Peoria, he was with old friends, and there was weed, petty arrests, and a lot of the usual shenanigans guys in their late twenties engage in. Smith, who is now remarried and goes by Danielle Davis, doesn't believe Nathan's woes resulted from hanging around the wrong crowd.

"I really can't say that because they're all people he grew up with," said Davis, whose family lived on Proctor, one block from the Nathans. "You're talking about people that were close like family. So, I really can't say that. At that point, he's an adult. He's not a kid so you have to make those right decisions for yourself. And knowing, 'OK I can do certain things if I want to get to this level, it may not be the best choice to go to certain places or be around certain things.' But I can't say it was being with the wrong crowd. He was just trying to find his way. And everyone knew him and it was like family. It wasn't like he was making new friends; these are people he grew up with."

There were some negative headlines in the Peoria *Journal-Star* and on local television during that period, but Peoria didn't give up on its sports hero. Not when he'd given them so much joy on the court and had been nothing but kind to folks off the hardwood. Nathan made some mistakes, to be sure, but his hometown remained in his corner.

"For me personally, it was dust yourself off and let's keep on going," Derrick Booth said. "It wasn't the end of anything for me. I always thought and believed it was just a matter of time before he was about to get called up again to the NBA. From the time he came home from the Hawks it was just stay ready. He never quit playing basketball. Never slowed down playing basketball. Every day, all day. That was always what he did. For me that was always an option for him."

In April 2001, Howard and Danielle had a baby girl, Aerial Jourdan. If that reminds you of Air Jordan, you guessed right. Howard was obsessed with Michael Jordan and convinced Danielle they should name their child after him. She gave in, with a condition.

"Yes, so corny," Danielle says with a laugh. "Her middle name is spelled differently, though."

As Howard struggled to find his place in a post-basketball star world, it took a toll on his young family. He knew he wanted to do something in basketball, but what?

"Basketball was his passion and his purpose, obviously," Danielle said. "Being who he was, he would have had no problem if he had the right mind and that's what he focused on with getting a coaching job, mentoring, or in that arena. Whatever that looked like for him. He could have easily. But you have to place yourself in a position, in the right environment and mindset to go that route. It wasn't that he didn't pursue other jobs but it always came back to basketball. And I knew that."

The couple eventually separated but maintained a cordial relationship for Aerial. Howard was an involved parent from the start and that never waned. His little Air Jordan loved basketball just like her daddy. Howard and Danielle divorced in 2008, and in 2010 she moved to the Atlanta area to start anew. Living in a wheelchair since late 2006, Howard was now about 700 miles away from his 9-year-old daughter.

Despite the distance, Howard remained in close contact with Aerial. A budding basketball player herself at the time, Aerial says they talked or texted almost every day. Howard, a Warriors fan, and Aerial, a Lakers fan, engaged in fun-loving basketball trash-talking sessions with regularity. Father loved Kobe, and daughter was a huge LeBron fan. Howard couldn't glide up and down the court anymore, but he still was thinking basketball all the time.

Aerial attended Centennial High School in Roswell, Georgia, a school that opened in 1997 and was named in honor of the Summer Olympics held in Atlanta the year before. It was the centennial anniversary of the modern Olympic games. For many years after the crash, Howard couldn't drive so he'd have to rely on Charles, one of his sisters, or a friend to drive him places. But later he was given the go-ahead to drive himself, and he loved traveling in his big, red Chevrolet Silverado truck.

Howard would make the 10-hour drive down to Roswell to watch Aerial play or elsewhere for her AAU games.

"Aerial would go with him and he just wanted to drive himself and she'd say, 'That's a long time to drive,'" Danielle said. "He could have flown. But I think he enjoyed that independence of driving. I told her don't take that away from him. If he wants to drive, let him drive. He came to as many games as possible while she was on the road and even here at her high school games."

Aerial says she didn't feel pressure to play basketball because her dad was Howard Nathan, Mr. Basketball.

"No, I've been playing for the longest," she said. "I really started playing on a team since I was three and I loved it since."

In the spring of 2019, Aerial's senior season at Centennial was coming to a close. Howard loaded up the red Silverado, took a couple friends with him, and hit the road to see his daughter's Senior Night game.

"It was great, I couldn't wait for the game to start," Aerial said.

And then a few minutes into the first quarter, she suffered an MCL injury in her left knee.

Howard Nathan and his daughter, Aerial, at her 2019 graduation from Centennial High School in Roswell, Georgia. Though he was nearly 700 miles away from his only child, Nathan was close with Aerial and made several drives south to see her play basketball. (Photo provided by Aerial Nathan)

"It was the worst, but I kept playing through," said Aerial, who averaged 11 points, 4.4 rebounds and 2.7 assists per game as a senior, according to maxpreps.com. "I had to (because he was there)."

• • •

When Howard was eventually able to leave the hospital after an extended stay, he lived with his parents for a while. From there, he and sister Stacey, four years his junior, moved in together. It was a surprise to no one that a family member took him in. That is simply how the Nathans operate. They lived in a townhouse about 10 minutes from Howard Sr. and Sue, with a wheelchair-accessible ramp so Junior could navigate his way in and out of the building. Stacey doted on him, making sure he had everything he needed whenever he wanted it. So did the other five siblings, who were frequent visitors. All the Nathans were living in Peoria and were willing to pitch in to help their brother.

"We all individually understood that our lives would change," Charles said. "We didn't want Mom and Dad to have to do all the work. We didn't want Mom and Dad to have to do any of the work. Because this is what we were taught, to be there for one another. And everyone did their part; we rotated days and times."

The basketball star now confined to a wheelchair remained upbeat. Always.

"It was easy for us to handle the situation better because he handled it," Stacey said. "Had he been a wreck, then we probably would have (too). So, seeing how he went about his day and his life encouraged us. We came to him with our issues like every day. I'd come to his room to tell him about something that happened, and he would just sit there and listen and be an ear to everyone."

That positive attitude manifested itself in different ways. Howard would lift people up in unexpected ways when they needed it most. In 2008, Sue was diagnosed with breast cancer and had to undergo chemotherapy. It was torturous and one day she phoned Howard hoping for some sympathy.

"I called him when I had to go to my treatments and I said, 'Junior, I can't take this. I want to die. This chemo is so bad I just wanna die,'" Sue remembered. "He said, 'Mama! As much faith as you got and you're gonna tell me. I'm paralyzed, I can't walk. And you can't take chemo?' He said, 'Mama, suck it up. Do it.' And I did it, but he had to tell me. I thought he was gonna pity his mama but he didn't."

It had been more than a decade since Nathan starred at Peoria Manual High School, the town's basketball powerhouse on the gritty south end. But after the car crash, neighborhood kids wouldn't get to see him playing pickup ball down at Proctor Center or run with younguns at open gym.

Still, the name Howard Nathan carried a certain cache in Peoria.

"I work at the detention center, and I know around the time when he played, those kids had never met him," Stacey said. "But with him being sort of an urban legend, who he was was passed down. It was as if *they* knew him. Like how they've never met Michael Jordan, they never witnessed Howard Nathan play, but they knew who he was. And when they met him, they would come back around because he was so humble."

Oh, they came back all right. Neighborhood kids became regulars at Stacey and Howard's townhouse. Picture that: a basketball legend in a wheelchair who voluntarily gave his time to grade school kids.

"At our house, there would be little kids who would knock on the door just to be around him," Stacey said. "And sometimes you would not even want to go outside because there would be kids coming up. He's feeding kids in the neighborhood, he's giving them popsicles, candy, money just to put in their pocket. That's just who he was."

Charles added, "He made the little kids feel like they were *his* best friends. Seven and eight-year-olds knocking on the door, 'Is Howard here?' I'm like you better go. And when you want to push them away, he'd say let them in."

They'd play video games, watch basketball, eat snacks, whatever. The kids were happy, and so was the basketball legend.

Little kids weren't the only ones enamored with Nathan. Nathan's rise and fame occurred in something of a sweet spot in Peoria's basketball dominance. Later in the 1990s, Peoria Manual gained national recognition as an elite powerhouse basketball school. Led by Sergio McClain, Marcus Griffin, and Frank Williams, the Rams became a fixture in the *USA Today*'s national rankings and were a huge draw wherever they went. Griffin, the six-foot-eight center and rare big man in a city known for guards, said Nathan paved the way for all the stars that came after him.

"There's not a person that grew up in Peoria in the last 30 years that played basketball who did not picture themselves being Howard Nathan," Griffin said. "There's not a guard in Peoria who did not want to be Howard Nathan. Not one. He touched so many lives. There's a lot of basketball players that came out of Peoria who owe everything to Mr. Nathan. I'm one of them. I owe him a lot."

● ● ●

It took some time, but Nathan eventually found his path. In the summer of 2014, his childhood friend Derrick Booth reached out with an opportunity. Booth had returned to their alma mater and was the head coach at Manual. He was looking for an assistant coach to fill out his staff and knew of a brilliant basketball mind in town with some time on his hands. For a while, Nathan had stopped going to basketball games. He thought the kids didn't appreciate it anymore. That they were spending too much time playing video games and not enough time sweating in the gym. But when Booth called and asked him to be a Manual assistant, Nathan was on board.

Booth vividly recalls the conversation as he stood in his living room looking out the back window of his house and told his childhood friend it was time to get back in the gym.

"I said you've been on the bench for too long, and he didn't really know where I was going with that," Booth said. "He said, 'You ain't never known me to be on nobody's bench.' And I said you've been on the sidelines for too long and I want to get you back in the game. I said life is about purpose. No matter what your situation is you have a duty to carry out your purpose. And I said your purpose is to pour into these young men. I said I want you to come help me coach. He was like, 'For real, D?' I said I'm serious, I want you to be my assistant and come help me coach. I said these young men need to hear from you. It didn't take a lot of arm twisting. He said I'm there. He started coming to open gym in the summer and he just never stopped coming."

For four seasons, Nathan accompanied Booth on the Manual bench. With the school buses unable to accommodate his wheelchair needs, Nathan would drive himself or get a ride from Stacey or a friend to road games. When Booth would offer gas money after a long trip to Danville or Chicago, Nathan shrugged him off. Booth said Nathan's dedication was evident as he hardly missed an open gym or practice.

As a coach, Nathan wasn't an Xs and Os strategist. He was still a player at heart and saw things from a player's perspective, something that can be lost on the average coach. Once during his first year on the bench, he pulled Manual freshman Da'Monte Williams aside during a late-game timeout against Morton. With the Rams down three points, Nathan told Williams to pump fake his defender in the air and then lean into him to draw a foul.

Williams, son of former Manual great Frank Williams, did just that, drew a foul and hit three clutch free throws to tie the game in the waning seconds.

"I was like dang, I would have never thought about that," said Willie Coleman, then a Manual assistant. "I'm thinking about a play, what we can do. Just those little things that he instilled in players made him a great assistant and he saw the game a different way than coaches do."

Derrick Booth, who had a very successful 11-year run as Manual head coach, was thrilled to get some extra time with Nathan.

"We had a ball. I really, really did enjoy having him there," Booth said. "It was like old times with Nate. Me and Howard had this connection that we can give each other a certain look and it's funny because we know what we're both talking about. We give each other a look and we both start laughing because we see the same thing. We don't have to say anything. And it may be some joke me and him had with each other 25 years ago and we'll give each other a look across the gym and we know what it means."

Wheelchair users often deal with chronic pain due to sitting all day, every day. That sedentary lifestyle can cause any number of problems, and general discomfort on a regular basis. Nathan was no different, but he largely kept this to himself.

"What (the Manual players) didn't know is that Nate would come into that gym most days in a lot of pain," Booth said. "And it wasn't anything he would advertise because he didn't want people feeling sorry for him. He would describe his legs and his feet as feeling like they were on fire. And being stuck with pins. That's what it was like being stuck in the chair. But he didn't let that keep him in the bed or anything like that. He still was there. And he wouldn't say it to everybody, I know I was one of the few he would feel comfortable saying it to."

Nathan was also active in a "Stop the Violence" campaign, trying to combat Peoria's gun violence and steering kids away from the street life. With coaching, mentoring, and helping kids, he was using his local fame for good.

• • •

When Nathan was young and dominating every level of basketball he encountered, it felt like a no-brainer in Peoria that he would be the city's first NBA star. Or at the very least, enjoy a long career in the world's best basketball league. For various reasons, that did not happen. Nathan made it, but only for those 5 games and 15 minutes with the Atlanta Hawks. Instead, a super skinny Peoria kid with otherworldly basketball talents and instincts carved out a long career in the NBA several years later.

Shaun Livingston, then a six-foot-seven beanpole, led Peoria Central High School to back-to-back Class AA state titles in 2003 and 2004. Like all basketball players growing up in the 309, Livingston looked up to Nathan. And when Livingston landed on the dynastic Golden State Warriors for the last 5 years of a 15-year NBA career, he made sure his childhood hero got a chance to experience some of the good life.

As 2015 turned into 2016, the Warriors were a fixture in American sports culture, an unbelievable team with a crowd-pleasing, freewheeling style led by superstar guards Stephen Curry and Klay Thompson. Livingston was averaging around 20 minutes per game coming off the bench for coach Steve Kerr's powerhouse, a key defensive cog and team-first role player who contributed across all statistical categories. With the Warriors, 32–2 at the time, traveling south to face the Los Angeles Lakers on January 5, 2016, Livingston flew Nathan, Stacey, and Nathan's daughter Aerial into LA to see the game. The three stayed at a lavish hotel near the Staples Center and shared a few meals with Livingston and his family, who were also in town.

Over dinner at Roscoe's House of Chicken & Waffles one night, Livingston's father, Reggie, approached Stacey. After a few minutes of chatting, Reggie halted the conversation for a moment to go grab Shaun's cellphone. "And his screensaver was Frank Williams and Howard," Stacey said. "And I'm looking at this like, 'Oh my god.' He says your brother is the reason why (Shaun) wears number 34."

The group stayed until Stacey had to return to work, which meant they weren't able to attend another game. Howard and Aerial were sure to remind Stacey of how her job was infringing on their fun. But it was still a trip none of them would ever forget.

On November 11, 2017, DePaul hosted 14th-ranked Notre Dame in the first game at sparkling new Wintrust Arena near McCormick Place just south of downtown Chicago. It was a massive upgrade from Rosemont Horizon and much closer to DePaul's city campus. Nathan drove up from Peoria for the occasion. Kleinschmidt was there too, as were Joey Meyer and David Booth, the latter two working for NBA teams at the time. Nathan was in the wheelchair section and during a break in the action he wheeled over to the NBA scout seats to see both his former college coach and long-time Peoria buddy.

"It was really sad, for one seeing him in the wheelchair was . . . that was extremely hard to deal with," Meyer said. "Two, how much he regretted not listening. And how warm and friendly he was. That will stick with me the rest of my life. He was in tears and was just very, very emotional. It was just hard for me to see him . . . when you see a guy who is so young and was such a great athlete sitting there in a wheelchair, it's hard to deal with."

Meyer doesn't remember the game at all, not even who DePaul's opponent was that day. It wasn't significant in comparison to seeing his old point guard.

"I can remember everything but the game," he said. "The interaction with Howard was much more important to me than what was happening on the floor, I can tell you that."

• • •

In early July 2019, Nathan and a friend were hanging out at the Peoria townhouse. Stacey was in the kitchen making food. At some point, Nathan went to the bathroom and was gone for longer than normal. When Stacey and the friend went to check on him he was on the bathroom floor, but they thought he was just playing a joke. He was a prankster, and it wouldn't have been out of character. "Get up, Junior!" Stacey said. They left the bathroom and a few more minutes passed. When they returned to see what was going on, Nathan was still in the same position. He had a pulse but was not breathing. The paramedics were called, and Nathan was rushed to OSF St. Francis, the same hospital he spent time in 13 years earlier after the devastating car crash.

At the hospital, Nathan's heart stopped, apparently for a second time. Doctors revived him, but he was induced into a coma. Word spread quickly that the great Howard Nathan was in trouble. Phone calls and texts flew around the country, informing Peoria's wide circle about the perilous situation involving one of the town's most famous sons.

The July 11 edition of the Peoria *Journal-Star* reported, *"The heart of former Manual High School basketball star Howard Nathan appeared to stop twice after he collapsed Tuesday night in his Peoria home. But medical personnel revived Nathan there and in the emergency room of OSF HealthCare Saint Francis Medical Center. That hospital is where Nathan, 47, remained Thursday in intensive care."*

The whole Nathan family basically began living at the hospital. Aerial flew in from Atlanta to be near her father. Everyone was swapping stories trying to figure out what happened. "I just talked to him yesterday and everything seemed fine" seemed to be the general consensus. Fine one day, on ice in a coma the next. Unbelievable.

One week passed. Then another. Nathan's six siblings, plus Sue and Aerial, slept in the hospital with Junior. Every night. (Howard Sr. was there all day and would make the short drive home each night to sleep.) One sibling was allowed to sleep in the room with Nathan; the rest of the crew slept on the floor or a couch in the waiting room.

"We never left," sister Stacey said.

Nathan wasn't improving. He was on a breathing machine with a feeding tube down his throat. Doctors said he had suffered severe brain damage due to going a prolonged amount of time without oxygen to his brain the day he collapsed. With no positive outlook in sight, doctors asked Sue and Howard Sr. the most gut-wrenching question a parent could ever hear: Were they ready to pull the plug? The Nathans agonized.

Yes. This was no way for their Howard to live.

"I said you take out the breathing tube and we'll take my baby home and we'll take care of him," Sue said. "Because I wasn't going to put him in no nursing home. What do you think he would want? A man who went everywhere, could drive, and do everything he wants to do for himself. And my kids worked in a nursing home, and it ain't no place to be. So, we had to make a decision and [with] my pastor, we pray this prayer, 'Our father God in heaven, hallowed will be thy name.' And at the end 'thy will be done' and so for me being in the Lord, I knew what thy will be done means. So, Bishop said, 'Sue, you talk to Howard?' I said yeah, we talked about it. He said 'What do the kids think?' And he asked all my kids what they thought and they agreed with me. He said, 'Sue, do you know what you're saying, Sue? Do you know what you're saying?' I said Bishop, I know what I'm saying. I said God is going to give him back to me or he's going to take him. But I said I'm not going to let him go to no nursing home. And so, I told the lady that's what I wanted to do. She said are you sure? I said that's what I want to do and I'm taking him home Friday."

But Junior wasn't done yet. The ventilator was removed, but he actually began to breathe on his own and even opened his eyes. Knowing how much he'd hate to look disheveled, sisters Tonya and Angennette gave him a bath using his preferred soap and then cologne. Sue would look down on her once strong and powerful son and plead with him, "You gotta fight, Howard. You gotta fight."

Derrick Booth asked Sue if he could give Howard a shave and she said, "Yeah, and make sure you cut that thing off on his chin. My kids were so mad at me (laughing). Derrick shaved him and my girls said, 'Mama! Junior is gonna be mad at you. You don't shave off his goatee. That's his signature.' I didn't like it but I knew he liked it."

With the breathing tube out, Nathan was moved to a new room, and Sue became encouraged when she saw his legs move. For three days it went like that with emotions swinging back and forth like tree branches in heavy wind. There was sadness, hope, anguish, prayer, and everything in between. On the third night after the breathing tube was removed, Sue told her son she was going home to sleep and attend Sunday school and church the next morning, but his sister Camisha would be there to stay with him.

At around 2 a.m. that night, Sue awoke to a banging at her door. It was her daughter Roberta (Bert) yelling, "Mama get up, get up! Something is wrong with Junior! I said, 'Lord, have mercy.'"

At 47 years old, Howard Nathan Jr. passed away on July 28, 2019. He lived a life full of highs and lows and was truly beloved. A Peoria legend.

"When you watch your child for three weeks laying in that hospital and no response, then you have to make a decision to let him go or pray that God bring him back," Sue said, fighting back tears. "Howard (Sr.) said, 'Sue, God didn't want him to live like that. He said God made the decision for us to take him because he didn't want to be a vegetable.' Nothing ever stopped him. To lose my child . . . (crying) every day I cry. I'm in one room, and Howard's in another room and he's crying. We cry and we cry. My heart hurts. I get the phone, and I dial his number and I talk to him because I miss him so much (sobbing)."

The funeral, held at Church of the Living God, was a massive gathering. The line to enter the church was so long that the service started well after the 10 a.m. time it was slated for. Basketball stars, politicians, and hundreds of people Nathan impacted over the years crammed into the church on an emotional late summer day in Peoria. A beautiful, eight-page program was handed out to attendees that included loads of photos and newspaper clippings of Nathan over the years. On one page, the clippings are arranged in the shape of his trademark 34.

Tom Kleinschmidt, now the head coach at his alma mater DePaul Prep (formerly Gordon Tech), was one of the speakers at the funeral. Like many others, the old friend from Chicago was emotional as he remembered his friend.

Sue and Howard Nathan Sr. hold up a sign honoring their son's Mr. Basketball award in their home on Proctor Street a little more than a year after Howard Jr. passed away. The Nathans turned the back room of their house into a mini museum dedicated to Howard Jr.'s basketball achievements. (Photo by John Grap)

"I remember talking to him the whole way down there (to the funeral)," he said. "I was talking to him because it was that ride that we took so many times. Two thirty in the morning on a Tuesday (for example). Got up that morning and driving down there on 55, I'm sitting there talking to him, saying, 'How many times did we take this trip?' That's when it really set in."

Despite their extreme sadness at losing Howard, the Nathans were in awe of the crowd that came out on that Saturday morning. They knew Howard made an impact on many, but seeing the seemingly endless crowd file into their church left an enduring mark.

"Just seeing the support and love from the people . . . it was wonderful," Charles said. "It was a feeling on the inside where if I pass away today, I would want my service just like this. Because people didn't only talk it, they showed it during the time he passed away."

As local newspaper and television stations ran stories on Nathan's passing, Shaun Livingston told more than one outlet that Nathan was the best high school player to ever come out of Peoria. High praise from a guy with 15 years and 3 NBA titles under his belt.

Jerrance Howard, who played at Peoria Central and Illinois before becoming a high-profile assistant coach at Kansas, may have said it best. In speaking to WMDB, Peoria's CBS affiliate, Howard said, "He gave us confidence to go around the world and say you're from Peoria, Illinois. Everybody knew that's where Howard Nathan was from. He was our superhero here in Peoria, and always will be. There will never be another Howard Nathan."

In the months that followed Howard's passing, the Nathans felt a huge void that would never be filled again. There always had been nine of them, and then suddenly it was eight. Even in the 13 years he lived in a wheelchair, Howard's presence loomed large, his positive personality always present. A deep sadness hung over the family as they struggled to become accustomed to a life without him.

"Since Howard has been gone, we haven't done anything," Sue said about four months after he died. "We're not going to celebrate any holidays for a while. Howard was our cook."

The walls of the Nathan house are lined with family pictures. You can see the crew of seven siblings as cute little kids, and then the progression of life's moments through the years, often with Howard Sr. and Sue right there with them in the frame. In the months after Junior was gone, Howard Sr. had a tough time seeing his oldest boy in all the photos as he solemnly walked through his house. It was just too much.

"My husband said, 'Sue, we've got to move these pictures.' I told him I ain't moving my baby's pictures," Sue said. "His picture got to stay. His truck is in our garage. I said Howard, 'We can't take the pictures down. He's going to be a part of us until the day I die.'"

In February 2020, about six months after arguably the greatest baller to ever emerge from Peoria had passed away, a celebration was planned in his honor. Derrick Booth, his close friend of more than 30 years, organized a street dedication near the Nathan home at the intersection of Proctor and Madison Park Terrace.

Speakers included Peoria Mayor Jim Ardis, Representative Jehan Gordon-Booth, Peoria First District Councilwoman Denise Moore, Derrick Booth, and some of Nathan's family members. Several dozen people gathered in the street on a chilly winter day as brief stories were told about what Howard meant to the community.

When it was her turn to speak, Sue Nathan was overcome by emotion. She'd been crying for months, and this day only exacerbated it. "Forty-seven years ago, that was my baby," she said. "That was my first son. Everybody loved my son, but I loved him more."

Howard Nathan Sr. stood tall near his family, a stoic face amid a tearful scene. Wearing glasses, a long black peacoat and black top hat, he cuts an imposing figure—easily taller than his star son was. Nathan Sr. is a man of few words but he did briefly address the crowd. "Losing Howard hurt our family but with the help of God, we'll get through it," he said.

When the speeches were done, Charles Nathan, with tears streaming down his face, pulled on a long string to unveil a new sign high on a light pole and just under the West Proctor Street sign. The new, blue street sign read "Honorary Howard Nathan Jr Court."

The de facto Howard Nathan Day continued that evening at the Manual-Peoria Central basketball game. Fans arrived early as Nathan's No. 34 was being retired. A who's who of Peoria basketball royalty were present, including the recently retired Livingston, and former Manual stars Sergio McClain, Marcus Griffin, and Frank Williams. They all looked up to Nathan as kids and each dreamed of becoming the next Howard Nathan. The gym was packed, as Manual-Central games often are, but there was an extra buzz in the air with the specter of Nathan's presence.

Manual's players warmed up before the game all wearing orange T-shirts with Nathan's likeness on the front and "Nathan 34" on the back. Around the crowd, several variations of Nathan shirts dotted the bleachers as community members paid tribute to the Peoria ballplayer.

A framed "Nathan 34" orange jersey with white numbers was given to Nathan's family, along with a black marble plaque displaying a picture of Nathan and a list of 10 accomplishments, led by 1991 Mr. Basketball, 1991 Illinois state runner-up, and 1991 McDonald's All-American. High atop a wall in Manual's gym, a large picture of Nathan racing upcourt in the orange Rams uniform, dribbling with his left hand was added. The image also includes Nathan's top accomplishments, this time Mr. Basketball, Hoop Dreams, and Atlanta Hawks. At the bottom of the frame it says, "A hero gets remembered but a legend never dies."

With dozens of Nathan family members in the gym, Derrick Booth addressed the crowd.

"I'm glad that after Howard poured years of his life into Manual, that so many of you came out to honor his legacy," Booth said. "It is fitting that tonight is a Manual-Central game, because I'll never forget one thing that Howard told me long after we both graduated. Peoria High was playing in the state tournament led by Brandon Lee and Shaun Livingston, and one thing Howard said was, 'We have to root for Peoria now.' That was the type of guy Howard was, he loved Manual, but he also loved this city and wanted to bring everyone together."

On the night they honored the greatest player in Manual High School history, the Rams led for most of the way in the late-season rivalry game. The tide turned when Manual's best player, Rolando "Pee Wee" Brown fouled out in the fourth quarter on an ill-fated steal attempt. Without Brown and his game-high 25 points, Peoria Central milked the game away at the free throw line for a 67–57 victory.

It was a disappointing finish for a Manual crowd hoping to rekindle some memories from the Nathan era. But as they all knew, there will never be another Howard Nathan Jr.

3

Mayor of the South Side

It is a classic McClain family story.

Brindeshie was an infant, about six months old. The second of Wayne and Robin McClain's two children, she is five years younger than brother Sergio. The family of four was living in the rented second floor of a West Bluffs neighborhood house in Peoria when Robin's motherly instinct kicked in late at night. Sergio and Deshe (pronounced De-Shay), as everyone calls her, were sharing a room and Robin either heard something or just felt that she had to check on her little girl.

When she arrived in the kids' room, Deshe, who was nursing a bad cold, had her face pressed up against the clear plastic sheet lining her crib. Her lips were forced up against it like a fish and there was a vapor on the plastic from her breathing. Robin ripped the plastic open to grab her baby, whose breathing was quite labored.

"I screamed for Wayne and he jumps up and tells me to just drive to Methodist (hospital)," Robin said.

In an instant, Wayne grabbed Deshe, wrapped her up and took off running. He quickly told Robin if she sees him en route, they'd hop in the family's brown Fiat Brava with her.

"I never saw him (on the drive) . . . he just took off," Robin said. "My whole plan was I thought I would be able to grab them when I was driving."

With less than a mile between their house and Methodist Hospital (now UnityPoint Health-Methodist Hospital), Wayne ran the whole way with Deshe in his arms, beating Robin and Sergio to the emergency room even though they had wheels.

Deshe had suffered an allergic reaction to Theophylline, a drug used to treat symptoms of asthma and bronchitis. It had caused a seizure, and the situation at the hospital looked dire. Doctors ushered the McClains out of Deshe's room as they treated her and a chaplain came to console them, shockingly saying their little girl might not make it.

"Wayne was yelling at the chaplain," Robin said. "We thought she was gone. It was very intense. He grabbed my hand and pulled me away from the chaplain. It was awful. We were all crying. She survived that, but she was in the hospital for a while. They had her all wired up. She had gone without oxygen for a little bit."

Deshe ended up being fine, but it was a scary time for the McClains. After being released from the hospital, she was put on the anti-seizure drug, Phenobarbital, for three years.

Looking back now, what does Robin think when she remembers Wayne running down Main Street with his baby the entire way and checking her into the ER before the car got there?

"He was just a real man," Robin said. "That's all I can say about him. His determination . . . there were no boundaries. He would just put in his heart and his head what he was going to do."

Deshe has a simple explanation.

"That's just who he was," Deshe said.

Running was a theme with Wayne. He religiously jogged five miles a day, tortured his basketball players with running drills and would just take off running if a family member was in need. Five years or so after he sprinted with his baby to the hospital, Wayne made another dash for Deshe.

This time, Deshe was a kindergartener at Roosevelt Magnet School on the south end. Her teacher had called the McClains to say their daughter was sick and needed to be picked up. The McClains only had one car at the time, and Robin had it that day at her job as homeschool facilitator (truant officer) for District 150, Peoria's public school system. Wayne was at Peoria Manual, where he taught physical education and coached basketball.

Despite the car situation, Wayne said he would go grab Deshe on his lunch break. He jogged the mile and a half to get her.

"I remember this like it was yesterday," Deshe said. "He comes in the classroom, gets me, and I'm sick to the point where I'm putting my head on the desk. I couldn't even move around. He picks me up and puts me on his shoulders and he tells me, 'Lay your head on top of my head.'"

Wayne then jogged with Deshe on his shoulders for three or four blocks to his mother's house, where he put Deshe on her grandmother's couch and then jogged back to Manual for the afternoon of classes and basketball practice.

. . .

Born in Peoria in 1954, Wayne McClain was one of eight children raised by a single mother, Rosetta McClain, whom everyone called Ruff. They lived on the south end, then a diverse lower and middle working-class community. McClain was a strong athlete and earned his street cred through sports.

"He was kind of like my protector to be honest," said Bobby Humbles, a lifelong friend who was two years behind McClain in school. "Coming from grade school going to junior high, he kind of protected me. He would tell me what to do in the lunch lines. Wayne was a character. He was kind of a bully in a sense, not a mean bully. But just a very tough guy that people respected. Strong personality, fun and he was a good athlete."

Humbles says even though McClain did not have a father in his life, he was not devoid of male guidance.

"He had older brothers who kept him in check. While he may not have had a father in the household, he had father figures."

McClain enjoyed an excellent athletic career at Peoria Manual, playing basketball and football. As a senior on the basketball court, he teamed with Humbles' older brother Mike to form a stellar backcourt in 1971–72. It was Coach Dick Van Scyoc's sixth season with the Rams and they were one of the best teams in the state.

Unfortunately for Manual, it ran into what many consider the finest team in the history of Illinois high school basketball in the Class AA semifinals—Quinn Buckner's Thornridge Falcons. McClain and the Rams lost to Thornridge, 71–52, and finished the year 25–8.

Thornridge went 33–0 to win its second straight title with an astonishing margin of victory of more than 32 points per game.

McClain's high school career was over, but his Peoria journey was just beginning. Next up: Bradley University and a short-lived college basketball career, plus a chance meeting in the cafeteria that would change his life.

Robin Montgomery was a freshman at Bradley and just wanted to find some dinner. A volleyball player, she had come to Bradley from South Shore High School in Chicago and was still getting acclimated at the new school when she was grabbing a quick meal in Geisert Hall on that fateful fall night in late 1974.

"I had just left volleyball practice and was trying to get food before they closed and that was the closest cafeteria that I could still eat in," Robin said.

"I had never been to Geisert before. I was getting my food in line and this man comes up and stands next to me and he's just staring at me. And I just kind of looked at him and laughed because I have a really good sense of humor. I just ignored him, and as I moved my tray, he moved with me. He never said anything, he just kept staring. I got my food and I looked back and he's still staring right next to me and I walked to a table to sit down, and he and all his friends sat down with me. That's how I met Wayne."

An unusual approach to be sure, but it worked. No one ever accused Wayne McClain of being shy.

Despite being an excellent practice player, Wayne did not see the court much at Bradley. According to the Peoria *Journal-Star*, McClain played just one year of varsity ball for the Braves, in 1974–75. "We had a lot of hard workers on our team and none of 'em worked harder than Wayne," Bradley head coach Joe Stowell told the *Journal-Star*. "He got the best out of himself that he could. He was a self-made, hard-nosed guy."

McClain graduated from Bradley with a physical education degree and embarked on a career of teaching and coaching.

• • •

As a varsity assistant for nearly two decades under Dick Van Scyoc, McClain developed a reputation as a ferociously tough coach on the court. He grew up in the same environment many of his players did, fatherless on the south side of Peoria. At the bottom of the city's infamous hill, an unofficial dividing line between Peoria's haves and have-nots. McClain knew the kids needed discipline in their lives, and he was there every single day to provide it in abundance.

"It was torture," Derrick Booth said of practices with McClain. "He was not only assistant varsity coach, but he was the sophomore coach. And those practices sometimes would be like six or seven of us, just sophomores. I was thinking, 'There's only six or seven of us, we can't go up and down full court, it's going to be easy.' Man, he would 3-on-3 you to death. Full court, 3-on-3. Oh my god, he was torture."

Willie Coleman, who starred at Manual in the 1990s, recalls that when McClain walked into practice, the players knew what kind of mood he was in based on where he put his keys down. If he set his keys up atop a nearby ledge, they were in trouble. If he gently set the keys down on the table, practice was likely to be tolerable.

"School ended at 2:25 p.m. and at 2:15 your stomach started hurting," Coleman said. "You can get that from every player. Because we were like, 'Man, we've got practice.' And practice was hell. The first hour was brutal."

Chuck Westendorf was an assistant alongside McClain for all those years under Van Scyoc, and then later when McClain became head coach. He laughs now thinking about the unrelenting discipline his friend thrust on players.

"The bell rang at 2:25 p.m. and at 2:35 they were on that baseline with their shirts tucked in and their shoes on the line," Westendorf said. "They weren't out in the hall talking to their girlfriends. And if they were, they were going to run sprints. First thing we did. Get on that line! We may run for 5–10 minutes. Now the next time Michael (for example) is out there talking to his girlfriend, you may want to grab him by the neck and throw him in the gym. Because if not, we'll be doing this again, that's what Wayne would tell them. '(Impersonating McClain) Everyone understand me? You know I love you guys, but that's just how it's going to be.'"

McClain was a fierce competitor, but he saw the big picture, too. He was teaching kids from the rough part of town how to work hard and, hopefully, prepare them for life after high school. He knew the streets could be tough, and he witnessed many kids swallowed up by gangs, drugs, and crime. McClain took an equal interest in non-basketball players as well, doing everything he could to keep Peoria's young people on a path toward success.

After tormenting players with sprints and grueling drills for at least two hours, McClain would immediately flip the switch after practice and become a coach of life skills and a mentor for players who needed to talk about anything. The door was always open, and the demanding coach always had time.

Derrick Booth had two parents at home, so he was better off than most, but he still says McClain played an integral role in his young life.

"There were conversations I had with Coach McClain that I needed to have as a teenager going through puberty and all these things that I wasn't having at home," said Booth, who graduated in 1991. "Uncomfortable (to have at home) but I was having them with Coach McClain. It wasn't because I was initiating it, it was because he would just bring this stuff up. 'Guys, guys' and he would just start talking about it. And it was needed. It was like perfect timing. Those are the conversations young men needed to have in a responsible way that are not common or comfortable to have at home, even if you've got a father at home. That's what was special about him. But it was appropriate. It was real."

In 1994, Van Scyoc won his 810th game as a head coach, setting the all-time Illinois high school basketball record. A stunning amount of practices, drills, players, road trips, academic check-ins, and more. Van Scyoc finished his career with 826 career wins and 399 losses over a 44-year coaching tenure. The old ball coach clearly knew his stuff, but a strong staff helped him immensely along the way.

During the school day, Van Scyoc was not a traditional teacher. Instead he was a "job coach" for the district's vocational training and career exploration program, where he spent one period at Manual and the rest of the day helping students land job interviews, driving them to interviews and checking on them after they were hired.

"Van Scyoc had one class, he would leave the building and come back for basketball practice," said Westendorf, who married Coach Van's daughter, Gwen. "In between, McClain's putting out fires all day long. I walk in and Wayne says, 'My head is spinning. So and so didn't do this, so and so was running down the hallway.'"

Van Scyoc, who won 543 games at Manual following stints at Armington and Washington High Schools, was well respected by his players. He had a proven track record of winning and treated players fairly. In an era when kids respected their elders, Van Scyoc returned that respect, and his players knew he cared about them. Sure, he was old school and demanded effort, but that is what coaches do. There was an interesting dynamic at Manual, though. In the 1970s, '80s, and '90s, how did an older white man relate to young, urban Black players?

"He had McClain," said Coleman, who succeeded Derrick Booth in 2017 as Manual's head coach. "McClain was on the south end. Van could relate but it's good to have an assistant that grew up in that. When you coach for Manual, you try to get a coach who played for Manual and can relate to kids. Because there's so much going on with kids that (outsiders) don't understand. I grew up in a house where you saw white powder that you had to put down for roaches. I seen that. I seen where you have to move the closet door to the side because the door broke. And a lot of kids go through that stuff and if you ain't been there, you can't relate. McClain was able to do that. If you've been on the south end, you have to understand what these kids are going through. That's what it's about. And you're trying to help them get out of the

Wayne McClain, right, poses with his children Sergio and Brindeshie in the 1990s. Wayne was the consummate family man and his wife and kids were never far away from him. (Photo provided by McClain family)

situation—that's the main goal no matter how you do it. Get an education no matter how you do it."

"Coach McClain lived like four blocks away from my house," said Courtland Tubbs, a terrific three-sport athlete at Manual. "We could touch him. Coach Van stayed up on the hill, not that it was far, but it was up on the hill. It was less than a mile away but . . . we never saw him. But we saw Coach McClain because he stayed right in the same area."

"You had Van, who was in charge," Sergio McClain said. "But Dad ran everything. He was the one that could control all the kids. And they feared him and respected him. And what Van couldn't get them to do, Dad could. He would always make sure they respected Van."

As he neared his 70th birthday in the early 1990s, Van Scyoc began telling McClain that he was ready to retire. This went on for two or three years, but each time Van Scyoc decided to keep coaching. McClain had been lead assistant for several years and was basically being groomed as the next head coach.

"Finally, Wayne came to me and reluctantly said, 'I'm going to have to leave,'" said Sandy Farkash, Manual's principal at the time.

Farkash had a dilemma on his hands. Force out a legendary coach and there would be considerable backlash from the community. Conversely, let a budding coaching star who players adored walk away and the Rams program would be thrown into disarray. It was a brutal spot for an administrator, but Farkash was determined not to lose McClain.

Then in March 1994, in Van Scyoc's 28th year at Manual, the Rams finally won that elusive state championship, in surprising fashion at that, with senior Brandon Hughes and juniors Coleman and Ivan Watson leading the way. Still, Van Scyoc proceeded through the spring as if he'd be returning for the 1994–95 season.

"All of a sudden, Van retired on the last day of school," Farkash said. "I was going to have to deal with the situation that summer but then he retired."

With that, Wayne McClain was recommended to Peoria's Board of Education to be the next head coach at Peoria Manual. He had some big shoes to fill in a community that expected winning.

• • •

"Most people would see what I'm about
to tell you as bad. But it wasn't."
—Sergio McClain

Taking over a program that just won its first state boys' basketball championship in 64 years is serious pressure. When that program returns a bulk of its talent and is expecting to contend for state again, the pressure only ramps up further. And when your son is one of the team's star players, let's just say a man's shirt collar can start feeling awful tight around the neckline.

This was the backdrop in the winter of 1994–95 at Peoria Manual as Wayne McClain took over the big chair after 18 years as an assistant to Van Scyoc.

Bob Leavitt, who covered high school sports at the Peoria *Journal-Star* for 30 years, wrote this about the cauldron McClain stepped into.

"You hear it said there is no heavier burden than a great potential, and that's what comes to mind remembering Wayne as a head basketball coach. Manual was at the pinnacle of its basketball prowess when he took over for a state prep coaching legend. But that position then was not unlike what people said when UCLA's incomparable John Wooden retired: 'I don't want to be the coach who follows John Wooden; I want to be the coach who follows the

coach who tried to follow John Wooden.' Despite graduating its two top scor-
ers from the '94 state title team, expectations for a repeat were as enormous
as the odds against any school in a two-class system repeating as champion.
But Wayne never whined about the pressure or blinked in the face of it."

Rest assured, it wasn't easy. Early on that season, Wayne and Sergio were butting heads. Sergio had played significant minutes as a freshman on the state title team and returned full of youthful swagger.

"That first half of that season was kind of tough for me because we were fighting as far as what I thought I could do, and what he knew I couldn't do," Sergio said.

Before the school day started at Manual, Wayne taught an early bird P.E. class at 6 a.m., which he made Sergio attend each day to put him through a workout. On one particular day, Sergio was kind of slogging through his early morning workout. Making matters worse, he had played poorly in a tournament the previous weekend and made the mistake of complaining about his father to Robin and some friends. Naturally, word got back to Wayne that his boy was running his mouth a bit.

"He says, 'You're going around telling everybody this and that. Look at you, you can't even make a damn free throw,'" Sergio recalled. "I'm frustrated and he's saying this in front of all these kids. And I'm pissed and I'm not focused, and I miss another free throw. He's like, 'Miss another free throw and see what happens!' I took the ball, he's jogging and he jogs past me, and I just threw the ball at the rim."

With that, Wayne stopped in his tracks on the other side of Manual's gymnasium. He looked down, blew snot out of both nostrils onto the gym floor and started running diagonal across the court toward Sergio.

"And he got in front of me and popped me (makes punching motion with hand)," Sergio said. "In front of everybody. In the face. And I grabbed the ball and threw it at his face and hit him dead in the face, and he started chasing me."

In this frenzied moment, Sergio, a 16-year-old sophomore, hastily planned on running out of school to Robin's workplace, some four miles away. When he got near an exit door, Wayne hollered for him to stop.

"And when that man called my name, I swear his voice shook the corridor," Sergio said. "It felt like God himself had called me and stopped me dead in my tracks. I'm sitting there crying. And he's like, 'Get over here! Get in this office now!'"

Father and son ducked into Wayne's tiny office inside Manual. Sergio thought he was dead. But there would be no more yelling and certainly no more physical confrontations. Instead, with the pressures of basketball and a city's expectations reaching untenable levels, Wayne delivered a speech his son will never forget.

"If you don't want to play no more, I'm still gonna love you," Wayne told him. "I don't care about this. If you feel it's too much pressure being coached by me, I will step down and I don't have to coach. At the end of the day, you're my son and I'm not about to let this tear our relationship apart. I'm not about to let the outside world tear our relationship apart. So, if you don't feel like doing this, or you want me to step down and you want somebody else to coach you, I will get out of the way."

Merely a handful of games into his head coaching tenure, Wayne McClain was offering to hang up his whistle. After waiting a lifetime to finally be a head coach and have a program to call his own, he realized something else dwarfed the importance of a shiny new job title. It would have been a stunner in the basketball coaching world but, of course, it did not reach that point. Instead, the moment was a true turning point in the relationship of a father and son who would go on to reach incredible heights on the basketball court.

Robin McClain: "I remember that. That's the side that I fell in love with of Wayne when I first met him. He's a very caring, very genuine, very loving person. And he saw that basketball was causing some problems between he and his son. He saw that Sergio was feeling pressure. He had a decision right at that moment, and I remember we talked about it right after at home, he made a decision that my kid's happiness is more important to me than me winning basketball games or me coaching. If my coaching strategy with my son is going to hurt our relationship, I'm not going to coach. If he doesn't want to play, I'm not going to make him. Whatever he wants to do, I'll support him and won't be mad at him. That definitely happened. And I think that was a turning point for Sergio. I think he understood then that his dad was just trying to make him better and get him where he needed to be."

For his part, Manual big man Marcus Griffin says he remembers the incident as well.

"Everybody heard about it but nobody knew (exactly) what happened," Griffin said. "It was none of my business. It wasn't basketball, that was stuff they had to work on."

● ● ●

When you ask former players or colleagues about Wayne McClain, two responses are guaranteed: 1) smiles 2) impressions of his high-pitched voice shouting instructions or simply leveling with a kid.

"The community looked up to Wayne," Coleman said before stopping in his tracks. "Wow. That's the second time I've called him Wayne (today). I've never done that before."

Sergio McClain had to share his father. When your dad is a father figure to the whole neighborhood, that is the deal. Wayne and Robin McClain may have only had two children, but their family was massive. Dinners at the house, rides to games, holiday celebrations, take-out Italian feasts from Avanti's—nothing was off limits when the McClains took you in. There was always enough food, always an open-door policy in the small wood-frame house on 1919 West Marquette Street.

Bruce Wayne McClain was from the south end and knew what it was like to grow up without a father. That is why he vowed to always be there for Sergio and Brindeshie . . . and many others. From Peoria Manual to Bradley to teaching in the Peoria school system, McClain's heart was always in his hometown.

Coleman, who would later become a Division 1 player and eventually head coach at Manual, grew up just down the alley from the McClains on West Antoinette Street. Coleman recalls looking out his kitchen window on Saturday mornings and seeing Sergio in his backyard doing yard work, working out, or doing drills on the backyard rim. When the kids were about 9 or 10 years old, McClain took them to the Shirt Shack in town. While the kids waited outside, Wayne emerged from the store with a pair of long sleeve white shirts, one with blue sleeves and the other with red sleeves. He had pre-ordered the shirts, blue sleeves for Sergio because he was a Cubs fan and red sleeves for Willie because he rooted for the Cardinals. (Coleman says he liked the Cardinals because two of their best players, Willie McGee and Vince Coleman, formed his name, Willie Coleman.)

On the back, the kids' names were emblazoned on the crisp, new shirts.

It was one of countless examples of Wayne going out of his way to take care of kids.

"I would see him go and buy underwear and blue jeans and shoes and socks (for kids)," Sergio said. "Hygiene products . . . he'd be like, 'Man I saw so and so today, and he was musty. He had holes in his shirts.' He was very observant of the kids. He'd say, 'When I get my check Rob, or if you have some extra money Rob,' and he wouldn't just get a shirt. He would go buy the kid five sweatshirts. He would get them two packs of draws, two packs of socks, hygiene products that would last for two to three months."

With a style that was brutally hard on the court, but loving off it, McClain was able to thread a needle that few coaches can achieve. Because all his players knew how much he cared about them as people, it allowed him to exert intense discipline without kids scoffing or walking off the court and quitting. On the south end, you can't just be a basketball coach. You're a chauffeur, meal provider, counselor, father figure . . . and coach.

"You have to understand you've got a bunch of hard-nosed kids from the inner city," Griffin said. "You needed somebody that was not going to let somebody blow smoke up their asses. Not saying we were all bad kids, but we were all inner city. I don't think you can have a coach from Normal West coming down to coach those kids."

Striking that balance with teenagers is a gift. Go after them too hard on the court and fail to look them in the eye or show compassion off it, and you've lost them. Allow them too much leeway or don't hold them to high standards, and the respect factor has been lessened. McClain was an absolute savant at this.

"It's very innate," said Bruce Weber, who was a head coach at Kansas State, Illinois, and Southern Illinois, and worked with McClain at Illinois. "He'd be hard on them but make sure they had lunch on their table. Or make sure they had a new pair of Nikes, or Adidas or whatever it might be. He cared about them. You didn't have to be just a Manual player either, and that's what I learned as I got to be around Wayne and got to go back to Peoria and saw his interactions and (attended) different events. I saw him and Robin and how much they cared for that community."

McClain also helped coach the Illinois Warriors, the Adidas-sponsored AAU team Sergio and Marcus played for under head coach Larry Butler. In the summer between the players' junior and senior years, they attended the Adidas Big Time Tourney in Las Vegas, with a who's who of star prep basketball players from around the country. The players and coaches extended their trip, visiting some sites in California in addition to the Vegas tournament, where the six-foot-eight Griffin had a great week and was named Open Division MVP (the tourney's top tier) in a field that included future NBA players Tracy McGrady and Lamar Odom, along with future Michigan State star Charlie Bell. The Warriors defeated Bell's Michigan Mustangs squad for the Open Division tournament title.

"The stuff that he did for me, you can't ever thank a person enough," Griffin said of McClain. "I can remember going out to Vegas, my Mom did not have any money. We were out (West) for I think, 14 days, and I took $50. That's all I had. That's all the money my Mom could give me. I was calling her saying I need more money, but Coach McClain made sure I was good. Like he went out of his way to make sure that we were good. Serg said he shared his father with a bunch of kids for a lot of generations. Coach McClain was that person in a bunch of peoples' lives."

McClain and assistant coach Chuck Westendorf had an agreement for many years. On Saturdays, Westendorf got to the gym first and opened the doors for the players. McClain, a music lover whose Saturday morning ritual included listening to Teddy Pendergrass and Al Green, would stay after practice or open gym until the last kid showered, cleaned up, and left the building. Almost every time, each of the coaches picked kids up, dropped them off or both.

"It was like a family affair," Westendorf said.

Toughness was the embodiment of Manual basketball, and McClain was the perfect leader of Ram strength. If you played against Manual, you needed to be ready for tough-nosed, full-court grinding defense rarely seen in high school basketball. It might not be pretty offensively, but there was never a doubt about the Rams bringing defense and discipline for 32 minutes every game.

The grueling drills in practice and relentless approach from McClain was purposeful. He figured practices would often be tougher than games for his young men, and the Rams carried an intimidation factor with them when they ran out of the tunnel before a game, a confident group of athletes in orange and black.

"He would always say if he got in a fight in an alley with you, he would tell you that he would or wouldn't want you with him," Sergio said. "He would tell you either way. 'I wouldn't want you in an alley with me because you would run away. You're a coward.' Or he'd be like, 'I would want you in the alley because I know you would fight till the death.' That's the mentality he had. And that's the mentality we had. When we got on the court, he'd say, 'You guys are not playing for Van. You guys are not playing for me. You're playing for the pride of the south side of Peoria, because everyone looks down on y'all. Everybody spits on you guys. And people say Manual, it's like the garbage of the city.' And we carried that chip on our shoulders. He was like, 'You're playing for your families. And you're playing for an opportunity.' So whatever measures it took for us to get a W, we were taking those measures. We didn't let anybody intimidate us. We didn't let anybody come in and outwork us."

Respect was everything to McClain. He was an educated man who grew up during the Civil Rights era and expected to be shown the proper deference by people regardless of their skin color.

"He was the type of guy who was not scared of a White man in a time when we were told to be fearful of a White man," Sergio said. "If a White man talked crazy to him in public, he'd say, 'Who the hell you talking to?' He was always showing me to stand up for myself. 'I'm an educated man with a masters, you're not about to sit up here and talk to me like that in front of my kid, my family. Or even if they weren't here, you are not going to talk to me like this. You are going to respect me like I respect you.'"

McClain was highly regarded in his community. A well-known man who knew generations of families in Peoria, scores of people have stories about McClain coaching their kid, teaching their kid, or simply giving a warm smile and hello in public when they approached him to talk basketball. In 2001, an 18-year-old girl named Jamie Epstein was a freshman at Indiana University, less than a year removed from graduation at Peoria Richwoods. Epstein was driving to New York City for a spring break trip with friends when a car accident on Interstate 80 in Pennsylvania ended her life just as it was getting started. Jamie's father, Shelley, was an editor at the *Journal-Star* and her mother, Marianne, was a teacher at Trewyn School on the south side. The Epsteins didn't have a personal relationship with McClain, but the high-profile coach still reached out.

"He sent us a note which I thought was very nice," Shelley Epstein said. "I saw him once in the Steak 'n Shake and had a brief conversation, but he didn't have to do any of that. So, nothing to do with basketball, but I was very impressed with his humanity to do that."

• • •

Though basketball was his passion, McClain had numerous interests off the court as well. A big one was clothes. McClain loved clothes. Suits were meticulously picked out, and he had shoes for days. For years, McClain, Bobby Humbles, and Dana Davis, another close friend, would go shopping together in Peoria.

"I used to tease Wayne and Dana that they shopped like women," Humbles said. "They loved it. Wayne was known for dressing. He was known for his suits. He was known for his shoes. He liked to dress, and he liked to shop."

It continued when McClain was hired by rising star coach Bill Self at Illinois in April 2001, where now he would be on national television 30-plus times a year. Weber, who kept McClain on the Illini staff when he replaced Self two years later, laughs thinking about it.

"Every game, it was his thing," Weber said. "He loved clothes and he loved shoes. I didn't use my locker much (at Illinois) and he literally used my locker (to store) shoes in there. It was unbelievable. He did so much for everyone else and very rarely spent on himself, but when it came to clothes, that dude . . . he loved it, he wanted to be stylish, shoes, shirts."

Weber was, ahem, not known for his stylish attire when he arrived at Illinois. A classic nose-to-the-ground Midwestern coach who had spent more than two decades in West Lafayette, Indiana, and Carbondale, Illinois, he was much more concerned with the intricacies of practice or an opponent's out-of-bounds plays than with fashion. Luckily, he had a trusty assistant to help him out.

"When I got to Illinois, I had JCPenney sport coats, I didn't have anything and the media was killing me," Weber said. "Wayne would joke with me that he would help me get some style. All of a sudden, I would find some shirts on my desk, and he would say I got a couple shirts for you that you might like."

• • •

In the spring of 2002, the head coaching job at Bradley University became open when Coach Jim Molinari was fired. McClain had just finished his first season as an assistant at Illinois, following a wildly successful seven-year run at Manual that included three state titles in his first three years.

McClain, 48 at the time, was extremely interested in the opportunity to coach his alma mater. In an April 3, 2002 article that ran in the Champaign *News-Gazette*, McClain was said to be one of four candidates interviewing for the Bradley job along with Michigan State assistant Brian Gregory, Yale head coach James Jones and Jim Les, a former Bradley and NBA player who was an assistant for the WNBA's Sacramento Monarchs. In the article, then-Illinois coach Bill Self said McClain is a "hand-in-glove" fit for the Bradley job.

Meanwhile, as the job search neared its conclusion, Deshe McClain decided to snoop around the online message boards to see what fans were saying about her father's candidacy. Bad idea.

"There was so much stuff being talked about my dad, about Manual, about Sergio, about Frank (Williams) . . . you know people don't care if they're right, they just want to say something," Deshe said. "And anonymously. I ended up getting on there and making an account using my full name. I started just jumping on people saying, 'That is incorrect information!' I was just jumping on people."

Deshe called home to vent with her mother about it; Robin put her on speakerphone with Wayne in the room.

"He would start laughing," Deshe said. "Finally, he said, 'Deshe, stay off the message boards. Those people don't have anything better to do. Don't worry about what they're saying. I'm good. I'm an adult, I can protect myself. That's not your job, I'm supposed to protect you.'"

Alas, the job went to Les, despite a coaching resume that featured only two years as a part-time assistant in the WNBA and one year as a player-coach in the now-defunct Continental Basketball Association.

"(Wayne) was really, really excited about the chance to be head coach at Bradley University, his alma mater," Robin said. "And after those (high school) championships, he felt that he had a very good chance of getting that job. I mean, we were banking on it. We were looking at houses. He was very excited about the possibility of having his own program in college. And he often said to me, 'It doesn't matter what university you're coaching at. Any university has the opportunity to make it to the NCAA (Tournament).' He wasn't worried or concerned about the fact that Bradley was a small D-1. He just wanted the opportunity to coach and to lead and to get some players to the tourney. He was highly disappointed."

Weber added: "I think that was his dream and goal. Obviously, I was sad for him because I know that was something he wanted. Life works in a lot of different ways and you feel bad. But he loved Peoria, it was everything to him."

• • •

Though he missed out on the head job at Bradley, McClain was part of some magical years with the Illini. Hired by Self in 2001, he was retained by Weber two seasons later when Self left Illinois for Kansas.

"(Former Illinois athletic director) Ron Guenther asked me if I would consider keeping Wayne," Weber said. "Everywhere I've gone I have tried to keep one of the (former staff) guys because I think it's good for the transition. Obviously, I knew Wayne. Just doing our homework, you felt like he had a good connection with the Illinois high school coaches with him there for recruiting. And he jumped right in. He had a great relationship with the players, and that was one of the reasons I kept him on our staff. He had a great knack of being able to get after them, but laugh with them after practice, and hug them and goof around. I think that's what made him special."

To outsiders, McClain always appeared stoic on the bench. Whether his team was on the verge of a Final Four or in a skirmish on the court, he kept a steady demeanor and rarely showed emotion. But Weber says he was plenty playful behind the scenes.

"He loved to play pranks, oh especially if you couldn't deal with it," Weber said. "He would always get the other assistants or players and trick them. He loved to wrestle, and he would wrestle the players and I literally would be scared. This was real stuff. I was with (Purdue) Coach (Gene) Keady all those years and he could cuss them out, yell at them, make them run but then he'd laugh with them after and Wayne had that same ability."

Even when he wasn't necessarily going for a laugh, McClain had the ability to be hilarious. During his time at Illinois, McClain grew close with Weber's family, including his three daughters. Once during a high school prospect's recruiting visit, the Illini staff gathered at Weber's home to spend time with the recruit and his family. As the visit was concluding, a young man arrived to pick up Weber's youngest daughter, Emily, for a homecoming dance. If the teenage boy wasn't already terrified enough about taking out the daughter of a high-profile Big Ten coach, now he had to deal with McClain, too.

"Wayne went to the car and said, 'I'm Wayne McClain, who are you?'" Weber remembered. "And he started interviewing the guy. The kid had a little bit of a loud muffler and you could hear it coming down the street. And Wayne goes, 'I don't approve of this car. Is this a safe car?' And we're just sitting there laughing our heads off. His face didn't change, there was no laughter and he was just scaring the heck out of this kid. We couldn't stop laughing, and we told our daughter the next day that that kid might never come to our house again."

In 2004–05, McClain was on the bench as the Illini spent nearly the entire season ranked No. 1 in the country and were less than two minutes away from a national championship. Illinois finished 37–2 on the year with two losses

Basketball provided the McClain family with some special experiences, including this occasion with all-time great Earvin "Magic" Johnson. Johnson is flanked by Sergio McClain, and Marcus Griffin, back left, when the two high schoolers were selected to play in Magic's Roundball Classic in 1997, a high school All-Star Game in Michigan. Also pictured from left to right are Wayne McClain, Deshe McClain, Robin McClain, and LaEisha Meaderds. (Photo provided by McClain family)

by a combined six points, including a 75–70 setback to North Carolina in the NCAA Final in St. Louis. Led by star guards Dee Brown, Deron Williams, and Luther Head, it was an Illini team that will be forever revered.

Part of McClain's duties as an Illinois assistant was doling out punishment if a player missed class. Players loved McClain, but this was one instance where they sincerely wanted no part of him.

"In college, you're going to miss a day of school, you're going to miss a class here and there," said Brown, who was a first-team All-American as a junior and graced the cover of *Sports Illustrated*. "Every college student does. We had a really good attendance rate and really attended all our classes and did what we were supposed to do off the court, because dudes didn't want to see Coach McClain at five in the morning. You just didn't want to see him. It would ruin your week."

Brown learned his lesson as a sophomore prior to the basketball season. It was a mistake he was sure not to make twice.

"I missed class one time and I had to go see him," Brown said. "When I got there, he was already in a sweat and he just started dancing. He was like, 'Yeeaah, I got you.' I was like this is going to be my last time seeing this dude. That 45 minutes was one of the worst . . . the stuff that he had you doing, it would blow your mind. Running, the wall sits, he'd just get real creative trying to break you. And the whole time, he's just talking to you and you're getting something out of it but it's a punishment. Life lessons. I can't make it up . . . when you go through that you don't want to see him again. And if you do, you'll want to go to his office and talk to him. You don't want to catch him in that environment because he's going to really try to break you and give you a life lesson. I was like, I don't know what I got myself into."

Despite working in a profession that required quite a bit of travel, McClain hated flying. When he first teamed up with Weber at Illinois, McClain told his new boss about his distaste for airplanes. Umm, bad news, Wayne. We have an upcoming summer trip scheduled for Sweden, Finland, and Estonia, Weber told him. Oh, and there's also an overnight cruise sprinkled in.

"He said, 'I don't do water and I don't do boats,'" Weber said. "I said well you've got to come on the trip. He just sat there and he was miserable."

It wasn't the first time McClain made his aversion to water known. Two decades earlier, McClain was a P.E. teacher and coach at Manual when he got to know a student named Greg Stewart. In addition to coaching lower levels of basketball and assisting on varsity, McClain was the freshman baseball coach. In the fall of 1983, Stewart was on the freshman baseball team and later, he had McClain as a P.E. teacher. Manual had a swimming pool in the building and part of each semester's gym class rotation included several weeks in the pool. McClain dreaded this but he knew where to turn. Stewart grew up with a pool in his backyard and was also a lifeguard at the local park district.

"I don't know if he couldn't swim or what his deal was, but Wayne hated the pool," said Stewart, who later became a Peoria *Journal-Star* sportswriter for 15 years. "He did not like going into the pool at Manual. It was hot, humid, and chlorinated. But every year I was in his P.E. class . . . and whenever we had swimming for that four weeks or six weeks, he wouldn't go in the pool. He would always just give me the clipboard and say, 'Stewart, don't let anyone drown in my class today.' And I basically ran the swimming program for him and he would go to his office or the gym or whatever. For three years (all except freshman year), I basically ran his swimming classes while he went and did who knows what."

• • •

On March 9, 2012, a day after Illinois lost to Iowa in the opening round of the Big Ten Tournament, the entire Illini coaching staff was fired by new athletic director Mike Thomas. A hired gun of sorts, Thomas assumed the AD job in November 2011 and proceeded to fire football coach Ron Zook and basketball coach Bruce Weber in his first four months on the job. According to Deshe McClain, Thomas called the basketball staff to his office and "all he said to them was thank you for coming, we're going to let you go, thank you for everything you've done. And shook their hands and walked out."

Deshe was at her job as an alternative high school teacher at Novak Academy in Champaign when the big news hit the Internet and local TV channels. She left Novak at lunchtime, drove her black Toyota Camry to the Illinois basketball offices and raced upstairs to see her father.

"He was just sitting in the office, packing his stuff up," Deshe said. "I saw him and I immediately started crying. My dad looked at me and said, 'Deshe, it's OK. It's OK. We're going to be fine. This is just a job, it happens all the time, I will find something else. You don't need to stress.' It was just typical of who he was. I was supposed to be there to comfort him, and he ends up comforting me and he was the one who got let go."

Twenty-three days later, Weber was introduced as the new head coach at Kansas State University in Manhattan, Kansas. Later that year, just prior to the 2012–13 basketball season, Weber and McClain were reunited when McClain was hired as Kansas State's director of student-athlete development. It was a different role for the veteran coach, but Weber wanted to add experience to the young staff he had assembled.

Weber said he was surprised McClain accepted the new job.

"He was heartbroken, we all were heartbroken with what happened (getting fired)," Weber said. "But I didn't think he'd leave (the state of) Illinois. He was there his whole life. I think because he was so heartbroken, he was just crushed for me, for him, for everyone, I think he wanted to go and have a good taste."

Mission accomplished. The Wildcats went 27–8, including tying for a share of the Big 12 championship with a 14–4 record. It was Kansas State's first conference title since 1977.

"Even though his role was different . . . he was a very important part of it," Weber said.

But after just one season in the Little Apple, McClain resigned and moved back to central Illinois. He accepted a job as head coach at Champaign Central High School, a move that surprised people at the time but some say makes sense in hindsight. After 10 years at the high major college level, McClain was back to his high school roots.

Now back in the area, McClain went to see Manual play in the Thanksgiving week Tournament of Champions at Washington, a town just east of Peoria. Coleman, then a Manual assistant, thought something didn't look right with his old coach.

"He walked down the stairs and Robin was holding him and he just didn't look like McClain to me," Coleman recalled.

Shortly thereafter, Coleman was out shopping at Walmart in Peoria. Then, out of nowhere, McClain turned around an aisle and surprised him saying, "Gotcha! Gotcha!" It was a funny moment but Coleman was again troubled by McClain's appearance. His hair was grayed, he had gained weight, and something seemed off with the proud man he had known his whole life. McClain told him the family was having a BBQ at Martin Luther King Park on the south end that weekend and he should join them.

"That's when I called Howard (Nathan) and (former Manual player) Ivan (Watson) and said, 'Y'all need to come over here and see McClain.' I could tell something wasn't right. To me, I knew he was sick."

Later, Coleman decided to visit the McClains in Champaign, and he spent the night at their house. He wanted to be around the man who had meant so much to him, both as a kid and young adult. At one point, Coleman asked McClain why he quit college coaching.

"And he covered up good, 'You know what, Willie. We're on the fucking plane, it was raining and I was like, God doesn't want us up there, why do we have to go up there?' He made it seem like flying and all that. But I think he knew . . . just to get closer (to family)," Coleman said.

It was the spring of 2014, and McClain clearly was not feeling well. He told Robin he had another lung infection, an ailment he'd endured twice before. The first was in 1994, shortly after his mother, Ruff, passed away at 72. The second occurred when McClain was coaching at Illinois, and each time he was prescribed heavy doses of Prednisone, a steroid used for many conditions, including breathing problems.

Several members of Peoria's basketball royalty gathered at a barbeque at Martin Luther King Park in the summer of 2014. Robin McClain, Ivan Watson, Sergio McClain, Wayne McClain, and Willie Coleman stand behind Howard Nathan. Wayne McClain passed away shortly after this photo was taken. (Photo provided by Willie Coleman)

"When he had lung infections he was back and forth to the doctor's office every week or so getting treatments," Robin said. "Breathing treatments. And he had problems breathing (this time); it was the same situation that he had with the lung infection. So that is what I felt was wrong with him. And even with his two other lung infections, it took a while but he got better. And he continued to work out then, he continued to work out with this. He was still running, still mowing the lawn. Wayne was still washing walls. This is a guy who liked to be moving all the time. I knew he was ill, but I thought it was a lung infection."

The breathing became so labored that Wayne had Robin drop him off at Urbana's Carle Hospital, saying he was going to see his doctor. Per usual, he told Robin not to stay and that she should go to work and pick him up at lunchtime. When she returned, there was no Wayne. She waited and waited, calling his cell phone several times but he wasn't picking up. After more than an hour nervously waiting in the parking lot, he called back.

"Rob, I'm in the emergency room," he said.

When Robin got to the ER, Wayne was coughing repeatedly and doctors said they wanted to perform X-rays to see what was going on. Wayne was asked to cough up some mucus so it could be tested, and when he did it came out dark. Pneumonia, Robin thought. After the fluid was tested, doctors confirmed it was indeed pneumonia and they wanted Wayne to stay in the hospital overnight. Robin called Sergio, who was working alongside his dad as an assistant at Champaign Central, and told him to come to the hospital. Wayne told Robin to head home and shower, check on her job, and then she could return later to relieve Sergio.

Sergio McClain was asleep in his father's hospital room with the covers pulled over his head. When he awoke, he heard a doctor telling Wayne, "The cancer is growing and it's uncontrollable now. And you only have 48 hours." One minute Sergio thought his pops had pneumonia, the next he was hearing that this powerful man, his best friend, had two days to live.

"What did you just say?" Sergio remembers asking the doctor.

"And the doctor says, 'Who are you?' I'm like I'm his son. What did you just say? Then my dad was like, 'Doc, I haven't told him anything yet. He doesn't know.' And I said don't worry about him, he can't do nothing to you, because he was kind of intimidating the doctor. I said what's going on (to the doctor)? So, the doctor takes me out of the room and says, 'Your dad has cancer, he got diagnosed with terminal lung cancer three or four years ago.' And this man has been going through chemo, everything by himself, not telling nobody nothing."

There are moments in life when it feels like the world has come to a screeching halt. When all the noise around you goes silent and everything is a blur. Wayne McClain is on his deathbed? This brick wall of a man who never showed weakness, who raised hundreds of kids on Peoria's south side was on his way out? Now?

"It knocked me off my feet," Robin said.

And how's this for a cruel twist? A man who never smoked was stricken with lung cancer. Heck, he didn't even drink and rarely ate red meat. What he did do was run five miles a day, every day, and lived as clean as possible.

Word spread quickly in Peoria's basketball community of McClain's dire state. Phone calls and texts rapidly flew across the country as players and coaches informed one another that their beloved leader was in trouble. Derrick Booth, who played on the 1991 Class AA state runner-up team and was Manual's current head coach, was in St. Louis for a getaway weekend with his wife when he found out. Booth immediately left the Lumiére Place Casino & Hotel and zoomed the 180 miles on highways I-55 and I-72 to Carle Hospital in his 2009 blue Cadillac DTS, calling Howard Nathan on the way. The two close friends arrived in Urbana at the same time to see their former coach.

McClain was already in a coma when Booth and Nathan crammed into the room with other loved ones.

"I remember all of us sitting in Coach McClain's room, and Howard was talking to Coach McClain, 'Come on coach, just like you used to tell me,'" Booth said. "Howard was saying stuff like that to him. I remember Coach McClain was in a coma, and Howard was talking to him and talking to him and talking to him and Coach McClain's body just like jumped like he was trying to fight out of that coma. But Howard was like, 'Coach McClain, you can't go! Come on you can do this.' It was very passionate. Howard was talking to him right on his bedside holding his hands. It was almost like Coach McClain gave a fight, like his body just jumped."

Griffin, a star on Manual's four-peat title teams under McClain, was working at Star Transport, a large trucking company in nearby Morton. Griffin was at work when his cell phone buzzed. It was a friend of Sergio's whom he knew, but she was cryptic, only saying you need to get to Champaign and see Sergio. Griffin pressed but that's all the mutual friend would reveal. After several unanswered attempts to reach Sergio, Griffin phoned Deshe McClain.

"Yeah Marcus, you should come," Deshe said.

Not knowing what he was driving into, Griffin left work and got behind the wheel of his pearl white Cadillac DeVille for the 80-mile trip to Carle. He says he remained positive and didn't let his mind travel to bad places as he stared blankly at the windshield ahead.

"I walked into that room and saw . . . (heavy sigh) yeah," Griffin said. "I didn't know anything. I didn't even ask. What's wrong, that's all I wanted to know? How can we get him back right? Then you start to hear that he had all this other stuff going on. As soon as they told me lung cancer, I'm not stupid, I'm intellectual, now it all made sense, everything that led up to that."

Leaving Kansas State after one year. Gaining weight (Prednisone). Having darker skin (chemo). Those close to him even said McClain had been more emotional in recent months.

When he looks back and thinks about it, Sergio saw signs too. Father and son would be at the gym and after 15 minutes Wayne would say, 'Come on, Serg. I gotta go. There's too much dust up in here.' Or when Sergio noticed bald spots on his dad's head and thought, *Why is this fool cutting his own hair?* The truth was that Wayne was intentionally messing up his hair with clippers to cover up the hair loss from chemo.

But why keep it all to yourself? Why fight a brutal cancer battle alone when you are loved by so many? For those who knew Coach McClain, and his circle was vast, everyone says they are unsurprised he chose to wage this war on his own. The main reason: he didn't want others to worry about him.

There was McClain precedent for this, too. Ruff went out the same way, not telling anyone she was ill before passing away in 1994.

"He's the type of person who doesn't want you feeling sorry for him," said David Booth, a former Manual great and now NBA executive. "If you aren't feeling sorry for him, he's happy. When he was at Kansas State he would have the ball boys take him to chemotherapy but Weber never knew that."

"I was more sad for my dad," Deshe said. "He protected us all the way to the end and that was just who he was. I was sad that he carried that on his own and we were oblivious to it. At the same time, I understand it because that was who he was. He never wanted us to worry. He had gotten sick at one point with the lung infection and they had him on Prednisone, and it made him gain weight which he absolutely hated, and he would be coughing. When that happened I was like, 'Daddy, you ok? Daddy, you ok?' And he was like, 'I'm fine, stop worrying.' He knew that had we been in the loop, all of us would have been nervous nellies, driving him nuts, wanting to rush him to the hospital at every second, crying nonstop."

"People were saying to me, 'Oh my god, aren't you upset that he didn't tell you everything?'" said Robin McClain, Wayne's partner for four decades. "No, I was not. Because I knew this man and that's the man he was. He never, ever, ever wanted any of us to suffer. He was the best husband ever. He never wanted us to worry or anything like that. And Wayne took that disease and he handled it on his own and that's how he handled life. He was a strong leader. That was his choice and I knew his reasons were the right reasons based on how he felt about his family. No, I was not angry with him. I showed him love until the end."

"I got a call from Robin," Weber said. "I still remember it was a Sunday morning and I was getting ready for church and she said, 'Wayne's not going to make it.' And it just totally shocked me and you wish you could say goodbye. But Wayne went out the way he wanted to go out. That was him. It was not about him."

After several days in the hospital, McClain took his final breath with his family holding his hands, on October 15, 2014. In the aftermath, the McClains learned that Wayne had been keeping a daily diary on his iPhone. The proud man may not have wanted to discuss his illness with loved ones, but they knew he never stopped thinking about them.

"It was a good thing to see it because it showed why he wasn't telling us," Robin said. "He didn't talk once about, 'I have cancer and I'm dying.' That was never in any of his posts. His day to day was a prayer, 'God, please take care of my wife. She's this, she's that. Please make sure my kids have this or that. I love my family so much.' That's the kind of stuff he was writing every single day. He was thanking God for the gifts he had given him during his life. He was thanking God for allowing him to touch lives, that's what he wrote about."

Unless someone is a heavy smoker who comes down with lung cancer or an extremely overweight person contracts heart disease, to name two examples, it can be impossible to know how one becomes stricken with disease. A nonsmoker in terrific physical condition such as McClain getting lung cancer is an example of life's cruel mysteries.

But McClain's lifelong friend Bobby Humbles has a theory. Back when McClain and Humbles were teammates at Bradley in the 1970s, Braves coaches would line up jobs for the players during the summers. It was all legal work for local businesses. Some paid well, some didn't. One such job McClain and others had was working for the Peoria school district.

"I remember those guys were working in the school district cleaning out asbestos," Humbles said. "Back then we didn't know (the dangers of asbestos). I was a meter reader, which was a gravy job. We had different jobs over the years, but I remember one summer Wayne and some of the other guys, that's what they did."

Wayne McClain was dead at 60, leaving the many tentacles of his terrific basketball life saddened and shocked. More than 1,000 people attended the funeral in Champaign, including Self, Weber, and scores of former college and high school players.

Back in 2009, Jerrance Howard, who graduated from Peoria Central and whom McClain vouched for keeping on the Illinois roster when Howard was playing sparingly, summed it up well. Howard had become a highly successful college assistant coach, working his way up from young assistant at Illinois to longtime sidekick of Self's at Kansas.

"He's a reason why I have been successful," Howard told the Peoria *Journal-Star*. "I wouldn't have graduated if it hadn't been for him. He raised the whole south side of Peoria."

Fast forward to the fall of 2019. It has been five years since McClain passed away. Robin and Deshe live together in the family home in Champaign with Deshe's two children, daughter Brindisi and son Qofee Wayne. Deshe was five months pregnant with her daughter when her father died. Wayne went to the ultrasound when they found out Deshe would be having a girl; it pains her deeply that her father didn't get to meet her children. Sergio lives in St. Louis with his wife and son, Sergio Jr. The family has gathered on a lovely Midwestern Sunday at a church in Champaign to raise money for the Wayne McClain Pipeline Foundation, developed by the McClains to provide leadership training, mentoring, tutorial services, and scholarships to young people in central Illinois.

Delicious plates of homecooked chicken, vegetables, macaroni and cheese, peach cobbler, and more were served for $15 a plate with the money going to the foundation. After a long day of working in the kitchen and running around making sure everything was running smoothly, Sergio McClain, wearing an apron proudly featuring his dad's name, reflected on the life they shared.

"We built a big house, we all have our own wings (in Champaign)," Sergio said. "We had a big enough house that had enough space, and we would wake up in the morning even if we had our significant other with us or kid or whatever, the house is big enough for all of us. We would see each other; we would come back to each other. My dad would always say, ever since he got to Illinois, 'Man, this is the best life ever. I get to wake up every day and be around the people I love. That's better than any money, that's better than anything. This is awesome to me.'"

"I don't have any regrets because we spent every day together. We talked every day. There wasn't a day we didn't have a conversation. There wasn't a day if he wasn't on the road that we didn't see each other. I don't have any regrets."

4

Legends, Titles, and the University of Illinois Pipeline

Marcus Griffin's mother did not care if he played basketball, but she made damn sure Marcus and his brothers were well-behaved.

Sergio McClain's father trained him to be a great athlete with the relentlessness of an Army sergeant from an early age, and Sergio relished the challenges, never backing down.

Frank Williams's mother worked multiple jobs to provide for her 10 children as a single parent and was the backbone of a family that adored her.

Three African American families who lived blocks from each other on Peoria's south side. Three players who will go down in the history books of Illinois high school basketball. Their individual tales are different, but the three friends' legacies will always be intertwined.

Before they were the most famous faces in a generation of Peorians and before they sold out gyms in central Illinois and beyond, they were just three kids from the south side. The trio played substantive roles in four consecutive state championships for Manual, a feat that had never been accomplished in state history.

Gentle Giant

Many young men growing up on the south side of Peoria, particularly in the 1980s and 1990s, dreamed of playing basketball for the Manual Rams and wearing the orange and black. Marcus Griffin was not one of those kids. Raised with an iron fist, as he puts it, by his mother, Ollie Bobo-Jones, Griffin was one of 11 children in a blended family. Griffin didn't have much of a relationship with his father and for most of his childhood, he grew up with Bobo-Jones and two younger brothers, Herbert and Roderick.

Living in the Harrison Homes public housing project, and then on the projects' outskirts, the family was poor, but the young men didn't know any different. There was government cheese, powdered milk that gets water added to it and peanut butter with a layer of oil on top from food pantries. They knew not to ask for anything except clothes for Christmas. Eating at restaurants? Not so much.

"There would be times where we didn't have food in the house and someone would bring us food," Griffin said. "There would be times that Mom wouldn't eat anything because the kids were eating all the food. She gave up everything for her kids to be fine. There ain't no food in the house but you're eating, and you look over there at Mom and she's over there smiling because we're eating. So, she gave up everything for her kids to be fine. Everything was about sacrificing . . . but that was the norm. We did not know anything was wrong. When you get older you realized she sacrificed *a lot* for us."

While much of the south side was hoops-obsessed, Griffin was absent from that sports culture, despite being quite tall. He did not grow up following Manual, or even knowing who its latest stars were. Griffin played a little bit during his grade school years, but not necessarily by choice.

"I was forced to play basketball," he said. "I lived in a very bad neighborhood, and my Mom wanted us to do stuff to stay out of trouble. So, I played basketball. I was thinking at that stage that was the only time I was ever going to play basketball. I didn't have any ambitions of playing basketball outside of that. It was just me playing, and then hopefully my Mom was gonna say 'OK, you did it. Leave it alone and go do something else.' Ehhh . . . it didn't work out like that."

Bobo-Jones was working hard to provide a better life for herself and her kids. She worked at Caterpillar, the city's construction machining behemoth, and went to school at night thanks to the company providing tuition reimbursement. During this period, Bobo-Jones married a coworker from Cat, allowing the family to move to central Peoria, a significant step up from the south end. That relationship later fizzled, so Bobo-Jones and the three kids moved back down the hill. Raising three young men mostly on her own, Bobo-Jones was a disciplinarian.

"If we weren't home when the streetlights came on (at night), she would track us down," Griffin said. "And wherever she found us, we got our butts whooped. In that time, you did whatever you had to do to check your kids. My Mom did not care. She was like, 'I'm raising three boys and I do not want

In a town of guards, the six-foot-eight Marcus Griffin was a rare star post player. Here Griffin goes up toward the basket against New Trier in the 1996 Class AA semifinals in Peoria. (Photo courtesy of IHSA)

them to be a menace to society.' I remember her saying that for so long . . . 'My boys will not be a menace to society *ever*.'"

Chuck Westendorf, a longtime Manual assistant coach, taught P.E. at Trewyn School, where Griffin attended grade school. Although Griffin makes fun of himself as being uncoordinated as a young player, Westendorf says he saw potential in the tall boy.

"When he was young in grade school, he looked like a player," Westendorf said. "He's in fifth and sixth grades and he was long, he could run the floor. In seventh grade he got better. I was thinking, 'Marcus is going to be the real deal.' He liked to play, could run the floor really well, could block shots."

In addition to Griffin's skills, Westendorf saw the personality traits in a young man that would continue to define him off the court for years to come.

"He was like a teddy bear in a big body," he said. "Just the nicest kid."

As a six-foot-six freshman at a school with precious few tall athletes, Griffin made the varsity team right away. He joined a talented group that included senior Brandon Hughes, juniors Willie Coleman and Ivan Watson, and fellow freshman Sergio McClain. Proving just how unattached he was to the passionate south side basketball community, Griffin grew up mere blocks away from McClain but didn't know his highly regarded classmate until they began high school together. And seemingly everyone in town knew about the young McClain kid.

Coach's Son

If Marcus Griffin was a relative outsider to Peoria Manual basketball when he entered high school, Sergio McClain had been on the inside of the Rams program his entire life. His father, Wayne, was a standout player at Manual in the early 1970s, and after graduating from Bradley, he rejoined the Rams program as an assistant to head coach Dick Van Scyoc. Sergio was born in 1978, and it wasn't long before he began tagging along with his pops to Manual practices, games, and open gyms.

From the beginning, Sergio was trained to be a tough young man and a hard-working athlete. Sergio says he was about six years old the first time he remembers his father taking him on a jog, which was part of Wayne's daily routine.

"I probably jogged like a mile and I think halfway through the jog, I had to use the bathroom," Sergio said. "I wasn't used to running like that . . . I had to use the bathroom and I was crying. He was like, 'Don't stop!' I said I have to go to the bathroom. And he says, 'What do you have to do, number 1 or 2?' I was like I gotta do 2. He said, 'Do a 2 and keep running.' So, I'm over there crapping myself because he told me not to stop. Drawers full of crap when we get back to the house, and I'm crying. I came out and he just looked at me and was like, 'Good job. Even through the issues that you had, you didn't quit. And that's what McClain men are.'"

The intense discipline was not reserved solely for athletics. Wayne was unwavering in his expectation that his son looked good, treated others with respect, and never slacked off. Part of that was having his shoes tied, his shirt tucked in and keeping his face clean, even if he had a runny nose. In about the fourth grade, Sergio was at Roosevelt Magnet School, and he wasn't adhering to one of his father's rules.

"Sergio was running around school one day with his shoes untied, tripping over his shoestrings and somebody called Wayne and he went up to the school and caught Sergio in the hallway with his shoestrings untied," Robin McClain, Sergio's mother, said with a laugh. "That's the firmness that his dad had. As a mother, I wanted my son to be strong and I wanted him to do the right thing. But I was the one that would grab him and hug him and say, 'Your dad loves you, he just wants you to do right.' There was no abuse in our household. We tag-teamed. He was firm, and I would give Serg his hugs and kisses and tell him how wonderful he was and how proud I was and you're doing a great job. It was a balance."

"It was that mentality of a village raises a child," Sergio says. "Anything I did, before I would get home the phone would already be ringing at my grandma's house or our house, 'I saw your son doing this.' There was no room for error."

In truth, Sergio had been coached by his father all his life. Not necessarily as his formal basketball coach, but as a 24/7 life coach. And now as he entered Manual, his father would be on the sidelines coaching him in a public setting. That was probably the only difference.

"Well, Wayne was really tough," said Westendorf, the Manual assistant. "And probably tougher on Sergio than anybody. But every kid you talked to, they loved Wayne. Wayne was hard on Sergio and he pushed him to the limit. And I think he got every ounce of talent he had, whatever that was, out of Sergio."

Sergio began his high school career with a reputation that preceded him. In basketball-crazy Peoria, it was well-known that the new McClain kid was a ballplayer. Nobody could have foreseen the heights the next four years brought, but Sergio carried expectations with him on those burly shoulders. In the 1993–94 season, Sergio made the varsity squad but didn't start right away, he says, because Wayne didn't want the community thinking his freshman son was getting preferential treatment. The Rams were solid, per usual, but they weren't expected to be a state title contender after going 23–6 the previous season and losing star forward Jerry Hester, who was now a freshman at Illinois.

On January 22, 1994, the 69-year-old Van Scyoc passed Centralia's Arthur Trout as the state's all-time winningest coach when he picked up his 810th victory, a 74–61 triumph over East St. Louis Lincoln in front of 2,000 fans at the Collinsville Shootout. *My players are great, my coaches great, my fans great,* Van Scyoc told the *Journal-Star* afterward. *Tonight was more than I ever expected.*

At this point, 45 years into a legendary high school coaching career, Coach Van was still without a state championship. There were several close calls, notably a second-place finish in Howard Nathan's senior year, 1991, and a pair of third-place medals in 1986 and 1988 with David Booth and Lynn Collins. Coach Van maintained that the lack of a title did not keep him up at night, but any competitor strives for that feeling of finishing on top.

With wins over Danville in the super-sectional, Chicago Westinghouse in the quarterfinal and Rockford Boylan in the semifinal, Manual was one victory away from its first state title since 1930. A talented Carbondale team, led by outstanding seniors Rashad Tucker and Troy Hudson, was Manual's last hurdle. Led by a trio of super guards—electric senior Brandon Hughes and juniors Willie Coleman and Ivan Watson—Manual held the ball, trailing by one point with less than 10 seconds remaining. Hughes, a first-team All-Stater who later played at Michigan, drove near the right corner and was fouled with 4.2 seconds left. The referees were set to have Manual inbound the ball near its bench when longtime Rams scorekeeper James Watson jumped out of his seat near Van Scyoc to tell the officials that Manual was now in the bonus and Hughes should be at the free-throw line for a 1-and-1. He was correct.

In front of 9,845 fans at Champaign's Assembly Hall, Hughes calmly sank both free throws, and when Carbondale missed a shot on the other end, that was it.

Manual 61, Carbondale 60.

Manual's bench erupts as the final buzzer sounds on its Class AA state title in 1994, the first of four straight state crowns. The 61–60 win over Carbondale was a thriller and ended up being the last game coached by legendary Dick Van Scyoc. From left to right, Courtland Tubbs, Tony Byrd (22), Ivan Watson (12), Marcus Griffin, (52) and assistant coach Tim Kenny. (Photo courtesy of Peoria *Journal-Star*)

Van Scyoc won his 826th game and first state title. It was the last game he ever coached, as he retired later that summer. "Coach went 45 years without getting a state championship," Hughes told the Chicago Tribune afterward. "We knew that meant a lot to him."

Watson, now in his mid-80s, kept the scorebook for more than 50 years at his alma mater. A 1955 Manual graduate, he attended and recorded stats for just about every sport, boys and girls, over the years.

"I've thought about it, but I don't know," Watson said about how many games he's seen. "Boy, I don't know. I tell people if I had been smart and kept $1 or 50 cents and put it in the jar for every time I heard the national anthem, I would be a rich man, let's put it that way. I've been around a long time and seen a lot of good players."

Manual coach Dick Van Scyoc speaks at a pep rally after the Rams won the Class AA state title in 1994. It was the last game Van Scyoc would coach, and he retired as the state's all-time wins leader. He is also credited with being the godfather of modern basketball coaches in Peoria. (Photo courtesy of Peoria *Journal-Star*)

The unexpected 1994 state title was a watershed moment for Manual's program. Long considered a terrific program with top players and coaching, the Rams now had hardware to back it up as Coach Van handed the keys to Wayne McClain with a young, talented roster.

Mama's Boy

The seventh of Mary Ann Morris-Williams's 10 children was always quiet. Frank Williams, as the cliché goes, let his play on the court do the talking.

"This one day we decided to go see him in grade school, I think it was his seventh-grade year (at Trewyn School)," said Vernon Morris, Frank's oldest living sibling. "I saw how he performed and I said, 'Man, this dude is gonna be special.'"

For the first few years of Frank's life, the large family lived in the Harrison Homes on Peoria's rugged south side. Later they moved to residences on Seibold Street, Lydia Avenue, and Stanley Street, but all were within spitting distance of the Harrison. There in Brick City, the Harrison's nickname because of the dark red brick buildings that seemed to stretch for miles, Frank's older brothers were heavily involved with the Gangster Disciples.

In 1986, United States Congress passed the Anti-Drug Abuse Act, establishing mandatory minimum sentences for the first time triggered by specific quantities of cocaine. Much tougher sentences were enacted for crack cocaine than for powder cocaine. Literally 100 times tougher. For example, distribution of just 5 grams of crack cocaine carried a minimum 5-year prison sentence, while distribution of 500 grams of powder cocaine triggered the same 5-year minimum.

A 2006 report by the ACLU laid bare the racist undertones of the Anti-Drug Abuse Act and the absurdity of the 100:1 ratio for crack cocaine vs powder cocaine.

"*This sentencing disparity is extremely arbitrary for several reasons*," *the report states. "First, the 100:1 drug quantity ratio promotes unwarranted disparities based on race. Because of its relative low cost, crack cocaine is more accessible for poor Americans, many of whom are African Americans. Conversely, powder cocaine is much more expensive and tends to be used by more affluent White Americans. Nationwide statistics compiled by the Sentencing Commission reveal that African Americans are more likely to be convicted of crack cocaine offenses, while Whites are more likely to be convicted of powder cocaine offenses.*"

The ACLU report further states that in 2003, Whites constituted 7.8% and African Americans more than 80% of the defendants sentenced under the harsh federal crack cocaine laws, despite the fact that more than 66% of crack cocaine users in the United States were White or Hispanic.

It was under these conditions that Morris was in federal prison for Frank's entire high school and college basketball career on a nine-plus year sentence for possessing 27 grams of crack cocaine with intent to deliver.

But when he was a free man, Morris said he and his brothers made sure to shield Frank and other basketball players from their illegal activity.

"With Frank, I couldn't let him hang around where we were active at," said Morris, who now lives in Houston. "Him and his other guys, I'm like, 'You all play basketball, that's what you all need to be doing. There's no reason to hang around while we're doing what we're doing.' That just really means wherever there's illegal activity going on, because of the ramifications that can derive from that atmosphere, I couldn't even have him hanging out there. Him and the rest of his guys, too. Same with Marcus, Sergio, all of them."

Morris says that despite the typically nefarious connotations associated with the gang lifestyle, there were positives, too. He says they would watch out for kids in the neighborhood, making sure they went to school and imposing curfews, encouraged kids to spend time at the local Boys & Girls Club, rewarded kids for good school attendance and held community clean-up days. Morris, who is 12 years older than Frank, would give his younger siblings $3 per A on their report card, a practice he still maintains today with his grandchildren.

"Well, we call it an organization," said Morris, who is no longer affiliated with any gang. "People call it a gang because they feel like it's disorganized and stigmatize the negative aspect of it. But there's more positivity than what people know. I don't condone it and I don't advertise it these days, either."

Frank Williams, who declined numerous requests to be interviewed for this book, joined Manual's varsity team as a sophomore for the 1995–96 season, when McClain and Griffin were juniors. With a slender frame and baby face that belied his mature game, Williams took over the reins as point guard for the back-to-back Class AA champion Rams. Silky smooth from the start, it could sometimes appear as if Williams wasn't playing hard, but that was just his stoic, nonchalant mannerisms. Coach Wayne McClain let Williams practice with the varsity twice as a freshman but kicked him out of the gym both times for his perceived indifference.

Shy and introverted on the outside, Frank Williams was a superstar on the court. Raised as one of 10 kids by a single mother, Mary Morris-Williams, Williams was electric with the ball in his hands. He won the 1998 Mr. Basketball award, Big Ten Player of the Year at Illinois, and was a first-round NBA draft pick. (Photo courtesy of IHSA)

"Frankie had a great mom," said Tim Kenny, then a Manual assistant. "If Frank had a bad practice, we would take Frank home and tell Ms. Williams, 'Frank wasn't very good today.' And that was the end of that. He'd be a new person the next day. It didn't happen much because Frank was a great kid. Never in trouble. He didn't have that motor as a young kid. But Frank was a great kid, so when he got older it clicked. By the time he was a sophomore, he was very responsible. You didn't have to babysit Frankie. He was a responsible kid, a great kid and well-behaved."

Mary Ann Morris-Williams worked hard, often two or three jobs at a time, to support her large brood. Her jobs included stints at local hospitals and restaurants, but it was hard providing for everyone. The matriarch of the family was one of 17 kids and grew up in Chidester, Arkansas, a town of less than 300 people.

"Yeah, she was constantly working," Vernon Morris said. "And then she had to come home and work as well. Being predominantly males, we weren't cleaning up the kitchen or any of that."

Because he was making an income, Vernon was able to help his mother financially. He was happy to ease the burden for the mother he and his siblings all loved. In turn, Morris-Williams would buy groceries or clothes for her kids.

Derrick Booth, a member of Manual's 1991 state runner-up team and later its head coach, remembers being in the Q & L barbershop near Carver Center with Howard Nathan when Morris would roll up in a black Pontiac Fiero GT with the license plate *GD360*. There were no acts of intimidation or tough guy persona— just young guys getting haircuts and hanging out.

"I remember Vernon coming in there with security, and he had two guys with him," Booth said. "One would always be by him and one would be by the door. Vernon was normal, he would come in there and speak and chuckle, small talk. Him and Howard knew each other very well. He would sit in his chair and get his haircut just like everybody else. There wasn't any aggressive meanness. But did I know that the two guys with him were his security? Yes."

It was a different era for gangs then. While drug deals were frequent, the dangerous element of gang life so prevalently portrayed now was not a regular occurrence on the south side of Peoria in the 1980s and early '90s.

"As prominent as gangs were in Peoria, primarily the Gangster Disciples and the Vice Lords, there was not significant gun violence," said Booth, who grew up on the south side. "Even though I knew Vernon firsthand and I knew he was the leader of the GD's, he was always approachable and had a pleasant personality."

After winning Mr. Basketball in 1998, Frank Williams was academically ineligible to play as a college freshman. He then embarked on a terrific three-year career at Illinois, where he was named Big Ten Player of the Year in 2000–2001 and helped lead the Illini, along with McClain and Griffin, to the Elite Eight that season with Coach Bill Self. After his junior year, in which he averaged 16.2 points, 4.7 rebounds, 4.4 assists, and 2 steals per game, Williams declared for the NBA Draft, foregoing his last collegiate season of eligibility. In June 2002, he was selected by the Denver Nuggets with the 25th pick in the first round and was sent to the New York Knicks as part of a draft-day trade. He signed a three-year contract for about $2.6 million.

Williams had trouble cracking the Knicks rotation, playing 21 games as a rookie and then 56 games in his second season, 2003–04. After he was drafted, Williams's mother, Mary, came to New York and spent a couple months with her NBA-playing son. Later, Williams bought her a house and some land in Chidester, the tiny southwest Arkansas town where she grew up. Mary moved south and was in the process of opening a restaurant with one of her sisters when she suddenly passed away in February 2004 from complications of diabetes and hypertension, according to the *Journal-Star*.

It's been a struggle since my mom passed," Frank told the Journal-Star's *Greg Stewart in 2007. "Something I've had a hard time dealing with. I've never talked about it until now. I looked at (buying her a house) as something I was supposed to do. After all the tough times we put her through, it was nice to see her get away and be back with her family. I know she was having a lot of fun.*

Morris was in federal prison in Duluth, Minnesota, when his mother died. He says he was approved to attend the funeral in Arkansas, but the night before he was set to leave he was told that could no longer happen.

"I had paid for the plane ticket and everything," Morris said. "Something transpired and I couldn't go."

Mary's death was a devastating blow to her nine living children. The family would have to move on without its beloved matriarch, who was only 55 years old at the time of her passing.

"She was loving, caring, she was a provider, she was stern," Morris says. "It's like the whole entire neighborhood loved her. And she was a hard worker."

Frank tried to carry on with his basketball career, but something was missing. For the first time in his life, his number one supporter and fan was no longer there.

"After she died, I just didn't have the same drive I had from when she was at the games watching me," Frank said in the 2007 Journal-Star *article. "I realized the reason I was (playing) was for her, to get her away from everything we were going through."*

He played nine games for the Chicago Bulls in 2004–05, the last of which came on March 9, 2005. At 25 years old, Frank Williams's NBA career was over.

Williams, who is considered one the greatest guards to ever play at Illinois, spent time in the now-defunct Continental Basketball Association and overseas in Italy and Argentina until 2010, when his basketball career came to an end. He has never been one to talk much, especially to reporters, but those who know him said Mary's passing likely had a major detrimental effect on his basketball career.

"I would say it contributed to it," Morris said. "It's like it killed his spark and his entire mannerisms as well. He still kept a level head, but the passing of my mom affected everybody. Frank was close to her, but we all were. He allowed her to experience life in a higher level, a higher degree. He has always been quiet, but I just don't know how he started perceiving life after that."

"It changed his whole life because he was in the NBA, doing good . . . and that literally changed everything for him," said Griffin, Frank's close friend. "I believe it changed his fight and it changed his mental outlook. Because I felt like he was doing it for his mom. When you grow up, I don't think a lot of people understand this, we play sports but sometimes we are doing this because we want to put our families in better positions. Meaning our mom first. If it never clicks over in your mind to do this for yourself, if that avenue is taken from you, it's going to fall apart. Unless you can change it in your mind that now I need to do this for me. And I don't know if it ever clicked in his mind after his mom passed. And this is just me speculating, but for so long it was, 'I want to make my mom live comfortably and take all her debt away.' And when that was gone from him, I don't know."

Recruitments

As juniors and into their senior year in 1996, Sergio McClain and Marcus Griffin were highly sought-after recruits for colleges across the country. From the start, the pair said they were a package deal; if you get one, you're getting both. Both were ranked among the top 40 or so players in the country and had dozens of scholarship offers. The pair were intrigued by some West Coast schools like USC and Fresno State, which was coached by Jerry Tarkanian at the time. But things were eventually whittled down to a group of Midwestern schools: Illinois, Indiana, Cincinnati, and Missouri.

Indiana wanted the pair in a big way, especially McClain.

"We wanted Sergio bad," said Dan Dakich, an Indiana assistant at the time. "Coach (Knight) thought Sergio could be the kind of guy you win big with. Kind of like he had with Quinn Buckner. Can he shoot? Not really. But he can guard everybody, he's tougher than hell, he's mature. That was kind of the way that Coach Knight looked at Sergio."

But things went off the rails for the Hoosiers in their pursuit of the pair when McClain and Griffin were in Bloomington for a visit in the fall of 1996. All along, Griffin felt like Knight mainly wanted McClain but was also recruiting him because they were a package deal. And as the pair of teenage basketball stars took in an IU practice, Griffin nodded off and fell asleep.

"Knight cussed me out and I cussed him out," Griffin said. "They wanted Serg, they really wanted Serg. I think with Coach Knight's background . . . Serg was a coach's son, tough, hard-nosed. But there wasn't a chance in the world that they were getting me."

When told of Griffin's perspective on the recruitment, Dakich said he understands that line of thinking.

"Yeah, I can see where he would think that," Dakich said of Griffin not feeling wanted. "We would have taken them both obviously and been very, very happy with both of them. I kinda felt that way recruiting him like, 'C'mon Coach, let's go.' Fake it till you make it (laughing). At least fake it here with this kid because he is going to have influence. Coach wasn't rude or anything . . . but you could tell. Marcus is probably right."

For his part, McClain did like Indiana and could have seen himself playing there.

"I liked Bobby Knight," McClain said. "Me and (former Hoosier) Luke Recker were good friends. The only thing when I went on that visit was they looked at Luke like I was being looked at in my state. And if it came down to playing time or position or who was going to shoot the ball, politics-wise I would get the short end of the stick. And I wasn't trying to deal with that."

Interestingly, Robin McClain, Sergio's mother, was completely sold on her only son playing for Bobby Knight. She says most coaches recruited the father, but Knight looked her in the eye and said, 'What do you want for your son, mom?' The legendary coach also gave her a big contact list of phone numbers and addresses of parents whose kids had played for him over the years and said call whoever you want. Some were parents of kids who had reached the NBA. Others were young players on the current team.

"You can call everybody you want on that list and you ask them what kind of coach I am, how I was with them, and if what I say I mean. And then you decide," Robin said Knight told her. "That was the first coach who did that. That is what convinced me about Indiana. It was huge. Because not only am I hearing what Coach Knight is saying to me but I also can call all these people and ask them what they thought. And they were giving me their honest opinions. And everybody didn't agree 1000 percent with Bobby Knight, but he felt secure enough with what he did as a coach and how he treated his staff and his players, and helping them get to the league and this and that. He felt secure enough that I could test it. And I appreciated that and I loved the campus. So really and truly at that time I felt that Indiana was going to be the best situation for Sergio. Coach Knight is honest. That's what I liked."

Although he went on visits and consistently told reporters he was undecided, Griffin had made a pact with his mother years prior. Because she was so busy as a single parent working and going to school, Bobo-Jones didn't attend many of Griffin's Manual games. But Griffin was intent on changing that when he got to college. After his freshman year when it became apparent he could play college basketball if he wanted, Griffin asked his mother if she would be willing to attend all his games if he went to a university nearby. Bobo-Jones said if he picked a school within a couple hours' drive, she would attend every home game.

"My Illinois decision was 98 percent about her," Marcus said. "I was a Mama's boy. I was 100 percent a Mama's boy, and so I valued her opinion a whole lot. I started to do my research on the history of schools. I knew about DePaul, I knew about schools up in Chicago. I knew we had other players from the past go to Illinois so I was like, 'Hmm.' I started watching videos of the Flyin' Illini and I'm like, 'Hmm.' So, I said, 'Mom, what about Illinois?' We thought about it, we talked about it, Champaign is not that far, it wasn't a bad town for gang violence. Champaign was just in my mind the whole time. It never left my mind. And then we started to get recruited and I knew."

The pair kept their intentions to themselves, though, and didn't sign letters of intent with Illinois and new coach Lon Kruger until the last day of the week-long November signing period. There was even a story in the *Chicago Tribune* saying the players made an 11th hour switch from Indiana to Illinois, which was probably not accurate but made for good suspense and newspaper fodder. At the time, Griffin had not yet qualified academically for a Division 1 college—and indeed, he would have to spend two years at a junior college—but McClain stayed true to his word and picked a school that his buddy also wanted to attend.

Illinois was not rolling at the time. About nine months before signing day in 1996, Lou Henson retired after 21 years as Illini head coach. Henson won 422 games at Illinois, but things trended downward after the magical 1988–89 Flyin' Illini team that reached the Final Four. In the seven seasons that followed, the Illini failed to make it out of the first weekend of the NCAA Tournament. So, the 63-year-old Henson stepped down, or was told to step down depending on what you believe, and Kruger was hired away from Florida to resurrect the Illini program. His first order of business? Convincing the Manual stars to stay home.

"Other places were already built as far as their programs, and Illinois wanted me to come in and help them build it," said McClain, who won Mr. Basketball in 1997, joining Howard Nathan as players from Peoria to win the award. "And that was very enticing for me. I never, ever wanted the easy way."

The good news didn't end there for Kruger and the Illini. On the same day McClain and Griffin signed, junior star Frank Williams verbally committed to Illinois as well.

A Trifecta of Thornton Battles

As the 1994–95 season began, a pair of first-year coaches inherited outstanding teams with state title aspirations: Peoria Manual's Wayne McClain and Thornton's Rocky Hill. Manual was the defending Class AA state champion and McClain, a long-time assistant, had taken over for Dick Van Scyoc, who retired as the state's all-time winningest coach. Hill, a Thornridge graduate, was a starter on the sophomore team at the school in 1971–72 when the

Falcons had arguably the greatest team in state history, led by Quinn Buckner. Hill began his coaching career at Thornridge, where he was a varsity assistant for two years and head sophomore coach for nine seasons. He then moved three miles west down Route 83, staying in Chicago's south suburbs, to fierce rival Thornton, where he proceeded to win 59 straight games at the sophomore level. It was enough to earn him a promotion to the big chair in 1994 when the head coaching job opened.

Hill inherited a terrific team, led by senior Tai Streets, who was widely considered the best all-around high school athlete in the state. Streets, a transfer from Rich South who later starred at wide receiver for a national title-winning Michigan football team and played in the NFL, had plenty of talent around him at Thornton; guard Chauncey Jones, forward James Johnson and super sophomores Melvin Ely and Erik Herring, among them. In the season-opening Schaumburg Thanksgiving Tournament, Thornton won its first two games before falling to host Schaumburg in the tournament title game.

Hill said some of his players were displaying poor sportsmanship after the loss, coming off the bench and acting wild. Before he could get to the locker room, Hill was approached by Thornton principal William O'Neal, who walked down from the stands.

"He said, 'Listen, Rocky. We're going to lose some games. But if we're going to lose, let's lose with class,'" Hill remembers O'Neal saying. "I said, 'OK, Mr. O'Neal.' He had just given me the damn job."

Little did either man know the Wildcats would hardly lose again over the next three seasons.

Following that late November setback, Thornton won its next 28 games, including an incredible 46–43 victory over Chicago Farragut and its rock-star tandem of Kevin Garnett and Ronnie Fields in the state quarterfinals. Three months later, Garnett would be selected with the fifth pick in the NBA Draft, but on a Friday night in March at Champaign's Assembly Hall, Hill's Thornton team ended the incredible 6-foot-11 talent's lone season of Illinois high school play short of a state title. (Before Thornton downed Farragut, Garnett's only loss at the Chicago school was earlier in the year to, you guessed it, Manual.)

The next morning, Thornton defeated a great Rock Island team with future Cincinnati star Pete Mickeal, 56–55, in the semifinals, setting the stage for the title game against defending champion Manual.

"I'm not perfect but I'm a pretty spiritual guy," said Hill, who now coaches at his alma mater, Thornridge. "I was praying and fasting when we got downstate because I wanted to win that thing and I wanted some divine help. But that turned out to be a bad decision. I was weak because I wasn't eating. I was so weak going into that championship game against Manual, I don't think I was in my right mind. I was woozy because I wasn't eating. I started fasting when we left to go down there (Thursday). And I was kind of a rookie to fasting so I didn't know, and I was just out of it. I'm not saying that that cost us the game, though."

Led by seniors Willie Coleman, Ivan Watson, and Darrell Ivory, plus super sophs McClain and Griffin, Manual handled Thornton 65–53 for its second straight title, and first under Wayne McClain. The Rams ended the year 32–2, while Thornton finished 30–2.

"Our best games were in practice," Manual assistant Tim Kenny said of the 1994–95 team. "We were loaded that year."

"They were tough," said Streets, who is now Thornton's head coach. "Those guys just didn't get tired (laughing). They just kept coming at us and coming at us."

The following summer, Wayne McClain called Hill and proposed the two powerhouses play a regular season game in 1995–96, even offering to travel to Thornton. Hill declined.

"I didn't want to see them dudes, man," Hill said. "That loss stung me so bad. I don't know, I just didn't want to see them. I wasn't scared. Looking back on it now, I probably should have played them in Chicago. Thornton's gym is a palace, it's probably one of the top two or three gyms in the state of Illinois. (Fans) would have been lined up around the corner trying to get in that game."

Thornton stormed through the regular season unbeaten in 1995–96 and entered the state tournament ranked No. 1 in the state AP poll, with Manual at No. 2. The two teams were on a collision course to meet again in the state final, this time at Peoria's Carver Arena as the state tournament moved from Champaign to Peoria after the 1995 tourney. Thornton and Manual each won its semifinal games by double digits and would meet in the Class AA final for the second straight year. Thornton entered the game 31–0, while Manual was 30–2. The talent was incredible on both sides, with Thornton boasting two future NFL players, Antwaan Randle El and Napoleon Harris, and a future NBA player in Melvin Ely. Wing player Erik Herring was also outstanding, and later became a double-digit per-game scorer at Division 1 George Mason. For Manual, McClain and Griffin were now juniors, and Williams, a sophomore, had taken over as point guard.

In front of a partisan crowd of more than 12,000 at Carver Arena, Manual again prevailed, 57–51, winning its third straight state title and joining East St. Louis Lincoln, 1987–89, with the second three-peat in state history.

"The defense they put up was pretty good, but the other key to that is we had to combat it on both ends because we did it the same way," said Randle El, who later won Super Bowl XL with the Pittsburgh Steelers in 2006. "On offense, you're trying to combat their pressure, now you go right back at them on your defensive side because we did man-to-man press, we did all kinds of 1–3–1 traps, we did all that kind of stuff against them. It was always how we did it, but it felt like we always ran out of gas (against Manual)."

"I didn't make a big deal about this, but I thought that was so unfair," Hill said of facing Manual in Peoria. "First of all, I've always thought Champaign is the downstate experience. And I'm not ripping on the great folks of Peoria, they're great people and great basketball fans. And Bradley is a great venue for high school basketball. But nothing compares to when you walk out on the floor at Assembly Hall. So, to have to play a team of Manual's talent, prestige, coaching, aura, tradition, the whole works, in their backyard . . . I just felt like it wasn't right."

In 1996–97, Manual was chasing history. No team in Illinois boys' basketball had ever won four consecutive state titles. It was now within reach for the Rams, as McClain and Griffin were headlining seniors, and junior Williams was also highly ranked nationally. Another showdown with Thornton loomed large, but this time the teams would meet in the semifinals because of a random seeding draw.

Manual took a 29–1 record into the heavyweight game, along with a No. 1 national ranking in *USA Today*. Thornton was 31–0, ranked No. 3 in America. It was a shame a game of this magnitude was not for the championship, but at least the schools would meet for a third time in three years. With another huge crowd at Carver Arena, the determined Wildcats, clad in purple, jumped out to an 18–4 first-quarter lead on Manual.

"They called a timeout, and I told my kids, 'Let's blow them out!'" Hill said. "And Peoria Manual's bench heard that. (TV announcer) David Kaplan referred to it on the telecast. I think it increased their focus. I hate that I did that. You're supposed to let sleeping dogs lie."

After the timeout, the number one boys' basketball team in America went on a 25–8 run to take a 29–26 lead into halftime. Williams, who was matched up with Randle El at the lead guard spot, scored 16 points during the mesmerizing run.

"One of the best first halves ever," Manual's assistant Tim Kenny said of Williams. "We were getting clobbered early. Of all of Frankie's state games, that was his best performance. He destroyed them for a half. Antwaan Randle-El won't forget him, I'll guarantee that."

A rebuttal, Mr. Randle El?

"Frank was good, man," said Randle El, now a Detroit Lions assistant coach. "He could shoot, he could handle the ball, he could dish the ball out. But we knew it wasn't just we shut down this guy and everything else was cool. You had to account for all of them."

"They had us beat that year," Griffin said. "If they would have just spread the floor and not tried to beat us by 30, they would have beat us. They were up big, but they wanted to blow us out. They kept on playing instead of slowing it down and when you keep on playing, you're going to give us opportunities."

The second half, fittingly, belonged to Sergio McClain. With the possibility of only 16 minutes of basketball left in his storied high school career, the kid who grew up practicing moves of Manual players on his backyard hoop knew he needed to make an impact. The kid who had been driven incredibly hard by his coach/father to be a warrior needed to go out on top. Workouts before school. Practices without a second of let-up after school. With another win over Thornton and thus advancing to the championship game, Sergio would be the first player in state history to start in four boys' basketball state title games.

But there was one problem: he could barely lift his left arm.

McClain had a torn left trapezius, a large triangular muscle in the back/shoulder region. He was being treated for it during the game, but with the pain rendering him ineffective, Wayne McClain sat his son with two fouls when the Rams were down by 14 points in the first half.

"I just remember he was like, 'You're done,'" Sergio said.

But when Thornton retook an eight-point lead early in the second half, something had to be done.

"There was probably five or six minutes left in the third quarter and I looked at Dad and said, 'Put me in. If we're gonna go down, I wanna go down on my own terms as a senior,'" Sergio said. "He debated it and curled his lips and he was like, 'Get back in there.' He respected me being a senior."

Sergio being Sergio, he scored 12 straight points in an 18–0 run as Manual seized control of the game. Thornton went nearly 11 minutes without a field goal as the Rams raced to a big second-half lead. Thornton furiously rallied late, cutting the Manual lead to three points, but it wasn't enough.

Sergio and Wayne McClain soak in the first four-peat in Illinois state tournament history after defeating West Aurora in 1997. (Photo courtesy of IHSA)

Manual prevailed 65–62 for its third win in three years over an incredible Thornton team that went 93–4 in a three-year period but never won a state title.

"That was probably the hardest game, just being so fatigued," Sergio said. "But Dad prepared us for that."

"The Manual-Thornton semifinal game in '97 is the best high school game I've ever seen," said Mattson, the Peoria TV reporter. "Above the rim stuff. Standing room only. The emotion. The Thornton kids were so fired up when they got ahead. Thornton wanted Manual so bad. I remember talking to them the night before, after they won on Friday, and the Thornton kids were like, 'We want Manual.' They were driven to play Manual all year. They played so well and they blew out to that lead. And then when Manual came back, you talk about theater."

On the other side, Thornton won 93 out of 97 games in a three-year period, including being ranked in the top 3 nationally, and never won a state title. Unfathomable.

"To this day, I can't believe we didn't win one," Hill said. "If it had been a few years later, I would have a state championship or maybe two or maybe three. It just wasn't meant to be. Even though I've got a good life, I have a great job . . . I just feel like . . ."

Hill's voice trailed off. His Thornton teams are inarguably one of the best and most talented teams in Illinois state history. Yet, fairly or not, they will be partly remembered for failing to win a title. Still, a huge part of that is the poor luck of playing at the same time as Manual's once-in-a-generation dynasty. He is able to laugh about it now, but Hill says when the team returned to Harvey after the third loss to Manual, some people in town were comparing him to former Buffalo Bills coach Marv Levy, who famously lost four straight Super Bowls.

Hill does have a theory on what separated the two powerhouses, and he partly blames himself.

"We weren't as close as we should have been," Hill says. "Because those Manual guys were really close. (I was told) they used to eat dinner over at Wayne's house and all of that. We never did that when I had those guys. That hurt us and I have to accept some of the responsibility with that because I should have created more of a family-type atmosphere. When I was coaching those sophomore teams at Thornridge, I would take them out and buy them pizzas after the games and stuff. We'd sit there and eat pizza and talk about the game and laugh, and just have fun. We didn't have that at Thornton and that's on me. And I don't know why I got away from that, taking my kids out . . . I don't know why I got away from it."

Later that night, one final game remained for the four-peat. The Manual Rams were dead tired from the emotional triumph over Thornton earlier in the day, but West Aurora entered the title game 29–3 and felt no sympathy for the three-time defending champs playing in their home city. West Aurora led by four points in the fourth quarter and was threatening to completely deflate the Manual hoopla and end the Rams' dynastic era on a sour note. Naturally, Sergio McClain had other ideas. Despite nursing the torn left trapezius, Sergio scored Manual's last 9 points, all in the final 2 minutes and 46 seconds of the game, and the sluggish Rams prevailed, 47–43. Sergio finished with a game-high 22 points in his final high school outing.

Four years. Four state titles. History made.

"I thought he was a heck of a boy today," Wayne McClain said of Sergio to reporters afterward. "I thought that he had three great games. Whenever we needed someone to step up, he did."

(*Manual's only loss in 1996–97 is remembered hilariously, or with incre-
dulity, by those who were there. It was at Chicago Carver, featuring its star
guard Nick Irvin, who was an AAU teammate of McClain's and Griffin's with
the Illinois Warriors. Griffin was out this game with an ankle injury so the
Rams were short-handed. Manual coaches and players said the refereeing
was outrageously bad, and multiple newspapers reported that coach Wayne
McClain grabbed the public address microphone and yelled into it, "You guys
shouldn't referee a biddy-ball game!" Manual trailed by 18 in the second half
but rallied to force overtime before losing 91–85 to snap a 32-game winning
streak.*

*"Me and Serg didn't talk for a while because of that game," said Irvin, who
later became a very successful high school coach at Chicago's Morgan Park.
"That game was a big deal.")*

As if four straight Class AA titles weren't enough, Manual was named
high school national champions by *USA Today* and invited to the White
House for its achievements. The Peoria community raised $16,000 to send
a 42-member contingent of players, coaches, administrators, and family
members to Washington DC, and a local attorney stepped up to pay for
the school's cheerleaders to travel as well. Manual was told President Bill
Clinton's schedule was too busy to meet him, but they would get some face
time with Vice President Al Gore.

> *"If I had to choose between visiting with the Chicago Bulls at the White
> House or being with the Manual Rams when they visit the vice president,
> I would take the Manual Rams any day," U.S. Rep Ray LaHood, R-Peoria,
> told the* Journal-Star.

As the trip loomed, Wayne McClain realized many of his players did not
own appropriate clothing for a moment like this. Of course, McClain sprang
into action.

"Our kids had nothing," said assistant coach Chuck Westendorf. "Wayne
went out and bought them socks and he bought them dress shoes. He said
you're going to Washington DC, you're going to look first class. You're not
going to wear blue jeans and a ragged shirt. You're going to dress up and look
nice and presentable. He bought them suits, he bought them everything.
They didn't have luggage. He had to buy them a small piece of luggage, too.
It was probably the trip of a lifetime for those kids."

In May 1997, the team from the south side of Peoria boarded a plane for
Washington and a whirlwind two-day trip. They took tours of the White

House, US Capitol, and Library of Congress; they met and posed for pictures with Al Gore. Sergio presented Gore with a basketball autographed by the team and principal Sandy Farkash gave the vice president a Rams jersey with "2 Gore" on the back and another with "1 Clinton" for the president.

The young men were a long way from the south side of Peoria.

Peoria to U of I Pipeline

In a three-season span from 1973–76, Peoria Richwoods went 83–6 behind a trio of future University of Illinois players. Richwoods did not win a state title, but it came close while also starting the Peoria to U of I pipeline. Mark Smith and Derek Holcomb went on to have excellent careers at Illinois (Holcomb went to Indiana first and transferred to UI); Smith still ranks in the top 10 of the school's all-time leading scorers. Later, in the early 1980s, Peoria Central's Tony Wysinger and Richwoods' Doug Altenberger took the 90-mile trek southeast on I-74 to play for Lou Henson and Illinois. Wysinger and Altenberger enjoyed outstanding Big Ten careers as well.

But the modern Peoria to UI train really got rolling in the 1990s. Jerry Hester was a smooth six-six forward at Manual and had scholarship offers from Illinois and Wisconsin, among others. While he was still undecided, Hester ran into Smith, the former Richwoods star, who offered some words of advice.

"I remember him saying that staying close to home and playing for a place like Illinois, that I wouldn't regret it," Hester said. "I went home and I asked my dad, 'Do you know a guy named Mark Smith?' He was like, 'Oh man, yeah.' I didn't realize how great of a player he was but he took the time to chat with me."

Hester liked Wisconsin a lot too, and the Badgers had an impressive coaching staff at the time with head coach Stu Jackson, who previously helmed the New York Knicks, and assistants Stan Van Gundy, Sean Miller, and Ray McCallum. Chicago King star seven-foot center Rashard Griffith was committed to Wisconsin, and the chance to play with him was enticing for Hester.

"It kind of came down to that conversation with Mark Smith and also a conversation with my mom," Hester said. "My mom knew nothing about basketball but she just wanted her son to have the best opportunity. She asked Stu Jackson if he would be there my entire four years. He said he thought he would be but he couldn't say for sure. That kind of helped swing it in Illinois' favor as well that he was honest with that, which I definitely appreciate because coaches aren't always honest like that, especially in recruiting."

Hester signed with Illinois and began an incredible streak of 19 consecutive seasons of a Peoria player suiting up for the orange and blue. Hester had a terrific college career, averaging nearly 15 points as a fifth-year senior, which was Sergio McClain's freshman year. Two years later McClain was joined by Griffin, who dominated at Lincoln College for a pair of seasons, and Williams, who sat out his first year as an academic non-qualifier. In 2000–01, Williams averaged a team-high 14.9 points a game; Griffin averaged 11.3 points and 6 rebounds; and McClain averaged 7.5 points, 5.5 rebounds, and 2.9 assists. This was all while the Illini won a Big Ten championship, earned a 1-seed in the NCAA Tournament, and reached the Elite Eight before being bounced by Arizona in a highly controversial game in which SIX Illinois players fouled out, including Griffin and McClain. It was their last game in Illini uniforms.

Peoria Central's Jerrance Howard was a freshman at Illinois when Griffin and McClain were seniors, giving the roster four Peorians in 2000–01. The following year, Williams led the squad again at 16.2 points and 4.4 assists per game, as Illinois took second in the Big Ten and reached the NCAA Sweet 16. Williams left for the NBA but Howard remained, keeping the Peoria streak alive. Two years later, athletic six-foot-eight forward Brian Randle of Peoria Notre Dame was passed the torch. Randle chose Illinois over Notre Dame and says the trio of McClain, Griffin, and Williams was a significant reason.

"I didn't go to Manual or Central or Richwoods, but I was still part of Peoria basketball," Randle said. "It wasn't necessarily an expectation that I went there, but it was almost like you kinda wanted to have an opportunity to bear the torch and carry the mantle of, 'I'm from Peoria and I'm part of this Illinois basketball lineage.' For me, that's what it was. Just seeing those guys on TV and the way they played with the edge they had, and the fearlessness, it made you want to be part of something great. And to their credit, they built that. That was one thing that they did not just for Illinois basketball, but for Peoria basketball. It almost felt like, 'I'm from Peoria, how can I not go there?' Look at what they're doing and how much fun they're having on the court, and they proudly represent this city. So, man, I want to be a part of this."

Two years later, Randle was joined by Richwoods' Jamar Smith. Smith lasted just two seasons in Champaign, but like clockwork just as he left, Richwoods' Bill Cole arrived for Randle's fifth-year senior season of 2008–09.

In Cole's junior season, he was joined by highly touted guard D.J. Richardson of Peoria Central. (Richardson played his senior year of high school at Findlay Prep in Nevada.) Richardson had a stellar four-year career, averaging double-digit scoring in three of the four seasons. And when he graduated after the 2012–13 season, the Peoria to U of I pipeline was officially dry after an astonishing 19-year run.

"Peoria is always a part of me wherever I'm at," said Hester, who started the streak. "I haven't lived there since I was in high school but it is still very much a part of me, and I still feel very strongly as I have conversations with former teammates or former rivals around the country. People that I talk to and have great relationships with talk about how great Peoria basketball was. To be a part of something that lasted as long as it did . . . I think (longtime sportswriter) Loren Tate put in the *Champaign News-Gazette* that I was the pied piper and that was just when Sergio came. It means a lot and all the great players that came to Illinois behind me, it definitely means a lot to be a part of that."

After Richardson's departure, Illinois went four seasons without a Peoria native on the roster. Coincidentally or not, it was also a disappointing four-year period without an NCAA Tournament appearance. But then in 2017–18, a Peoria presence returned to Champaign. It was a familiar last name, too. Da'Monte Williams, son of Frank Williams, followed his father's Manual to Illinois path and joined first-year coach Brad Underwood's club.

A six-foot-two guard, Da'Monte had a solid, if injury-plagued, career at Manual under coach Derrick Booth. Williams's mother, Tanejah Keeton, was a Manual point guard herself so his basketball bloodlines ran even beyond his All-American father. He wasn't a big scorer, but Da'Monte became an invaluable defender and leader in his junior and senior seasons as Illinois returned to the upper echelon of the Big Ten. Continuing the Peoria to Illini pipeline was fun for the soft-spoken son of a legend.

"Just being able to go to school for free at the University of Illinois and you graduate with that degree, it says a lot," Da'Monte said. "Being able to make it out of your city and still be fortunate enough to play the game that you love is always a blessing. But to do it up the street from Peoria and to be able to play on a high level and on TV is always a plus. I mean what's better than playing at home?"

5

How the Seeds of Struggle Were Planted

Violent crime is not a rarity in Peoria. To understand why this became so and why the south side of town has long been the epicenter of the violence, one must go back almost 100 years. It involves systemic racism, laws that disproportionately affected the African American community and the type of cringeworthy governmental practices that went on for decades as Whites prospered and Blacks were further hamstrung.

Simply put, Peoria is a violent and segregated place. Saying otherwise would be sugarcoating it or fudging the numbers. The city has held steady population-wise for many years, hovering in the 110,000 to 115,000 range for decades. Even as far back as 1940, Peoria had just over 105,000 residents. A mid-sized city by any measure. And yet, Peoria is mentioned with cities much, much larger in a category it wants no part of.

> From a December 2019 article in the *Journal-Star*: *"The murder rate in 2018 in Peoria was higher than that of Atlanta, Cincinnati, Dallas, Houston, Indianapolis, Miami and Pittsburgh, among other places."*

In 2019, Peoria was ranked as the 24th most dangerous city in America by the financial news website 24/7 Wall St. According to the site, "Peoria has one of the highest violent crime rates in the country, with 1,044 reported violent crimes for every 100,000 people in 2019. It also has the 15th highest murder rate among large US cities, with 23 homicides per 100,000 residents. Nationwide, the murder rate is 5 per 100,000." Furthermore, 24/7 Wall St ranked Peoria as the seventh worst city for Black Americans in 2019. Three years prior, Peoria actually ranked as *the* worst city for Black Americans.

> *While nationwide, 84.9% of black adults have a high school diploma—4.4 percentage points less than the white high school attainment rate of 89.3%—*

in Peoria, Illinois, 79.6% of black adults have a high school diploma, 13.4 percentage points below the area's white high school attainment rate of 92.9%. This is one of the largest such gaps in the country. Those without a high school diploma are more likely to struggle financially, and in Peoria, 34.5% of black residents live below the poverty line, nearly four times the 9.3% white poverty rate in the area.

Homeownership is one way many Americans build long-term wealth and avoid the cycle of poverty. In Peoria, just 32.6% of African American households own homes—less than half the 76.1% white homeownership rate.

In the late 1930s after the Great Depression, the US federal government tried to find a way to stimulate the economy and prevent foreclosures, so it established an agency called the Home Ownership Loan Corporation (HOLC). It would refinance mortgages for people who were facing foreclosure at a rate lower than one would get at a major bank. The government was basically subsidizing mortgages. An average person might go to Bank X, for example, try to get their loan refinanced and Bank X would turn them down, saying they looked at the algorithm and you're too risky and they would lose money on you. That same person could then go to the federal government and would have their mortgage refinanced, and the government more or less assumed that risk. The program existed for about 20 years before the agency closed down.

By the 1950s, the federal government had made loans to over 1 million homeowners in the United States. Data indicates they prevented 800,000 foreclosures, and even though it was assuming more risk and maybe had riskier algorithms than the banks, the agency made $14 million for the federal government—in 1940s and 1950s numbers. At the time, it was heralded as a very successful government program that kept people in their homes and generated revenue.

So, what's the catch? Well, shocker, the federal program was not intended to help *everyone*. Peter Kobak grew up in Cincinnati and moved to Peoria in the mid-2010s to work for the city. As he learned about the racial disparities of the city, he dug in and researched the history of Peoria, becoming something of an expert on the city's racial divide. What he found was quite troubling.

"Looking back on it you can paint this agency in a really positive light," Kobak said of the HOLC. "But research unearthed in the last few decades showed that (there were) some disturbing consequences. One of the ways that the government tried to guard against risk is they created risk assessment. They would go into cities, they actually hired hundreds of these risk assessors, and over 200 cities throughout the United States had these people come through. They would go into your neighborhood and look at the quality of your house, how much houses were selling for, to assess should we refinance homes in this neighborhood. And they were unfortunately also including the racial makeup of the neighborhood. Almost entirely White neighborhoods were rated very well. Even neighborhoods with just some people of color were rated much worse because they were seen as deteriorating just on the basis of race. So, race knocks you down points if it was a neighborhood that was not completely White. If it was a majority Black neighborhood then it was almost guaranteed to be in this category that was painted red. As a very high risk where the government would not refinance these mortgages."

This was redlining, a troubling practice of systemic denial of governmental services for areas outlined in red on the map. In Peoria, that's the south side.

This was from a 2018 article in the *Washington Post* with the headline ***"Redlining was banned 50 years ago. It's still hurting minorities today."***

Racial discrimination in mortgage lending in the 1930s shaped the demographic and wealth patterns of American communities today, a new study shows, with 3 out of 4 neighborhoods "redlined" on government maps 80 years ago continuing to struggle economically. The study by the National Community Reinvestment Coalition, shows that the vast majority of neighborhoods marked "hazardous" in red ink on maps drawn by the federal Home Owners' Loan Corp. from 1935 to 1939 are today much more likely than other areas to comprise lower-income, minority residents. "It's as if some of these places have been trapped in the past, locking neighborhoods into concentrated poverty," said Jason Richardson, director of research at the NCRC, a consumer advocacy group.

The south side of Peoria is living with just what Richardson described. And many residents who, sadly, have attended far too many funerals for young people. Sometimes you can see the trouble coming. Other times, the guys are just playing basketball in broad daylight . . .

Roberta Nathan, one of Howard's younger sisters, was hanging out at the Proctor Center outdoor courts with her young son as crowds of people lined the courts, watching Peoria's top basketball talent play heated games to 16, where every basket counts as one point and winners stay on the court. There were at least 100 people at Proctor on this day in June 1992, and Roberta saw a

A couple kids shooting hoops at Proctor Center on a late summer day in 2020. For many, many years, the best players in Peoria played intense games here on the south side. Some believe that a tragic murder in 1992 down the street from Proctor made it no longer a desirable place for pickup games. (Photo by John Grap)

lot of strange faces, which was unusual for a south sider accustomed to being around basketball. Howard Nathan, fresh off a successful freshman year at DePaul, was out there playing. So was Willie Coleman. And many others.

One of Howard's best friends, Maurice "Reece" Armstrong, was hanging out but not playing ball that day. Reece, 21, lived with his grandmother a couple blocks from Proctor.

"I had just left to go to work and I'm telling him to come on I'm going to take you home, there's too many people out here that we don't know," Roberta said. "Reece said, 'I'm good, I'm good, I'm ok.'"

Shortly after Roberta left Proctor, Reece was messing around and throwing M-80 firecrackers onto the ground, according to the *Journal-Star*. One hit the back of a 21-year-old St. Louis man named Chester Wilson. It is unclear exactly what happened next, but a confrontation ensued, and the evening turned violent as gunshots were fired and Reece was shot three times. He was taken to OSF Saint Francis where he lived for 10 more days before dying of internal injuries from a bullet wound in the back.

There are some people in Peoria who believe the mystique and allure of the summertime outdoor games that doubled as hangout spots were forever altered after Reece was murdered.

"After he got killed, it just wasn't right (to play at Proctor anymore)," said Charles Nathan, Howard's younger brother. "To this day, they don't play like they used to."

Coleman, who was a starting guard on Manual's 1994 and 1995 state title teams, remembers being on the asphalt court at Proctor that day. A high schooler at the time, Coleman went on to play at DePaul and later became Manual's head coach.

"After seeing that, we never went back to Proctor," Coleman said. "It was never the same. I don't see any people on the courts anymore."

Reece and Howard had gone to Tyng School together as kids and been close friends for years.

"He wasn't a troubled kid," Charles said of Reece. "He was raised by his grandma. He was a ladies man, so he might mess with your girlfriend and you don't know. But when you find out, now you want to beat him up. He wasn't a fighter. He didn't care how big or little you were. He messed around with guys that were big and they would chase him. We were at Proctor Center one time playing ball and the game was stopped because these guys are coming to get him. These guys were probably about six to seven years older than him. He was messing with their girlfriend."

Nathan's family members say Reece and Howard had been together at DePaul that week, and Reece convinced his friend to head home for a couple days. No one could have known then how life-altering that seemingly frivolous decision would become.

"Through his car wreck and everything, I never saw Howard shed a tear," said Angennette, the oldest Nathan sibling. "But I saw him shed a tear for Maurice. That's the only time. Maurice . . . he was hurt by that. He was angry about that. That was like someone took his life from him, because they were together every day. Maurice stayed at our house. They were like brothers. That really did something to Howard."

Admitted gang member Mark Williams, 18, of Chicago, was found guilty of murder, aggravated battery with a firearm, and aggravated discharge of a firearm and sentenced to 50 years in prison. Another Chicago man, Iven "Mushy" Brown, 21, pleaded guilty to aggravated battery with a firearm and was sentenced to 30 years. Wilson, the St. Louis man hit with a firecracker that started the deadly confrontation, also was charged with murder, but the charges were later dismissed.

The death of Reece Armstrong was an ugly chapter in a city that has seen its share of bloodshed.

On the surface, Jim Ralph is as unlikely an expert on Peoria as one could imagine. A native of Amherst, Massachusetts, Ralph has been a history professor at Middlebury College in Vermont since 1989. He is currently a dean at the idyllic New England college and teaches American History and Culture, while specializing in the Civil Rights Movement. While completing his PhD in history at Harvard University, Ralph wrote his thesis on the racial justice efforts in Chicago, and later wrote a book called, "*Northern Protest: Martin Luther King, Jr., Chicago, and the Civil Rights Movement.*"

It was from there that Ralph's curious eyes wandered slightly south and he began a fact-finding journey of Peoria and its role in the Civil Rights Movement.

"One of Dr. King's chief lieutenants, an impressive man named C.T. Vivian, had gone from Macomb, Illinois, to Peoria and then he was at the Carver Center in the late 1940s and early '50s, and in the mid-1940s he was involved in some direct action, but it got no national attention," Ralph said. "But that's what led me to Peoria. And then I found out that there was a much larger movement in the 1960s in Peoria, [a] quite phenomenal movement in many ways and that's what I've been studying."

Ralph has made numerous trips to Peoria in the last 20 or so years, sometimes staying for a month at a time. The research never ends, as the saying goes, and Ralph has discovered a midwestern city with many layers and an interesting history that continues to evolve. According to Ralph, Peoria was only 3 percent African American around 1940, but that figure grew dramatically in the '50s and '60s and is now near 30 percent.

Ralph says Peoria's Black population increased starting in the 1940s as people from Tennessee, Alabama, Mississippi, and Arkansas migrated north essentially along the Mississippi River and where train lines were located. Northern cities offered better job opportunities, including Caterpillar in Peoria. Oftentimes, there were connections, as families knew one another and found a common landing spot.

"You're getting an intensification of segregation in the '60s, '70s, '80s and '90s," Ralph said. "We'd hoped in the 1960s when you got fair housing ordinances plus the Fair Housing Act of 1968 that there would be dramatic reduction in racial segregation, but that has not happened in Peoria. So that's one of the things that's troubling. Peoria is not alone in that. It's been a reality in a lot of northern cities."

(Sports have not been part of Ralph's research, but he has spent a lifetime around basketball. Growing up in Amherst, Ralph's father was the team doctor for several teams at the University of Massachusetts, including men's basketball. One player Ralph got a chance to be around was future Hall of Famer Julius "Dr. J" Erving, who played two varsity seasons at UMass from 1969–71. As an adult, Ralph has played in weekly pickup basketball games at Middlebury for many years.)

As for his research, Ralph said redlining certainly took place in Peoria and very likely had lasting effects on the city.

"Many of these ideas were actually first articulated and elaborated in Chicago and they spread outward as the principal way of doing business," he said. "That had a lot of effects, the legacies of this, in terms of homeownership, where African Americans can live and also the value of homes. Essentially, Peoria had this urban explosion. From the 1950s forward, you had a large number of Whites who moved to peripheral areas. It is absolutely true that in the initial moves, White Peorians had the opportunity to take advantage of these moves, and African Americans would not have been able to."

John Stenson was born in Peoria in 1945, grew up a couple blocks from the Carver Center on the south side, and graduated from Manual. Stenson joined the Peoria Police Department in 1966, and in 1997 he became the city's first Black police chief. He retired in 2004 after 37½ years on the force and enough stories to fill three books. Stenson and others remember a time as recently as the 1980s when the south end was a diverse community with Blacks and Whites comingling and kids riding their bikes from one friend's house to another without any safety concerns.

But at some point, that changed. Businesses left the area. Homeowners fled and renters took over. And then the influx of crack cocaine and gangs started creeping in, turning the community into something very different than the safe lower-middle class neighborhood it once was.

"With coke and marijuana, to distribute that you just can't be a drug dealer standing on the corner with a pocketful of money," Stenson said. "You're going to get robbed or you've got to get protected to keep from getting robbed. You have your gang elements. You gotta have an apartment where you can go in and get it or a window that you can watch it, that type of thing. All of that stuff started occurring. And as you addict people to drugs, they've got to do something to feed that habit. One thing leads to another as far as crime goes. The other part is people who were trying to raise their kids, trying to do the right thing, find that sometimes it's easier to flee an area than fight to keep it clear of crime."

Many of Peoria's basketball stars grew up in the city's impoverished south side, a swath of town just west of the river that has been largely ignored by city leaders for decades. With a modern poverty line hovering close to 45 percent, the 61605 zip code is sadly associated with major gang violence and a stern "don't go down there at night" warning from those in town. Small row houses line the streets near Manual High School, and the infamous Harrison Homes housing project is a little more than a mile south down Griswold Street from the school. It is in this neighborhood that some of Peoria's finest hardcourt stars lived, attending grade schools on the south side before heading to Manual.

"Unless you're there you don't see how far behind people are," said Hedy Elliott, a Peoria teacher for more than 20 years who runs a GED program in town. "Harrison Homes is seven decades behind the other side of the city. People hang out their laundry still, people don't have a car, people don't have a working phone."

Whites fled for other areas of Peoria or the suburbs. Meanwhile, the remnants remain of government policies from decades ago when Blacks were basically pigeonholed into living on the south side. However, if there is a positive in any of this, it is the round ball that bounces on the hardwood and fills the hearts of residents of all races. Basketball. The great equalizer. Because when Peorians are devouring their local hoops on a chilly Friday night in the winter, the only colors that matter are orange and black at Manual, maroon and black at Central, or green and white at Richwoods.

"It might be the only time that African Americans and Whites in Peoria get together and cheer for the same thing," said Shelley Epstein, the *Journal-Star's* former longtime reporter and editor. "When I would go to those games at Robertson (Memorial Field House) or Peoria High or Richwoods, yeah there were a lot of Blacks and Whites and it was endearing. Peoria is not as segregated as Chicago, but it would be a stretch to call it fully integrated."

6

The Tragedy of Mud

Marshall Dunnigan Jr. was a happy, jovial kid. He loved basketball, hip hop music, girls, pizza, candy, hamburgers, and cereal—usual teenager stuff. "He wasn't picky about no foods or nothing, if it was there he'd eat it," his mother Beverly March says.

March says her boy was crazy about candy; Jolly Ranchers, Snickers, PayDay, and Milky Way were his favorites. Like so many young men growing up in Peoria, Dunnigan also was basketball-obsessed.

When he was about five years old, his aunt, Flora March, handed down a family nickname.

"We were calling him Mudbone, and we stopped calling him Mudbone and started calling him Mud," Beverly March said. "It just stuck with him."

From then on, everyone called the smiling boy Mud.

March and Marshall Dunnigan Sr. had two kids together and were never married. March was often working two cleaning jobs at hotels or offices, and Dunnigan Sr. was a police officer with the Peoria Police Department. In the early 1990s, March and Dunnigan Sr. were no longer living under the same roof, but each was involved in the lives of Mud and older sister Marsha. (Mud also had two half-brothers, Lasion March and Timothy Keeton.) When Dunnigan Sr. built a backyard basketball court for Mud at March's house on Scenic Drive, the parents were pleased that they'd know where their boy was most of the time.

A hoop in the backyard? Perfect.

"They'd be out there until like 12 or 1 a.m. playing ball," March said. "That was like every day. It wasn't just [every] so often, it was every day. If they wasn't there, they was going to a school to meet and play ball. That's just the way he was all the time. The only time they came in was to get a drink or use the restroom or whatever. Eat and then right back out there. Long as he was at home and wasn't in any trouble, I had no problem with it. No problem. I was glad that his dad set it up for him out there, so he would be home and most of the time I'd know where he's at when he's not at school."

Future NBA player A.J. Guyton was one of the many kids who spent day after day in Mud's backyard playing basketball. The two even competed together for several years on the same 3-on-3 Gus Macker team.

"He was a little more mature than I was," Guyton said. "I kind of looked up to Mud; I looked at him for leadership and confidence in some ways at that time. There was something about him. He had everything, he was spoiled. His dad was a police officer, and he had all the newest shoes that we couldn't have. We always loved hoopin' with Mud. The one thing we had in common was we adored basketball."

Guyton, who later starred at Peoria Central and Indiana, also shared a love of hip hop music with Mud. When the two hung out, if they weren't playing basketball, they were almost certainly listening to music.

"He was a Big Daddy Kane fan," Guyton said. "I was a fan of OutKast, 8Ball & MJG, and West Coast. He was really West Coast and Big Daddy Kane. He used to wear a little flat top with the little part in it . . . he thought he was Big Daddy Kane."

Living with his mother on Scenic Drive on the north side of town, Mud spent his first three years of high school at Peoria Richwoods. The Knights were a solid basketball program, and coach Wayne Hammerton's system was centered around prolific scoring forward Mike Robinson. Robinson, who was in the same grade as Mud, was a prodigious scoring machine and therefore got the lion's share of shots. A five-star recruit, Robinson went to Purdue and played professionally overseas for more than a decade. Twenty-five years after his high school career, Robinson's 2,944 points at Richwoods stands as the city's all-time record.

It can be overlooked, but playing alongside a scorer of Robinson's stature is not necessarily easy. Every kid wants to get shots up, but there aren't many to go around in a 32-minute game when one player is averaging 30 points. Mud, among others, struggled to coexist on the Robinson-era Richwoods teams. Perhaps more than others, he also struggled to keep his frustrations quiet. The result was a highly talented junior who saw very few minutes on Hammerton's squad.

"As a sophomore, he should have been on varsity," said Charles Nathan, Howard's younger brother who attended Richwoods his last two years of high school. "As a junior, he should have been starting on varsity. So, I think he was frustrated with the (lack of) playing time. He wasn't getting a lot of minutes at all. The offense ran through Mike. So, no matter what, get Mike the ball and everybody else get out of his way. And a lot of guys didn't understand that. They didn't like that. Guys would get in the game or get in practice and they wouldn't do what coach asked them to do. And he wouldn't play you."

Nathan, who transferred to Richwoods after two years at Manual, was the starting point guard and didn't mind deferring to Robinson. But there were others like Mud who wondered when they'd get to shoot the rock.

"I think most guys complained about it (to teammates), but they wanted to play," Nathan said. "Mud was a different type of guy. He was more vocal. He would let you know how he felt. And most guys kept their mouths closed."

Robinson says he had a great relationship with Mud. Now a successful high school coach in Virginia, Robinson is also astute enough to understand it wasn't always comfortable being his teammate. But he says Mud never voiced any issues with him or the Richwoods system.

"Mud was a helluva guy," Robinson said. "One of the funniest guys and easygoing guys that you're ever going to meet. We had a blast. I had classes with him and we couldn't stop laughing. I can still remember his laugh to this day."

Even though he wasn't playing much, Robinson also remembers his former teammate as a talented ballplayer.

"Oh, he was smooth," Robinson said. "He had a helluva hesitation (dribble). Could get to the rim and finish. He wasn't really a shooter, but he was so smooth slashing to the bucket and finishing with either hand. He was really good."

Despite this, Mud hardly saw the floor as a junior at Richwoods in what was Hammerton's 25th of 26 eventual seasons as head coach of the Knights. Hammerton declined to comment on Mud other than to say, "He was a terrific talent. Very talented individual." Whatever happened, Mud was kicked off the Richwoods team as a junior. Neither Nathan or Robinson can recall exactly why, but the situation clearly wasn't working for player or coach.

"I think I pretty much saw it coming because it wasn't the first time that they had bumped heads," Nathan said of Mud and Hammerton.

Across town, Manual was a powerhouse in the midst of its unprecedented championship run. Mud decided he wanted to become a Manual Ram. To do that, one of his parents would have to move to the south end to be within

Marshall Dunnigan Jr. drives to the hoop against Thornton in the 1996 Class AA state title game. A transfer student from Peoria Richwoods, Mud, as everyone called him, was a key contributor to Manual's third state title in the 1990s. (Photo courtesy of Dunnigan family)

Manual's boundary. March acquiesced, and in 1995, she, Mud, and Marsha moved into a one-bedroom house at 1613 S. Arago St., one mile south of Manual.

When Mud enrolled at Manual for the 1995–96 school year, the Rams were coming off back-to-back state titles. Led by star juniors Sergio McClain and Marcus Griffin and budding sophomore point guard Frank Williams, Manual was a force and hungry for more. Nathan, who was a grade ahead of Mud and at college when his former teammate enrolled at Manual, remembers catching up with him that fall and laughing about the Richwoods days.

"He felt like he was at a school where he was supposed to be," Nathan said. "He felt comfortable."

Not one to back down from challenges, Mud entered the fray and became a contributor off the bench for coach Wayne McClain's team. In the 1996 Class AA state title game against an absolutely loaded Thornton team boasting two future NFL players (Antwaan Randle El and Napoleon Harris) and a future NBA player (Melvin Ely), Mud played the entire second half at Peoria's Carver Arena in front of more than 11,000 fans, pulling down key rebounds and playing solid defense. A trusted cog on Coach McClain's team—no small feat—Mud's steady ball handling and decision-making under pressure helped Manual withstand Thornton's press defense and win a third consecutive state crown.

"He was a key component to us winning our third state championship," Griffin said. "He was a transfer student from Richwoods. I don't know what happened or why he came to Manual, but I was happy he did. Me and him had a great relationship."

In the aftermath of the state title, Mud was riding a high like never before. Being part of the big show in town was thrilling for the 18-year-old, whose top basketball achievements prior to Manual was winning Gus Macker 3-on-3 tourneys with Guyton.

"He just felt invincible after that," Dunnigan Sr. said. "Nothing else mattered. It was like he had lived his life."

Less than six weeks after the exhilarating state championship, Mud was at the home of his girlfriend, Dareth Perry, in the Harrison Homes public housing complex. Dunnigan Sr., a Peoria police sergeant at the time, used to warn his son to steer clear of the Harrison but Mud was undaunted.

"He said, 'Dad, they know who I am. They won't bother me,'" Dunnigan Sr. recalls. "I said stay your butt out of the Harrison Homes, it's dangerous.

'No, dad, they won't bother me. They know who I am. They know I'm your son.'"

After 3 a.m. on the morning of April 25, 1996, Mud left Perry's home and started walking the three to four blocks to his mother's house on South Arago. He didn't make it nearly that far.

About an hour earlier that same April night, a member of the Black Disciples gang named Anthony "Cheesy" Metcalf was murdered near the Warner Homes, a housing project known to be BD territory. Thinking the murder was done by a member of the rival Gangster Disciples, the BD's sent a pair of 17-year-olds to the Harrison Homes to exact revenge in GD territory. According to court documents, Dennis Mosley was the driver and Nikia Perry (unrelated to Dareth Perry) rode in the passenger seat with a handgun, a pair of teenagers in the middle of the Peoria night searching for blood.

Nikia Perry approached Mud, who had no gang affiliations and was simply walking home, and shot him twice in the chest, once in the head, and once in the leg. Marshall Lynne Dunnigan Jr., 18 years old and merely weeks away from high school graduation, was pronounced dead around 4 a.m.

From the Peoria *Journal-Star: As Peoria County State's Attorney Kevin Lyons sketched evidence he would have used at trial, it became clear that a familiar Peoria theme ran through the killing—payback among street gangs battling for drug sales turf. "The Black Disciples control Warner Homes; the Gangster Disciples control Harrison Homes," Lyons said.*

But Dunnigan was neither in a gang nor the original target of the hit. Lyons said, according to Perry's statements, Black Disciples leader Frank Tyler was angered that fellow gang member Anthony "Cheesy" Metcalf had been shot dead earlier the night of April 25 near Warner Homes, allegedly by Gangster Disciple Rico Jackson. Tyler ordered Black Disciples Perry and Dennis "Zoonie" Mosley to "kick in (Jackson's) door and take care of him." If Jackson was not there, the pair's instructions were to "find somebody to take it out on."

Around 4 a.m., the phone rang at Beverly March's home. It was the Peoria Police Department, and they wanted to know what clothes Mud was wearing that night. "Why are you asking?" she said. The voice on the other end said someone had been shot near the Harrison, but they weren't dead, and March says she was told it wasn't her son. At some point, March started walking toward the Harrison to find out for herself. Dunnigan Sr. was driving from the shooting scene at the same time and picked her up.

"He said you don't need to go. He said I just left there and identified the body and that was him," she said.

In this pre-cell phone and social media era, most Manual students arrived to school the next day with no clue of what occurred hours earlier. But when they found out . . .

"It was just hysteria," said Sandy Farkash, Manual's then-principal. "It was just so difficult. And the faculty was traumatized as well. We have had several losses of lives, but this one . . . the way it happened, when it happened, to whom it happened, all those things were like a perfect storm. As a result of that, it was very traumatic. In a community like Manual, everybody knows pretty much everything. These kids were not strangers."

Farkash had received his own middle-of-the-night call from Peoria Police Chief John Stenson, telling him one of his students had been gunned down. Farkash called counselors, assistant principals, deans, and some teachers to prepare them for the daunting day ahead.

"I don't know that much education took place, but we had counselors there and counselors from other schools there," Farkash said. "We had staff to try to deal with it. You had kids who were just screaming in the hallways. Grief in a community like Manual is very demonstrable. You know it's happening. Kids are bawling, they're screaming. You think to a degree they are almost overreacting but they're not."

"Probably one of the most difficult things was because he was one of us," Griffin said. "You see people dying and everything, but it hits home when it's somebody who you see as you. Going to school that day . . . it was a bad day. Just consoling so many people. There was so much crying. I didn't focus on school for two weeks. It made school seem so minute. He's not here . . . I have classes with him. Teachers say something and you've got a tear coming out of your eye. It was just so crazy. Then it was how do you bounce back from something like this? It was rough. That shook everybody. Every time I see his father I give him a hug."

In the aftermath of the killing, Mud's family struggled to comprehend what had happened to their beloved son and brother. As March tried to pick up the pieces and simply get through the days that followed, her house was quiet with mostly just family members at her side. With one exception. Wayne McClain, Mud's basketball coach at Manual, stopped by the house on South Arago to check on March and ask if there was anything he could do.

Marshall Dunnigan Jr., right, celebrates the 1996 Class AA state title with his Manual teammates, including Marcus Griffin (holding ball). (Photo courtesy of Dunnigan family)

"It was really heartwarming and soothing," March said of McClain. "He took the time to come and be with me during that period of time. It really meant a lot when he came to the house and he was there for me."

"Here's the thing, you knew that he didn't have a bad bone in his body and couldn't be mad at anyone," said Robinson, Mud's former Richwoods teammate. "And you find out it was a mistaken identity. He wasn't into anything (gangs, etc.). That wasn't his personality, that wasn't him. It angers you but yet you become scared because we all grew up in that same area. So, it's like man that could have been me. That's the first thing that goes through your mind when something like that happens."

About 2,000 people attended Mud's funeral at Mount Zion Baptist Church five days after he was killed. He was laid to rest at Lutheran Cemetery in his Manual Rams warmup uniform. The day was so emotional that two people were taken from the church by ambulance. Coach Wayne McClain spoke at the service, and Mud's Manual teammates served as pallbearers, sitting in the first row at one of Peoria's oldest churches. *"Just 11 school days before he was scheduled to graduate, Marshall Lynne Dunnigan Jr. was laid to rest by friends and family members Monday afternoon,"* was the lead of the *Journal-Star's* article the next day.

"It was the largest funeral I've ever seen, and I was a police officer for 33 years," Dunnigan Sr. said.

Although most of Peoria's basketball community attended the funeral, one major star did not.

"I remember it was so shocking, it really hurt," Robinson said. "I didn't go to his funeral because I have this thing. A couple years before that I went to my first funeral, and it was just a terrible experience seeing somebody that way. Out of respect for Mud, I didn't want to remember him being in a casket. I didn't want to go. I couldn't do it because I experienced one a couple years earlier and I told myself I'd never go to one again unless I absolutely have to."

The next season, 1996–97, Manual retired its first basketball jersey in school history. A home white jersey with "12 Dunnigan" on the back still hangs on the wall in the beautiful gymnasium, some 25 years later. Until the spring of 2020 when Manual retired No. 34 for Howard Nathan, Mud's No. 12 was the school's only retired number.

It took many years, but Dunnigan Sr. eventually came back to Manual's gym. And in 2020, Mud's nephew Brian Tyler was a starter on Manual, and he was able to look up into the stands and see his mother, Marsha Harris, and grandparents at most games.

Three generations of Dunnigans pose for a photo in Manual's gym, with Mud's retired No. 12 jersey in the background. From left, Marshall Dunnigan Sr., Beverly March, Marsha Harris, and Brian Tyler. (Photo by John Grap)

"For a while I wouldn't go," Dunnigan Sr. says. "Time heals (wounds) and now I'm able to walk in there and look up and see his jersey. I wanted nothing to do with Manual basketball for many years. But I love watching my grandson, and I go to all his games."

(Author's note: Dunnigan Sr. was interviewed in February 2020, and in September 2021, he passed away at his Peoria home. He was 68.)

March, too, enjoys seeing her grandson play ball. She said Tyler reminds her of Mud when she's watching him compete. Visions of her son are never far away in the Manual gym.

"It's a good feeling," she says of seeing the No. 12 jersey. "It lets me know that they cared a lot for him to still have it up there. I have a good feeling with that. Very proud."

On January 10, 1997, Nikia Perry was sentenced to 60 years in prison for Dunnigan's murder. From the Peoria *Journal-Star: "Sixty years," Judge Robert Barnes said to the defendant in Peoria County Circuit Court. "The defendant has forfeited his right to live among men in society."*

Peoria County State's Attorney Kevin Lyons opted to use the facts of another murder—the 1993 killing of Anthony Foster—at Perry's sentencing for the Dunnigan slaying. As a result, Lyons said Friday he will drop the Foster murder charges against Perry.

Mosley was tried separately and convicted. He received 40 years in prison for his part in the murder, but had his sentence reduced and was released from prison in May 2019, just before his 41st birthday. Mosley served 22 years behind bars. According to court documents, Perry is eligible for parole in October 2024, which would be the halfway point of his 60-year sentence.

Meanwhile, the sadness will never disappear, but Mud's older sister Marsha Harris says she long ago reconciled her feelings regarding her brother's killers.

"It ain't going to change the fact, regardless of how much time they got, they're serving their time and they're going to have to deal with God from there," Harris said. "There ain't nothing more I can do. It ain't going to change my feelings. I still don't hate nobody. I was upset and I was hurt because I lost my brother, but I didn't have the type of attitude like I wished they were dead."

Every year on December 7, the family gathers at March's house to celebrate Mud's birthday. March brings a picture of Mud to Kroger and the grocery store makes a large cake with his picture atop it. Even though it's winter in the Midwest, the crew of about 20 hangs out in the backyard or the porch and listens to Mud's old music favorites. March will cook or sometimes her son Lasion makes barbeque. Some years, the group demands pizza.

"I don't like pizza but they'll be like, 'This party ain't for you, it's for him,'" March says with a laugh. "OK, go ahead and get the pizza then."

Remarkably, April 25, 2021, was the 25th anniversary of Mud's murder.

"I can't believe it's been that long," his mother said.

7

Finding Oscar Mack

It's a chilly Midwestern day in Peoria in February 2020, and one of the best players this basketball-rich city has ever produced is standing on an outdoor court that helped mold his game. David Booth was a self-made star at Peoria Manual, a lithe six-foot-seven forward with a nose for the ball, a knack for scoring, and a round-the-clock work ethic. Standing on the gray concrete at Proctor Center on the south side (one of the legendary Peoria courts where the who's who of River City hoopers went hard day after day in the summer), 1988 Manual graduate Booth looks around with a slight smile and a knowing air—he used to own this place. Now 50, Booth still looks like he could give you a couple buckets if your team needed it.

After Manual, he went on to score 1,933 points at DePaul University, still good for second all-time in the Chicago school's record books. Only 13-year NBA player Mark Aguirre (2,182 points) has scored more. Booth had several near misses with NBA teams but instead carved out an excellent 13-year career of his own, albeit overseas. Knowing he wanted to stay in basketball, Booth became a scout for the Memphis Grizzlies for four years, then a DePaul assistant for one season before latching on with the New Orleans Pelicans. He worked for the Pelicans for nearly a decade, the last six years as director of player personnel. In the summer of 2020, Booth was named the NBA's vice president of basketball operations.

All the while, Booth kept an eye on his hometown. With the majority of his family still in Peoria, including younger brother Derrick who served as a Manual coach for 16 seasons (11 as head coach), getting intel on Peoria's basketball scene has always been just a phone call away for David. The brothers have also run a free youth basketball camp in Peoria for years, so David has kept a close watch on the area's basketball talent. Derrick recalls David telling him four times over the years that he'd seen a young prospect he tabbed as a future NBA player. They were players either in middle school or early in high school that just had *it*. They were Springfield's Andre Iguodala (9th pick in the 2004 draft) and three Peoria kids: Frank Williams (25th pick in 2002), Shaun Livingston (4th pick in 2004), and . . . Oscar Mack.

Wait, who?

"He definitely could have played professionally, I was pretty sure about that," David Booth said of Mack.

"He's a kid that could have made money playing. He was one of the top kids in the area in terms of instincts and abilities. He didn't have to work on his game. Everything came natural to him. Very similar to Frank (Williams). I had to work for it, but those guys were born to play. I saw him play a couple times (as a high school freshman), and I told him you've got a chance but I just think he didn't have good mentorship around him and his surroundings got the best of him. It's kind of sad because he could have been the next great one after Frank. Point guard—could have also played the 2 (guard). His ball-handling skills, his court vision, things just came so easy to him. It was a shame that we didn't get to see the finished result because he was a special kid, I thought."

More than likely, you have never heard the name Oscar Mack. The reasons for that are complicated yet simple, confusing yet sensical, and self-destructive yet understandable. Born on January 3, 1988, Mack was the eighth of 12 kids for Ramona Mack and Oscar Williams. The couple was unmarried and Williams wasn't around much, but they had 12 children, each a year apart. Mack grew up in a Harrison Homes housing project apartment, sharing a bedroom with older brother Deondrae and younger brother Deothius, whom everyone called Bob. The bedroom had two beds for the three boys.

"If I was sleepy first, if me and Bob went to sleep first, Deondrae was on the floor," Oscar recalls. "If Deondrae and Bob get the beds first, I'm on the floor or I'll sleep downstairs on the couch in the living room. That's terrible. My older brother got friends over all night and my sister has her friends and they're running in and out all night. You better hope you get tired first and go upstairs and get that bed."

"Being at the zoo with the animals, caged in," Deondrae said of the family apartment. "It was a mess. Kind of hard for us all to get along in that one apartment."

Under the best of sleeping circumstances, the Harrison Homes was a rough place to grow up. Built in the early 1940s and nicknamed Brick City for the dark red brick buildings, the Harrison had hundreds of nearly identical, two-story apartments that went on for multiple blocks on acres and acres of land. All entrances were on ground level, where one would walk through a steel screen door and immediately into the living room. Next to the living room was a kitchen with a nearby staircase that led up to one or two bedrooms. Located about a mile and a half south of Manual High School down South Griswold Street, the housing projects were known for gangs, violence, and downtrodden living conditions for many of Peoria's impoverished, and predominantly African American, residents.

Mack offers that growing up, he heard gunshots every day. "Not almost . . . every day. I got accustomed to it."

Gangs and violence didn't stop outside Mack's door. Several males in Mack's family were members of the Gangster Disciples, one of the feared gangs in town. Mack has seen multiple siblings sent to prison, an older brother killed by a truck at the age of seven while running for a ball in the street, and had a four-year-old nephew shot in the leg when a 45-caliber gun accidentally went off in the Harrison apartment.

"Every day I'm worried about what I'm going to eat, what I'm going to wear to school, all that became a factor," Mack said. "And on top of that, when I go outside I'm seeing gangbangers, I'm seeing thugs, I'm seeing people get shot, I'm seeing people get killed, my brother is gangbanging, his friends are gangbanging . . . we stayed on a street that's notorious for gangbanging. So, it's like I want to go home and not stress about stuff because home is where the heart is and home is where you're supposed to go to relax, but it's like when I go there, that's where all the problems are at. Whether it's just getting home, or whether it's getting in the house and what am I going to eat tonight? Everybody else probably already ate so what am I going to eat?"

Mack found refuge a few blocks away in the home of his godmother, Brenda Bobo-Breedlove. A nurse at OSF St. Francis, Bobo-Breedlove had five children of her own, but she was friends with Mack's mother and sensed she could use some help. When Mack was about three or four, Bobo-Breedlove took him in, and he spent many nights at her home in the following years. While there on Westmoreland Street, only a few blocks from the Harrison, Mack felt safe and secure, like he was in a whole different world despite still being in the throes of his familiar neighborhood. Mack's first tattoo, on the left side of his neck, says "Brenda" in cursive.

"Every Sunday we sat down as a family and ate dinner (at Bobo-Breedlove's)," Mack said. "I wanted all that (with my biological family). I want to hear how your day went, sis. I want to hear how your day went, brother. And I want to tell you about my day. I never got that. I feel like I was (robbed) out of a lot of family values that would have made me a better man than I am today. I feel like I missed out on all that. I feel in my heart that things would have been 10 times better if I just had that a little bit. Yes, I got it from Brenda and I accepted it, and I love her more than life itself. But it's just different if I would have got it from my biological mom."

Teneal Johnson, the third of Bobo-Breedlove's five children, says Mack was treated like he was part of the family. Bobo-Breedlove also took in a niece around this time, so even though this was another crowded house, there was plenty of love (and food) to go around.

"She loved Oscar and Oscar loved her," said Johnson, who now lives in Detroit. "She took him in and Oscar called her mom. We all just had a relationship. He was just like one of the family. He addressed my aunts and uncles as aunt and uncle. He was part of everything. He never was a bad kid. Respectful, and yes, he was very appreciative."

By middle school, Mack's basketball talent was becoming apparent. Playing for Trewyn School, he was dominating middle school games, just too skilled, too smooth, and too advanced for his peers. Mack and his older brother by one year, Deondrae, were regulars at Manual's competitive 3 p.m. open gym runs in the summer, and coaches were excited about the possibility of a Mack tandem in high school. Before Oscar's growth spurt prior to high school, some coaches even pondered if Deondrae could be the better prospect, as he, too, displayed excellent skills.

"Deondrae was smaller but he was special too," said Derrick Booth, then a Manual assistant. "But then Oscar started growing and getting long in his seventh- and eighth-grade years. So, then you start to see how special he is going to be the more you watched him. Then I would watch his grade school games . . . and it was just too easy for him."

This was a strange time at Manual, one of the state's most storied high school basketball programs. After a fabulous seven-year run, including three state titles, Wayne McClain left Manual in 2001 with a 177–35 record (.835 winning percentage) to take an assistant job at the University of Illinois under Bill Self. Manual turned to Andrew Johnson, who had recently been fired from Proviso East. Johnson had been successful, but his teams regularly came up short in the state tournament. Johnson's two-year stint at Manual was an utter disaster. Allegations of player mistreatment, run-ins with his

P.E. students during the school day, and a 28–28 record marred Johnson's brief and unpleasant stint in Peoria.

> From the Peoria *Journal-Star* on February 20, 2003: *Manual boys basketball coach Andrew Johnson was suspended with pay Wednesday, pending an investigation by District 150, a school district source said. The action is because of an alleged physical altercation with a student. After an initial allegation that Johnson had choked a student, as well as claims that he verbally abused his players, a group of parents met Feb. 6 with school administrators. This week, Johnson allegedly threw a male student against a wall. Sources close to the program said Johnson has had difficulty gaining the respect of his players since his arrival before last season, and recent practices have had incidents in which player and coach were cursing at each other.*

Still, with Oscar Mack and fellow freshman big man Breland McKnight set to enroll in the fall of 2003 under new head coach Tim Kenny, there was reason for optimism among the Rams faithful.

Mack and McKnight both started on varsity from day one under Kenny, a longtime Manual assistant who was now tasked with bringing the program back to prominence. In addition to playing varsity, Mack also got a chance to compete in a few freshman games against his peers. It was on that level, against rival Peoria Central, where Mack may have cemented his standing as Peoria's Next One. Manual coaches were not shy about telling Mack that he reminded them of the great Frank Williams, who won Mr. Basketball in 1998, Big Ten Player of the Year in 2001 and was an NBA first-round draft pick in 2002.

Meechie Edwards, a former stellar Central player in his own right, was coaching the freshman squad at his alma mater when Mack put on a show.

"How do you coach against that? Oscar Mack was a smooth player," said Edwards, now Central's varsity girls' coach. "Had different gears. He was hard to scout because he could go left or right. He had a jump shot, he could shoot midrange, he could drop you off left or right and he had the tenacity of guarding you. That's what was different. You look at a lot of players and they might have these elements . . . he was a kid where I was like, man, the sky is the limit. He was so smooth and his awareness of the game and his knowledge of the game was on a different level. If he just stayed focused, we would be talking about (Oscar) with the Howards (Nathan) . . . he was one of the exclusive players. Coaching against him? Oh, my goodness, it was a nightmare."

And so how many points did Mack score that day?

"Oh, my goodness, you really want me to tell you?" Edwards asked. "I'm gonna stop counting at about 30. I'm a competitor myself (laughing). Awesome player. He's one of those players, you just find yourself watching him play. As a coach I'm very competitive and all up in your face, but I'm like, 'Jesus, how do you stop that?'"

"When he got to play against his peers it wasn't even fair," said Derrick Booth, who was keeping the scorebook for that freshman game against Central.

On the court, whether at practice or in games, Mack was focused, driven, coachable, and displayed a genuine love of playing ball. In the classroom, well, ahem, that was a different story. Mack says he basically did nothing academically at Trewyn and was still allowed to play basketball. So, he figured, why would high school be different?

"My whole life, I got away with shit because I was a good basketball player," Mack said. "I blame the school system, too. Middle school had a big effect on spoiling me. My sixth-grade year, I passed with all F's and I didn't miss one game. I didn't take nothing serious and I still did not miss one game."

"He was a great kid to coach," said Kenny, the varsity coach. "Not a good one, a great one. High motor, played hard, there every day. Great leader too, not a good leader, a great leader. Frankie (Williams) was quiet, Oscar was more like Howard (Nathan). Everybody around him was going to be better if he was there, I guarantee it. And the coaches loved him. Sometimes you have a kid who doesn't make it who drives the coaches nuts and is hard to deal with. But he's not that case at all."

With this highly talented freshman player on their team, Manual coaches were extremely proactive in monitoring his academics. And there were problems from the very start. It was strange, though. When Mack speaks, he sounds intelligent, looks you in the eye, etc. He's funny, engaging, never impolite with adults or teachers. And yet . . .

"His issues during the day, they're hard to explain because it wasn't the disrespect and it wasn't the violence," Derrick Booth said. "It was just silly behaviors. Not going to class, talking while he's in class, cracking jokes while he's in class, getting kicked out of class. So, it was a lot of just constant, 'Can you make it through this class? Can you make it through this class?' Talking to the teacher, can you call me or email me and let me know how he did today? It was nonstop, every day. And this was his first semester of high school. We learned really quick before Thanksgiving when the season starts, he has to be monitored and managed. Because those first couple weeks of school, you hear teachers talking about Oscar Mack. But it was never volatile, just disruptions. Constant disruptions."

Manual was a rebuilding program starting two freshmen, and it struggled that year. Mack, who wore No. 31, averaged about 12 points and a handful of assists per game, but the Rams were outclassed on most nights. Still, there was a future star in their midst, a transcendent six-foot point guard who would grow to be six-foot-three and was sure to lead Manual back to its rightful place among the state's elite.

But that never happened.

In the second semester of Mack's freshman year, he did not pass five classes, the requirement for athletic eligibility in the following semester. That meant he would be ineligible at the start of his sophomore year, but if he took care of school business that fall, he wouldn't miss too many games. Again, that didn't happen either.

Coaches were optimistic about Mack regaining eligibility. At that time, a student could record all D's and be eligible to play sports under Illinois High School Association rules.

"No, it was never close," Derrick Booth said of Mack regaining eligibility. "When I look at his grades all of sophomore year, I don't know if he passed a core class after that. But when I (heard) his perspective it makes sense to me. He just thought it was going to happen. Because it had happened all through his middle school years. He's showing up every day and just waiting on us to say, 'OK, go ahead and get dressed to play.' And it never happened. It didn't work like that in high school. You have to pass. The time and effort of walking into class and encouraging and motivating him, it took so much energy, even his freshman year. The teachers saw we were trying to work with him and help him, and they were trying to give him the benefit of the doubt. I think there came a time at the end of his freshman year where they couldn't give him the benefit of the doubt anymore because he was putting forth less and less effort."

So, what gives? Here was an intelligent kid who dreamed of playing in the NBA and was the one in a million who actually had that chance. He possessed all the skills you'd ever want and paired it with a terrific basketball IQ, along with effort on the defensive end that young stars usually rebuff.

"He's still a mystery to me," Derrick Booth said. "He loves the game, and I know he loved basketball more than anything back then. So even after you find out, 'OK they really are not going to let me play until I hit the books,' he never buckled down and hit the books. And that's the disconnect for me.

Because he could have done it, easily. Going into the sophomore year, he could have done it first semester and been playing by the Pontiac Tournament (around Christmas). That was the second blow to us as coaches. We were thinking we could get him back on track by the Pontiac Tournament. And we slowly started to realize that he's not taking care of business, and it's getting harder and harder to get him to go to class and stay in class and do the work. By Pontiac Tournament his sophomore year, that was a reality for us as coaches that we're about to lose this kid. Right after that, it was downhill for him. Second semester sophomore year, that's when we lost him."

Mack toggles back and forth between taking responsibility for all this and saying if he just had a better support system, things would have turned out differently for him. No one disputes the latter point. Just a *little bit* of stability and this is a different story. During middle school, Oscar and Deondrae played for the Champaign-based Ft. Sooy AAU program under coach Verdell Jones II. The program was big time in those days and boasted players like Shaun Livingston, Richard McBride (Springfield Lanphier and Illinois), Brian Randle (Peoria Notre Dame and Illinois), Daniel Ruffin (Peoria Central and Bradley), Brandon Lee (Peoria Central and Northwestern), Justin Bocot (Bloomington and Southern Illinois), and Verdell Jones III (Champaign Central and Indiana). Mack recalls the excitement he felt before a tournament in Florida when Coach Jones told the whole team that they could bring five family members on the trip, expenses paid.

But no family members attended. Mack says his mother never saw him play a game at any level.

On another AAU trip to Houston to play in the well-known Kingwood Classic, Mack recalls a feeling of emptiness as he gazed into the stands and again didn't see a family member present.

"I probably cried a couple times on a couple trips," Mack says. "I know I cried when we went to Houston, I cried my eyes out. Because everyone's family was there, and it's like goddamn, I'm the star player and I don't have a piece of family here. I know people who sat on the bench and never played and their mom and dad flew to every fucking trip. Their mom and dad flew to every trip, and he doesn't get a lick of time unless we're up 30. And here I am the best player, can probably get you 30 or 40 (points) if I wanted to, and I don't have nothing in the stands. It starts dawning on me like what the fuck am I doing it for?"

Jones II, now the head coach at Urbana High School, would make the approximately 200-mile round trip drive twice each practice day to pick up and drop off Oscar and Deondrae in Peoria for Ft. Sooy workouts back in Champaign-Urbana.

"But you know, that's what you do," Jones II said. "That's too far for them to ride their bike. I'm a firm believer of when kids commit to you, you commit to them. If you have the resources and the ability, you shore up those areas of deficit. Knowing those kids wanted to play for me, that's not a problem, I'll come up and get you, practice, take you home, feed you. I just felt you owed that to the kids."

As for Oscar's game, Jones II echoes many others in his effusive praise of the young guard.

"Oh, he was phenomenal," Jones said. "Defensively, he was a juggernaut. He could put it on the floor and get to the basket when he wanted. He was hard to guard. He had a motor. He was skilled."

Mack's last game in a Manual uniform was the final contest of his freshman year in a regional playoff loss against Canton. He performed brilliantly and displayed the type of promise and future greatness everyone expected of him. If only.

"In 30 years at Manual, it's the most disappointing story I have," said Kenny, who now serves as the school's athletic director. "There's hardly a time I come into the gym and don't think of Oscar. He would be on the wall (a place for retired numbers or All-State/Mr. Basketball honorees), he was that good. I loved him. He was going to be something. It's hard to go through that gym and not think about him. He would be on that wall and he would have made money playing basketball. It was gut-wrenching, him not playing. For him, the community, the school."

Mack often returns to his family and environment when he thinks about what could have been.

> "I can't sit here and blame anybody else for my actions and what I did . . .
> I hate to put something on family, but if I just would have had somebody
> in my family, an uncle, anybody, that was nonstop, constant on my ass
> . . . my mom was nonchalant about a lot of shit," Mack says. "I'm in this
> environment, you want me to be accustomed to that. So, then it goes
> back to me where I should have just been woke and I don't want this for
> myself. Which at the time I didn't. I knew I wanted to go to college. But
> then it's like when I leave school, I'm in the Harrison Homes. So many
> bad influences and so many things to grab your attention."

Mack should have been a member of Manual's graduating class of 2007. But starting sophomore year, he hardly passed another class. He did not walk the stage and graduate with his classmates. Despite being part of a loaded Illinois prep class that year, which included a pair of future top two picks in the NBA Draft, former coaches and teammates don't hesitate to say Mack would have been in the discussion for Mr. Basketball. According to the recruiting website Rivals.com, Illinois had seven players ranked among the nation's top 125 that year: Derrick Rose (Chicago Simeon, ranked No. 3 overall), Nayal Koshwal (Chicago Boys to Men Academy, No. 18), Beas Hamga (Decatur Christian, No. 26), Evan Turner (Westchester St. Joseph's, No. 49), Demetri McCamey (Westchester St. Joseph's, No. 72), Brandon McGee (Chicago Crane, No. 116) and Mike Tisdale (Riverton, No. 125).

"When he came on with Ft. Sooy and played on the national circuit, you got to really see how dominant he was," said Verdell Jones III, who was ranked No. 126 in the class of 2008 and enjoyed a solid career at Indiana. "I saw him play against some of the top guards in his class and he would hold his own. Yeah, he was next up for sure. Oscar was definitely one of the most fun guys to play with. Great personality, always laughing and smiling. Being on the court with him, you knew you had a dog with you the whole time. Pick you up when you fell, help-side defense, you just knew when he was on the floor, good things were going to happen with him."

It can be startling to hear coaches and peers say a kid who hardly played organized basketball was once in the same stratosphere as a pair of Mr. Basketball winners like Manual greats Howard Nathan and Frank Williams. But it's not like there is an agenda in making the analogy; nobody benefits or gains a thing from exaggerating. Nathan's prestige and legacy speaks for itself in Peoria and beyond. The name Frank Williams is rightfully spoken in hushed tones by Manual people. A six-foot-four point guard with a wiry, strong body type like Mack's, Williams was electric with the ball in his hands, and he was named Illinois' top player in 1998 ahead of Fenwick's Corey Maggette and Whitney Young's Quentin Richardson, a pair of players who combined to play 27 years in the NBA.

Tim Kenny coached both Williams and Mack. You might want to be sitting down for this next part.

"When I say Oscar was better than Frank, that's not a putdown of Frank," Kenny said. "That's just how good Oscar was at that same age. Frankie got better over the years. In Peoria we call the first names, you don't have to say the last name: Shaun, Frankie, Howard, Oscar. And they're not saying who? And that's a small group, too. Frankie had that incredible court vision and so did Oscar. He was physically stronger (than Frank).

He was a player, golly was he a player. You don't see guards going to the hole like he did, dunking with his left hand, dunking with his right hand. He was unbelievable. Shoot the ball, pass the ball like Frankie Williams with Howard's motor. And a great mind and knew the game. Probably a better feel for the game than Frank at that same age."

With high school basketball out the door, Mack hung around town, unable to break away from the destructive tentacles of his family. Like the majority of the Mack family, Oscar lacked a high school diploma. Unlike most of his kin, however, he yearned for more. Mack played in the Moonlight Basketball League, a league founded in 1994 by George Jacob, a Peoria City Council member and president of Brewers Distributing Co., and Junior Watkins, a Peoria County Board member and longtime Peorian who played ball at Manual in the 1960s before working at Caterpillar and then Brewers Distributing. Jacob and Watkins developed the Moonlight League to give at-risk kids an outlet late at night when they could otherwise be getting into trouble. Each year, there were 8 teams with 10 players per team between the ages of 17 and 26. Games began at 10 p.m. on Thursdays, and for the first several years at Carver Center and the YMCA, there was only one court, so it was 2:30 a.m. when the volunteers helping run the league sleepily exited for the night.

"At that time Peoria was kind of shaky," Watkins told *Peoria Magazine.* *"Guys were fighting . . . gangs and everything. We came up with the Moonlight League to get them off the streets. They would play in the evening after everything had closed up. The rationale was to get everybody tired so they'd just want to go home and get some rest." (laughs)*

The league was a hit, and one year 157 players tried out for 80 spots. Scott Meister was one of the first people that Jacob and Watkins tabbed to help out with Moonlight basketball. A classic behind-the-scenes basketball guy in town, Meister followed his father into the heating and air conditioning business, but really he spends most of his time helping kids. In addition to raising five children of his own, Meister loves building relationships with young kids and trying to help steer them in a positive direction.

"People used to ask what do we do, and I said we play basketball," Meister said of Moonlight. "We don't claim to do miracles. We just get kids together and play basketball. My thing was I made it a point to shake every kid's hand every night when he came through that door. I wanted to get to know the kids and spend a lot of time talking to them. I can't honestly say if we did anything special. We had one gentleman that came up with the slogan, 'This is a drop in the bucket.' What we're doing is nothing more than a drop in the bucket, this is our drop. But if everybody puts a drop in the bucket, the bucket will fill. And when he said that at one of our meetings, it just really hit home. We were hands-on. We enjoyed it, we were talking to kids and meeting kids and building friendships. It's truly what we did."

Volunteer coaches held a draft each year to select teams in Moonlight, and players came back a week later to find out if they were picked and what team they were on. With the random grouping of players, there's no doubt rival gang members sometimes became teammates.

"But we never had one fight," said Meister, who also spent seven years as a volunteer assistant coach at Illinois Central College in Peoria. "I remember my parents and my brothers and sisters when I said I'm getting involved with this, and we're going down to Carver Center to play basketball until two in the morning, well that (conversation) didn't go real well. But we never had one fight, not one car window busted out, not one car tire slashed, nothing. I think the word was on Thursday nights between 10 p.m. and 2 a.m., Carver Center is off limits, or the Y is off limits. Because there was never, ever an issue."

Along the way, the league brought in longtime Peoria teacher Hedy Elliott to help kids without a high school degree to prepare for the GED. There was no minimum number of kids required; league organizers decided that if one kid wanted to earn his GED, they would help. Elliott would arrive at the gym at 10 p.m. and tutor kids for an hour, either before or after their game. Elliott grew up on the south side and graduated from Manual in 1988. It was during a stint as teacher at Harrison School in the late 1990s that she became closely acquainted with the Mack family.

"I would probably say the minute I laid eyes on him I loved that kid," Elliott said of Oscar. "He's memorable. As a little kid he had this reddish-blonde hair. And he has these light-colored eyes. Imagine him 6, 7, 8 years old, he was positively precious. The family . . . they were wild. Especially his twin sisters that I had (laughing). They were a piece of work. But Oscar, he was unlike the rest of the Macks. He was very quiet, gentle, and probably didn't get a word in edgewise, there were so many kids. His look was so striking and he was so sweet. The first day I met him I was like, 'Oh my god, I love that kid.'"

Then several years later, Mack enrolled in Elliott's GED class. Elliott, who freely admits to knowing nothing about sports, recalls Mack's answer when they went around the room and each student talked about their hopes and dreams.

"Oscar says I want to get my GED and go play basketball somewhere," she said. "I'm like, well, I can talk to my friend Scottie Meister, maybe Oscar is good. I don't know. So, I call Scottie and Scottie's like, 'Oscar Mack? Oh yeah.' And goes on and on."

The GED is a 7.5-hour test, similar to the ACT, and comprising five parts: writing/grammar, history/social studies, science, reading, and math. A person has to pass each portion of the exam to earn the degree. If someone is weak in math, for example, but passes the other four parts, he or she can retake just the math portion to work toward passing the exam.

"People have it in their mind that it's a basic competency test," Elliott said. "And it's like no, it's not just a basic test. It's very involved, it's very long. It's not easy."

The year was 2011, and Mack was 23 years old. He was four years removed from when his high school class graduated, and he hadn't been in a school setting in several years. Elliott's GED class met three times a week, and she remembers working a lot outside of those set hours with Mack, driving to his apartment with practice tests and returning later to pick them up. During this time, Meister had worked his basketball connections to get Mack placed at Black Hawk East Junior College in Galva, an hour northwest of Peoria. But it was contingent on Mack passing the GED. With his sights set on finally getting out of Peoria and rejoining the organized basketball world, Mack was motivated.

"Oh yeah, that was his dream was to get to college," Elliott said. "He was putting in the work."

Like many others, Mack did not pass all five parts of the test his first time taking it. The writing portion was the last subject he had to pass, and the clock was ticking to enroll in time at Black Hawk East. He passed just in time and would be able to become a college student, although he'd have to sit out his first year of basketball before becoming eligible as a sophomore. Meister and Elliott worked together to pay for Mack's apartment, in addition to buying him groceries and providing rides back and forth from Peoria to Galva. Elliott recalls one ride in particular when she was driving Mack back to campus after he came home for a weekend.

"He said, 'Can we go to this liquor store on Madison Park (Terrace) next to Kroger?'" Elliott said. "And I'm like, mmm k. I hope I'm not taking this kid to buy some liquor, you know. He comes out with a pair of shoes. From

Oscar Mack poses for a photo in the fall of 2020 in Springfield. Mack was tabbed as the next great Peoria guard from a young age, but a difficult childhood and lack of focus in the classroom resulted in him only playing one year of high school basketball. (Photo by Jeff Karzen)

being around my students and my GED students, when middle class people say, 'They have the latest shoes . . . ' No, they're knockoff shoes they bought for $15 from the back of the liquor store. I remember that. That was a learning experience for me. Like, oh that's where all of the nice tennis shoes come from. They're just knockoffs from the back of the liquor store."

BJ McCullum was the head coach at Black Hawk East, a Division 1 junior college program. He said at that time, the team did not have other players with similar backgrounds to Mack. Additionally, the rest of Black Hawk's roster was mainly comprised of 18–20-year-olds, and here was a 23-year-old who had not played organized basketball since his freshman year of high school.

"To be honest, the living conditions we had for players in the off-campus apartment they lived in, they weren't deplorable, but they weren't anything that you'd love," McCullum said. "I think the whole thing together had an effect: not being able to play, getting rushed into classes at the last minute, then living with eight other guys in a house that he didn't know and he was older than them."

On the court, McCullum says he did not see the electric version of Mack that Manual coaches talked about.

"By the time I got him, you could still see the flashes of what they talked about him being," McCullum said. "But physically, he wasn't strong anymore. And his skills weren't diminished, he could still really handle the ball and his first step was really unbelievable. But physical-strength wise, I think nutrition may have been an issue in his life. Being out of school, you don't get the school meals anymore. When I got him, physically he had diminished a little bit."

Mack was able to practice but not compete in games.

Though Mack says he enjoyed his time at Black Hawk, he didn't stay long. Less than a year, in fact. Since he was ineligible during his one season with the team, he never played in a college game. McCullum says he thinks Mack would have been eligible to play if he stayed another year, but the transition proved too difficult.

"I don't think mentally he was focused on making the academic transition to come back to college yet," McCullum said. "Not that he couldn't have, because he was bright enough to do so. But I don't think he was ready to make the commitment. And I don't think after being out of competitive basketball for so long that he was quite ready to step back into that either."

Mack's career in organized basketball was over and the resume was short: a couple years of AAU, one season at Manual, and one season of practice in junior college. He returned to Peoria, to a life surrounded by drugs, gangs, gunshots, police sirens, and poverty. Yet Mack did not succumb to his surroundings. It took a while, several years in fact, but he eventually got out of the River City. In early 2020, Mack moved to Springfield to live with his girlfriend, Phantayesia King. He also has a four-year-old son, Aiden, who splits time with Mack in Springfield and his mom in Peoria. From all accounts, Mack is a doting father. Elliott, the GED teacher who helped fund Mack's short college experience, has no regrets about trying to enrich his life.

"I'm not naïve," Elliott said. "You try your best and you hope but I'm certainly not naïve, either. I know the family; it was a shot in the dark. You try your best and do what you can do. But to me, I kept in touch with Oscar. And OK he didn't get a degree, but I think that the experience sets him apart from a lot of people that he was involved with or was raised around. He seems to always be working. Up until 2014, I taught night classes at the county jail so I know his family really, really well. It seems to me that (college) was an experience that actually changed his life. And whether he got a degree or not, I see how he's so different from the rest of the family. I just think that experience changed his life. It showed him there's a different world out there. And he got a little taste of it anyway. He met people outside his sphere. I just think it really enhanced his life. So, I feel good about it."

Mack knows Meister, Elliott, and another Peoria teacher named Candace Quinn went out of their way to get him into college. Money, time, car rides, phone calls on his behalf. And he is appreciative of their efforts. He's quick to credit people from outside his community who helped him more than those who were closest to him. On their end, Elliott and Meister have both helped countless kids over the years, and neither seek a lick of credit. They know the range of outcomes and that sometimes the stories have a happy ending, sometimes they don't, but life is not a tidy palate of black and white. More often, it's much more complicated than that.

"On one of our rides up to the school, I said, 'Let me tell you something Oscar, if for whatever reason this doesn't work out, I said I'm still going to love you,'" Meister recalled. "'I'm still going to give you a hug when I see ya.' Because so many times with the young men that I dealt with, and the reasons are always different, it doesn't always work out. It doesn't mean that now all of a sudden now they're going to get a four-year degree and be the vice president of something. It doesn't always work that way and in fact the odds are it doesn't. But that's OK. Because you can still be a solid person. If something for whatever reason doesn't work out and you come back, you can still be successful and do well in life and be a good father."

Mack knows all too well that things could be much worse. Back in early 2010, Oscar's 18-year-old brother Deothius, the one who shared a Harrison Homes bedroom with Oscar and Deondrae as kids, made a decision that would alter his life forever. Deothius and another man robbed the Family Food Market on Peoria's south side, and Deothius shot the store owner, Maged el-Sayegh, hitting him in the collarbone and left arm. Deothius, whom everyone calls Bob because he looked like his grandfather, Robert Washington, pleaded guilty to aggravated battery with a firearm just before his trial began. Charges of attempted first-degree murder and armed robbery were dropped.

In January 2011, Deothius Mack, then 19, was sentenced to 24 years in prison by Circuit Judge Glenn Collier.

> *"We get many people in here for guns or robbing people but not many who actually pull the trigger," said Collier, as reported in the Peoria* Journal-Star. *"This wasn't a warning shot. You intended to hit the victim and you did."*

Oscar, who is three years older than Deothius, shakes his head when asked about his brother. He hasn't visited him at Lawrence Correctional Center in Sumner, Ill., even though it's less than 150 miles from Oscar's Springfield apartment.

"My sisters have visited him, but I just can't," Oscar says. "I'm so used to my little brother being upbeat. If you knew Bob, then everyone knows Bob is upbeat. He's smiling, he's laughing, he wants you to laugh. Seeing him like that . . . he tries to put on this aura that he's OK, but deep down inside, he's hurt. I'm hurt, the family is hurt. I don't want to see him like that. It hurts me that if I go visit him, I know I gotta leave him. That's my little brother, and I don't want to see him walking me out of the jail and he has to stay. I never really wanted to take him through that and put more stress on him."

It is now the summer of 2020 and Oscar Dwayne Mack, once considered a teenaged can't-miss basketball prospect, sits at an outdoor table at a Dairy Queen in Springfield, occasionally munching on french fries stuffed inside a brown bag. Mack is 32 years old now, and though he says he probably hasn't shot a basketball in about a year, he still cuts an athletic figure. He talks about how moving to Springfield was the best decision he's ever made, how he no longer has to look over his shoulder because the Harrison Homes and Peoria's south side violence are miles and miles away. Still, he can't help but think about how a better family life could have changed his path in so many ways.

"I hold a bunch of grudges against my family," says Mack, who delivers packages for FedEx. "Not necessarily grudges, but it's like why can't you guys just be the family that family is supposed to be? I feel like if we were the family that family is supposed to be, or we were loving and caring, we probably wouldn't be here having this interview. We'd probably be somewhere else in a mansion or on my patio having an interview because I'd be in the (NBA) bubble down in Orlando or something like that."

"In a sense, he has still overcome (his family)," Derrick Booth said. "Just by working at FedEx and never giving into (crime) and never having a criminal charge, taking pride in that. Understanding that that way of life he grew up in is not it. And he's not as much a failure as he thinks he is. It's just not the NBA, but he still beat the odds by getting out of there."

8

The First Family of Peoria Central Basketball

A.J. Guyton had just graduated from the eighth grade when his mother, Rhonda Ruffin, laid out her plans for him in the summer of 1992.

"I think A.J. needs to get a job," Ruffin told the family in their living room on Callender Avenue near Bradley University.

The request was utterly sensible. Lots of kids are told it is time to get a summer job when they become teenagers. Rhonda wasn't expecting a dissenting opinion from husband Dan, but that's exactly what she got.

"Dan was like, 'His only job is to get a scholarship. That's all you do. We want you to play basketball,'" A.J. recalled. "I'm with you on that. I want to play ball all day long."

Dan Ruffin wasn't anticipating an NBA career for his basketball-loving stepson. Heck, Guyton was only about five foot nine at the time. He did, however, have the foresight and perspective to consider what basketball could do for his family.

"You don't have to go to a Big Ten school, you can go to an NAIA school, you can go to a Division 3 school, you can go to a Division 2 school," Dan said. "But the bottom line is you're going for free. And that's all I was thinking about. You can go to school for free for playing basketball, and that's a job. You really don't have time to be working—be hitting the books and working on your game if you're going to be a scholarship athlete."

At the time, Rhonda was working at Walgreens, and Dan was a security guard in Peoria Public Schools. The family of five—including older sister Keysra and youngest child Daniel—were doing OK, but as Rhonda says, "at that age, they want so much." So, it was natural for her to think it was time for A.J. to start buying some of his own wants.

"I didn't think that was a job," Rhonda said of basketball. "I just thought that was like recreation, I didn't see it as a job. And now I do. You're a man telling another man that's his job. That didn't make sense to me. I don't think we argued about it. He was like, 'If he focuses on his game, he can go to college, you won't have to pay no money. That's a job.' That's how he broke it down to me."

"No, you don't have to go get a job at McDonald's," Dan said. "For what? The $3 or $4 (per hour) they were paying then. For what? Are you going to work at McDonald's the rest of your life? We hope not. So, do stuff now to prepare for then. It would have been the same if he'd been a computer nut. Whatever you do is my thing. For him it was basketball, and for Daniel it was basketball. Keysra, we didn't know. You try to allow your kids to figure out what they want to be and then support them in that endeavor."

Twenty-two years later, Guyton narrated that story with fondness while standing at a podium in Bloomington, Indiana. The reason he was back on his college campus? He was being inducted into the Indiana University Athletics Hall of Fame.

"Big Dan was clutch in that moment," Guyton says now with a smile.

Dan Ruffin entered the lives of Rhonda's two oldest children when Keysra was five and A.J. was three. Dan was from a big sports family, the second oldest of eight siblings, many of whom had standout athletic careers at Peoria Central. He grew up across the street from Carver Center, playing pickup basketball in the summers and then football, hoops, and baseball in high school. He was in his mid-20s when he became a father figure to the two kids, and the family lived in the Warner Homes public housing project.

"Yeah, it was easy," Dan says of the early days with Keysra and A.J. "I liked them and they liked me. We had fun."

Dan was still playing pickup basketball then, and pretty soon the little boy in the house was tagging along. The kids' biological father, Arthur Guyton Jr., was in their lives, but they quickly warmed up to Dan, gruff on the exterior but with a kind soul.

"Yeah, we'd go to the park," Dan says of the excursions with A.J. "Then we'd go to Carver Center at night. I'd take him wherever I went to play. When I went to the gym, I'd take him. He'd be down there with the other little guys."

A.J. says this is where his love of basketball was born. Later, Dan began coaching basketball at Trewyn School, and A.J. would join him there, too, hoisting up shots while his stepfather coached.

Asked if he considers Dan his father, A.J. says, "Yeah, yeah, he raised me. He was my father figure. He seemed very strict, but he was really a teddy bear. He was the most generous guy that I had known. Me being a father now, I understand how difficult it is to step into a situation and take care of someone else's kids and treat them as your own. You can always be there, but do you treat them as your own? He took care of us financially and was the father figure for us since I was 3."

"Without him, I don't think I would have fallen in love with the game as much as I did," A.J. said.

When A.J. was almost seven, a baby boy joined the Ruffin crew. Daniel was the first child for Rhonda and Dan together, and it wasn't long before he was shadowing his two older siblings wherever they went. It was typical sibling stuff as Daniel just wanted to be near his older brother and sister.

"Daniel was just kind of the nuisance," A.J. said. "Him and my sister fought a lot; I never fought with him. My sister is a year and a half older than me, so I'm the middle child. He would irritate her, he was an irritant. He was the type of kid if you sit in the living room with your friends, he'll just come sit real close. Until she would be like, 'Would you go?!' He would just be picking at her and it was ongoing. It was love, he just wanted to be around. That's what he was known for as a kid."

As the young men grew up, A.J. became protective of Daniel. He taught his little brother how to ride a bike, took him to McDonald's for lunch, and was generally accepting of the little fella who wanted to be near his brother at all times. When they got a little older, the two would square off in fierce video game battles of Coach K College Basketball on Sega Genesis, and Daniel became A.J.'s rebounder when the tireless worker was putting up shots at the playground or gym.

"My brother was a gym rat," Daniel says. "I wasn't necessarily a gym rat but I was always in the gym, just because my dad coached and A.J. played. A.J. always wanted to go to the gym and work out."

As A.J. began his sophomore year on the Peoria Central varsity, a familiar face joined head coach Chuck Buescher on the Lions' bench. After working his way up the coaching ranks in Peoria grade schools and then a couple seasons as a Peoria Notre Dame assistant, Dan Ruffin became a varsity assistant at Central. The Lions had gone 25–4 the previous season and 176–31 over the past seven seasons, so A.J. entered a winning program with lofty expectations.

A.J. had played a little on varsity as a freshman, but he mainly was a J.V. player. Now, he was joining the big boys on Friday nights, and his stepfather was also on the bench.

"It wasn't weird at all," A.J said. "He did what assistant coaches do. They are the big brother figure when head coaches get on you, they calm you down and make sure you don't jump off the bridge."

At first, A.J. was timid in finding his way on the varsity level among more experienced teammates and a ramped-up pressure level.

"My nature at that time was passive," he said. "I was just a nice kid, I would shoot when I'm open, but I wasn't trying to attack and get mine."

Like he had done a few years prior in the family living room, Dan Ruffin stepped up to give his son a confidence boost.

"He was a sophomore and he's playing on the varsity, and you've got juniors and seniors saying why is he playing," Dan said. "I told him in order for them to understand why you're playing, you've got to show them why you're playing. You've got to make shots. You can't make shots if you don't shoot the ball. When you're open, shoot the ball."

"He would always pull me aside and tell me, 'You gotta go get yours.' Not in a selfish way but you've got to be aggressive," said A.J., whose brother Daniel served as ballboy, making for a three-pronged Central family affair. "You've got to look to score. He would say that, say that, say that, and it finally clicked in my sophomore year when he got there. He would say that off the floor, but he got the job my sophomore year and I became aggressive after that. I think a piece of that is the comfort of knowing I had my father figure on the bench, so you get a little comfortable in trying things and maybe making mistakes."

A scorer's mentality was born. Despite being slender and shorter than six feet at the time, A.J. started to hunt shots and gain confidence. Peoria Central went 22–6 his sophomore year, and 22–7 his junior year when he knocked in 47 percent of his 3-point attempts.

Without a doubt, A.J. was overlooked in town by the misfortunate of playing at the same time as Manual's championship behemoth. Newspaper and television stories centered around Sergio McClain, Marcus Griffin, and also Peoria Richwoods' high-scoring Mike Robinson more than Guyton. It was an absolutely incredible era of talent in the River City, but the lanky guard at Peoria Central was not at the media forefront. In that 1995–96 season, Robinson and Griffin were first-team Associated Press All-State selections. McClain made the second team, while Guyton and East Peoria's Mark Vershaw made the third team.

(In March 1996, the *Chicago Tribune* wrote an article on its 17th annual All-State boys' basketball team and declared that Peoria had indeed overtaken Chicago as the state's basketball mecca. For the first time in the newspaper's 17 years of publishing All-State teams, a downstate city, Peoria, had more first-team selections than Chicago. McClain, Griffin, and Robinson gave Peoria 60 percent of the *Tribune's* first-team All-State team. Guyton was on the third team.)

"A.J. Guyton (normally) would have been a once-in-a-generation player and he never got out of the Peoria Sectional," said Jim Mattson, a veteran Peoria sports TV and radio personality. "Guyton was funny. I'd bring a camera to a game and shoot the first half and he'd have two points. Then the coach would call in and say he had 30. He was so streaky. When he got hot, there was no stopping him. He could really score, but he was very overshadowed."

"I do think A.J. was overshadowed," Robinson said. "Here's the thing: he might have been overshadowed (by media), but we as players knew how good A.J. was. I knew how difficult he was to guard."

Colleges were aware of Guyton, who had grown to six-foot-one by his senior year, but he wasn't appearing on national top 100 recruiting lists. Still, he had options. Missouri and longtime coach Norm Stewart offered. Bradley and Coach Jim Molinari did, too. Michigan State, Indiana, and Saint Louis were also interested. Guyton decided not to sign during the NCAA early signing period, which occurs in November of a player's senior year. He had a great senior season, averaging 24 points a game but was the Lions' only returning starter as the team struggled to a 14–14 record.

In the spring, Guyton shifted his focus to recruiting.

On Bradley: "I thought about going to Bradley but the recruitment with Jim Molinari was horrible. He was literally like flipping through a book while I'm sitting there (on an official visit). No attention at all. I could have told him when he was ignoring me at the table that I ain't going to Bradley."

On in-state Illinois: "I wanted to go to Illinois, but they never really recruited me because Lou Henson felt I wasn't a Big Ten player. Crazy part is I probably would have went to Illinois just 'cause. Yeah, I would have went to Illinois if they recruited me."

He narrowed his choices to Michigan State and Indiana, with plans to visit both. The Hoosiers held off on offering a scholarship for a considerable amount of time. Ron Felling, a longtime IU assistant who recruited the state of Illinois for the Hoosiers, wasn't particularly enamored with Guyton, according to fellow assistant Dan Dakich. Indiana also didn't have an available scholarship until late in the recruiting cycle when starting guard Sherron Wilkerson was kicked off the team. When that happened, they ramped up interest in Guyton.

Guyton liked Michigan State as well, and new coach Tom Izzo made a positive impression. The now-Hall of Fame coach made two or three trips to Peoria recruiting Guyton—Izzo and Buescher ate a late dinner at Agatucci's Italian restaurant on University Street after one game—and Izzo's pitch resonated with Guyton. But Guyton also saw that the Spartans were bringing in star in-state recruits Mateen Cleaves and Charlie Bell, and there would be a logjam at the guard spots in East Lansing.

In front of Dakich, Felling, and Izzo in a 74–60 sectional semifinal loss to Manual at a raucous Field House, Guyton solidified his status as a priority recruit.

"A.J. was great that night," Buescher said. "In the locker room afterwards, end of the season, I'm just talking for 60 seconds and there's a knock on the door and it's Dakich. I said I'll be right there. Basically, Dakich told me whatever it takes. Not cheating-wise, but what do we have to do? Dakich loved him, he was great that night."

"I know Ron didn't really like him, and Ron had a great eye (for talent)," Dakich said. "But then we went back (for the sectional against Manual) and he was great, he was phenomenal. We were looking for someone who could get it in the bucket, and it was pretty clear he could get it in the bucket. And had a toughness to him that belied how he looked."

Dakich says he learned something from legendary basketball coach Pete Newell—famously a confidant of Bobby Knight's—many years earlier that resonated when he watched Guyton play.

"He could shoot it, you could tell he could shoot it, that stuck out," Dakich said. "But I'll tell you what, Pete Newell told me this a long time ago. Really good offensive players that are guards, when they go down the lane in traffic, they're the only ones that jump. A.J. did that two times in that game. Marcus Griffin could block shots, Sergio was there, they had three great players obviously. But when he went down the lane, man, he was the only one who jumped. He laid it in, and no one was around. In fact, I can still see the two plays in my mind."

IU coaches convinced Guyton to schedule an official visit to Indiana's campus. During the visit, former Peoria Central and Indiana guard Chris Reynolds dropped in to see A.J. and his mother. Reynolds, who graduated high school in 1989 and played in the 1992 Final Four with IU, was now a law student in Bloomington after earning his bachelor's degree.

Reynolds spoke to A.J. and Rhonda about what a great experience he had at the university.

"I knew academically and athletically it was a great opportunity to be a part of a culture of winning," said Reynolds, who now serves as Bradley University's athletic director. "Those four years at Indiana, it changes you. It makes you expect to do well. It's challenging so you feel once you graduate from a place like Indiana and after four years of being around Coach Bob Knight, that there's nothing in life that you can't do."

Guyton's visit went well, and as Dakich drove him and his mother back to Monroe County Airport in Bloomington for their private flight back to Peoria, Guyton turned to Dakich at a stoplight in the coach's Ford Taurus and delivered some major news.

"He's like, 'I really want to come here,'" Dakich remembers. "I couldn't wait to get back and tell Coach (Knight) this kid was going to commit."

"I ended up going to Indiana because I saw the opportunity to play," Guyton said.

He never could have guessed the range of emotions, historical significance, and lingering effects, on and off the court, that awaited in Bloomington.

Despite not being a heralded recruit, Guyton enjoyed a marvelous career at Indiana. He started 122 of 128 games over 4 seasons, never averaged less than 13.6 points per game, and was a superstar as a senior. In that 1999–2000 senior campaign, Guyton averaged 19.7 points and was co-Big Ten MVP along with Michigan State's Morris Peterson. He was also a first-team All-American.

Even with the individual excellence, Guyton's Indiana teams never made it out of the second round of the NCAA Tournament. And near the end of his senior season, things got really weird. A sports television producer at CNN/SI named Robert Abbott had spent months investigating Bobby Knight's alleged mistreatment of players. Abbott interviewed dozens of sources, many of whom were too fearful to put their name on the story, but the prevailing notion was evident that Knight had acted inappropriately on several occasions. One of Guyton's teammates, Neil Reed, told Abbott that Knight had once choked him in practice.

With the Hoosiers preparing for the Big Ten Tournament later that week in Chicago, Abbott received an unmarked package at his house containing a VCR tape. The tape would alter the perception and legacy of one of the winningest and biggest names in the history of college basketball. It was a grainy video of an Indiana practice, shot from way up high at the top of Assembly Hall, showing Knight briefly putting both of his hands around Reed's neck. (In 2018, Abbott directed an outstanding ESPN 30 for 30 documentary on this, titled *The Last Days of Knight*.)

As this played out in 2000, Abbott and CNN/SI broke the story, and it was immediately a monster. Without question, it appeared in every major newspaper in America in the following days and was a huge story on sports television. Part of the strangeness was this: the choking incident had occurred three years earlier when Guyton was a freshman. He was now at the tail end of his senior year and it was dominating the news cycle. At any rate, Guyton and the Hoosiers were left to pick up the pieces and try to salvage what had been a solid season.

But it was too much of a distraction.

Knight was missing from the court during the next few practices, Guyton says, and the Hoosiers had trouble focusing. They lost in the first round of the Big Ten Tournament to Illinois and were upset in the first round of the NCAA Tournament, losing by 20 points to Pepperdine. Indiana overachieved all year, knocking off three top 10 teams along the way, including eventual national champion Michigan State. But now it was over, and so was Guyton's outstanding college career.

"It ruined my senior year," Guyton says of the Knight distraction.

Twenty-plus years have passed since the incident that rocked college basketball and, to an extent, the entire sporting world. Guyton was there for all of it. Here are his recollections of the most infamous day in Indiana practice history:

> It happened so fast, (snaps his fingers) he did it . . . I saw the whole thing. I heard Neil say something. Coach Knight and Neil was into it because of me. With me being there, me and Michael Lewis, the other freshman, Neil became expendable. He would be complaining about Coach Knight . . . and Coach Knight was riding him. (Reed) had a right to complain, I can't even lie. Coach Knight was ALL OVER HIM. I didn't understand why because Neil was tough. I loved playing with him, great shooter, great free throw shooter, could get to the rim, get to the line. He was just a tough dude, played through a separated shoulder his freshman year. Coach Knight, once he figured that he didn't really need you, he would ride you. And he hit Neil with that. But I think he made a mistake because we needed him. He was the toughness that we needed at that other guard position at that time.

"We were in practice one day and he said something to Neil about something he did, yelling at him. Neil turned around and mumbled something. And I'm walking back because I'm thinking I was either guarding him or on his team. I heard . . . and I said 'Oh shit.' I heard (Knight) say, 'What the fuck did you just say?' and he started walking toward (Reed). And it just happened so quick. The video (seems) like all day, but it was really like one second. It was like he pushed him. It's like if I came and just pushed you by your throat. Knight went away and we just practiced again. I didn't think nothing of it. I was like, 'Oh shit, does this happen all the time?' I never saw it after that. I think for Coach Knight, that was his wake-up. It never happened after that. I'm not defending it. You should never put your hands on a player, but it was more likely to happen back then than it is today. You shouldn't be doing that, but that was the nature of coaching. You get fired up, grab your kid by the jersey and shake them."

Despite the topsy-turvy nature of his final month in a Hoosiers uniform, Guyton walked away with fond memories of Knight. They are feelings that persist to this day. In a way, Guyton was more prepared than most for the type of discipline that defined Bobby Knight's program. Chuck Buescher wasn't necessarily a Knight disciple, but Peoria Central's basketball program was absolutely Bish's way or the highway.

No facial hair. No earrings. No visible tattoos. Jersey tucked in. You could play by those rules or see yourself out. The end.

"I hated it when we were doing it, because I didn't understand," Guyton said of Buescher's rules. "If you came in the locker room with a mustache, it was clippers turned on and, 'You cut it off right now.' We didn't understand it back then, but I thank him for that discipline because understanding how we have to get jobs out here, you have to prepare yourself. You gotta do stuff you really don't want to do. His reasoning for doing it was seeing if you would sacrifice to play."

"I had kids do things that I wouldn't do today," said Buescher, who retired in 2004 after back-to-back Class AA titles and a 528–184 career record. "I wouldn't try. At Bradley when I played, Coach Stowell let the Black kids have a mustache. I had a lot of White players come to me and say that's not fair. When I went to Central, I thought either let them all have mustaches or none. So, I just said no facial hair. Couldn't have their hair fancy. Couldn't put a Z in their hair, couldn't put their number in their hair. I told them I want (spectators) to go home and say No. 25 was a helluva player, not the guy with a Z in his hair. That's how I want people to talk about you."

Former Peoria Central and Indiana University star A.J. Guyton, left, poses for a photo with his stepfather, Dan Ruffin, and mother Rhonda Ruffin, in front of the family's barbeque restaurant. (Photo by Jeff Karzen)

Another of Buescher's policies was requiring kids to wear dress shirts and ties to games. The varsity team would all sit together in the stands for the first half of the J.V. game, home or road, and then head down to the locker room at halftime to change into their uniforms for the nightcap. But as they sat in the stands, it was shirts and ties with everyone sitting together. No horsing around and jumping over chairs. No sitting with your girlfriend.

"Look, that was the best thing that ever happened to our kids," Dan Ruffin said. "It taught you how to be part of a group. As the season goes on and we go from one place to another, and they're sitting there in the stands and they have people coming by commenting how nice you look, what school do you go to? You go to Peoria High? I thought Peoria High was . . . and then they walk off. And it made the kids feel good. That might not be your everyday attire. But for this instance, I need to spruce up a little bit. First impressions."

Buescher and Ruffin had an excellent working relationship. Widely regarded as a terrific basketball mind, Buescher stayed in his coaching lane, concerning himself with practice plans and game preparation, not the complaints of unrealistic parents. As is often the case on a coaching staff, an assistant—Ruffin in this case—was the one players turned to with their girlfriend problems or issues at home.

"Bish, he wasn't about that," said Ruffin, who spent 12 years as a Central assistant. "That wasn't something that fell in his bucket. And that was cool. He felt out of his element and I didn't. I dealt with the parents. It was a good relationship."

"Big Danny was great for me," Buescher said. "I never had parent problems. Most kids we had were Black and most (parents) were very appreciative of what we did for the kids. Most of them had just a mom, probably more than 50 percent. They were appreciative. I really believe if something was said in the Black community, that (Ruffin) had my back. Big Danny was important to our program."

Central practices were tightly run and every minute held purpose. In November before the season started, practices went about two and a half hours. After the season-opening tournament, they were down to two hours. By Christmas, it was an hour and 45 minutes. But the Lions went hard. The first 40 minutes or so were fundamentals: drills on passing, ball-handling, shooting, fast breaks, and defense.

The primary goals were to have the team reach its peak in March and do so with fresh legs.

Although Ruffin could be perceived as ornery to outsiders, both coaches agree he was probably the one who stuck up for kids on the edge more often than not. Ruffin says one issue in which the two didn't always see eye to eye was with Buescher's handling of referees during road games in hostile environments. Ruffin thought his head coach should have been harder on officials when it seemed like the Lions were being hosed.

"You're getting cheated and he'd say don't worry about it, it builds character," Ruffin said. "And I'm like that shit only goes so far. Let the kids know you're standing up for them. I told him the one thing young Black kids don't need is somebody giving them hell to build character, because every day is hell. Every now and then you have to let the kids know you feel their pain. I feel we're getting stroked here."

One of those Black kids, Meechie Edwards, says Buescher was absolutely there for him and the others he coached over the years. Back in the early 1990s, Edwards was considered the next big star in Peoria when he left Loucks Middle School and enrolled at Central. Edwards fathered a child at 14 and had a solid high school career, but not the stardom that some had projected. To this day, he speaks highly of Buescher, while also acknowledging he was very demanding.

"People talk about the south side and how Wayne McClain was a father figure and I'm not knocking that, but Coach Buescher was the same way," said Edwards, who is now Central's varsity girls' coach. "He was there for us. I don't care what it was, I don't care if you were evicted, whether a kid went to jail or whatever it was, he was always there to tell us the right way. And a lot of times he would show you tough love and say I've got to let you go because you didn't do what you were supposed to do."

Reynolds, the point guard on Central's terrific teams in the late '80s who went on to Indiana, agrees. Reynolds remembers watching the NCAA Final Four on television at Buescher's house and how it helped bond the player and coach.

"Coach, he was tough on us but he cared about us," Reynolds said. "And he'll tell you this: you can get a lot out of young people if you care about them. And you can push them harder if you care about them. We spent time at his house and that's where he showed us the other side of him. And that was really important in terms of our chemistry as a team and our relationship with him. Developing that relationship with him was important, just to understand him better and for him to understand us. And those things carried over to the court."

Buescher, who was known for his trademark foot stomp on the sidelines, won 18 consecutive regional titles despite playing in a highly competitive basketball area. He was a central figure, no pun intended, in the classic Central-Manual games at Bradley's Robertson Memorial Field House that regularly drew 6,000 fans or more. For a long time during this golden era of Peoria high school hoops, Buescher was as recognizable a name or face as any in the local sports community. He says the 1987–88 games versus Manual, when an astonishing 11 future Division 1 players suited up for the two teams, is an enduring memory.

"It was too big," Buescher said of the rivalry. "It really was too big for kids. I remember the first game in the Field House, and Mike Hughes was a really talented sophomore for us. Now, Mike Hughes was one of the most talented kids I coached. Very talented, six-foot-seven, and very smart on the floor. Great instincts, could handle the ball, pass it, score. Score any way, drive it, shoot it. I remember coming into the locker room after the game and he was really upset, almost crying. Just wired. It was too big. We got beat and it wasn't that close. And he was just wired."

"It was an unbelievable atmosphere," Buescher said. "It was a great place. I've been to Duke and I've been to Kansas and I'm telling you the atmosphere was every bit as good. It really was."

Charles White was part of the outstanding Peoria Central teams of the late '80s, and he was one of the 11 future D-1 players on the court in 1987–88. The Lions lost three games total in White's junior and senior seasons, and his career ended with a heartbreaking triple-overtime loss to East St. Louis Lincoln in the 1989 Class AA state final in Champaign. White, Hughes, Chris Reynolds, and Tyrone Howard formed an incredible group that was oh-so-close to giving Buescher his first state title. White scored 20 points in that state championship game and later played four years at Bradley, averaging double digits his last two seasons.

To this day, the terrific athlete, who played much bigger than his six-foot-one frame, perks up when talking about playing in front of massive crowds against Manual at the Field House.

"For one night, in central Illinois, you were the center of attention. Period," White said. "It was must-see basketball and I know people came from all over. The exciting part was the Field House had an elevated court and they turn the lights out in the crowd, so the only lights were on the court. It was all eyes on you."

During this period from the late 1980s through the late 1990s, if Buescher and his wife Barb were going through a McDonald's drive-thru during Manual week, he'd nudge her and say "watch this" as they pulled up to the window where a Central student was working.

"And I'd say, 'You going to the game this week?' She'd say, 'Oh, coach, I got a new outfit, I'm getting my hair done Friday afternoon.' I'm not exaggerating. Kids would not work that night because they wanted to go. It was unbelievable. When you went back to your locker room after the game you couldn't hardly get back there because there were so many people."

A true student of the game, Buescher was always eager to learn more. After playing basketball and baseball at Bradley in the 1960s, Buescher's first coaching job was an assistant role with Manual's Dick Van Scyoc. For three seasons by his side, when Van Scyoc hit the road to scout an opponent, Buescher rode shotgun. When the head coach would work out players before school, Buescher was there, too.

"Coach Van, I think, taught me how to win high school basketball games," Buescher said. "I think he taught me how to win and how to coach high school basketball. Just the work ethic."

Years later when he was the head coach at Central, Buescher furthered his basketball education by attending a Bobby Knight coaching clinic at Indiana. It was the early 1980s and Knight ran the clinic himself. For high school coaches, this presented an incredible opportunity to learn from someone who was in the discussion as the foremost basketball mind in the country in those days.

"On Friday night he'd talk a little and you'd watch Indiana practice," Buescher said. "Saturday, same thing. He said teach them how to play, how to read screens. Don't teach them to go here, don't teach them to go to A to B to C. Teach them *how* to play."

Buescher, who was an assistant coach at Bradley from 1971–79 and again for a couple years after he retired from Central, was a big proponent of the Dean Smith "four corners" method late in games. If Central was ahead late in the fourth quarter, more often than not they went into stall mode. The Lions usually had good guards who could protect the ball, and why shoot if you don't have to without a shot clock? They worked on four corners for the last 5–10 minutes of every practice and Buescher says if he ran it 200 times over the years, his team lost only one or two of those games.

"Chuck Buescher is probably the best Xs and Os coach ever to come out of Peoria," said Greg Stewart, the former *Journal-Star* sportswriter. "You talk about time, clock and score. If any Buescher team has the ball and lead and maybe the bonus or possession arrow with a minute or two left in the game, they're not going to lose. I don't care who you are. Managing the game, managing the clock, and protecting the ball, excellent at it. They won a lot of games against more talented programs just because he was a better coach."

During the 1987–88 season, the Lions went 27–2, losing only to St. Francis de Sales (with 1988 Mr. Basketball winner and future Indiana star Eric Anderson) and Manual in the sectionals. Led by the junior quartet of Hughes, Reynolds, White and Howard, Central earned a top 10 national ranking during the season and, naturally, the teenagers were feeling their oats with that attention. When the team showed up for a Saturday morning practice following a sluggish victory the night before, they noticed a towel draped over the clock on the wall. There was one water bottle near the court, and the gym doors were locked after the team arrived.

"I'll never forget it," White laughed. "And practice was brutal. I don't remember what he was mad at us for, something about not playing as a team. 'Go ahead and get as much water as you want to, but once that water bottle is empty, it's over. We're not filling it up again.' So, you weren't going to leave your teammate hanging (by drinking all the water)."

Message received.

As Buescher's coaching career headed down the home stretch in the early 2000s, he handed the point guard reins to Daniel Ruffin, the sibling pest turned ball boy turned excellent ballplayer in his own right. Daniel, despite standing only about five-foot-five as a freshman, came off the bench for the Lions and played about 10 minutes per game. By his sophomore year, Daniel was getting major minutes as a point guard on varsity on a Marcellus Sommerville-led Lions team. As a junior, he averaged about 16 points a game, but that was just an appetizer for what was to come as a senior.

Things got very interesting for the basketball program on 1615 N. North Street along Interstate 74 during the summer of 2002. The previous two seasons, Daniel's sophomore and junior years, the Lions finished 19–10. It didn't take a basketball expert to know things would be better the following season. Shaun Livingston, the tall and lanky basketball savant who was tabbed for stardom as a middle schooler, transferred from Richwoods to Central. Brandon Lee, a terrific left-handed guard, transferred in from Manual. Buescher and Central now had arguably the three best players in the city on the same squad: Ruffin, Livingston, and Lee. (Peoria Notre Dame's Brian Randle, who later played at Illinois, could also lay claim to being in that top group.)

Central's first event that summer was the Richwoods Shootout. Buescher and assistant coach Chuck Westendorf sat in the stands as Dan Ruffin coached on this day. With the school only a couple blocks from Buescher's house, his wife Barb walked over to check on her husband's new-look team.

"She is standing near the end in the doorway for about three minutes, then she comes over and sits down next to me and she says, 'Merry Christmas," Buescher said. "Two great gifts (Livingston and Lee). She's seen a lot of games and that's a great line. She watched about three minutes and says Merry Christmas."

Central tore through its summer schedule with the new powerful three-headed monster. Livingston, who had struggled quite a bit at Richwoods, was a completely different player in his new surroundings. Central attended tournaments around the state, including a couple in Chicago, and hardly lost a game all summer. The Lions had won the first ever Illinois state boys' basketball championship back in 1908 and then another in 1977. Now, the second oldest high school west of the Allegheny Mountains looked poised to be a legit contender for a third state title in 2002–03.

Central began its high school season of big expectations with the Decatur Thanksgiving Tournament. After routing Decatur Eisenhower and Mt. Zion, the Lions lost the tournament championship 48–47 to Bartonville Limestone, led by Wisconsin recruit DeAaron Williams, who had a game-high 21 points to earn tourney MVP.

It would be the last Central setback of the season.

The Lions proceeded to rattle off 29 straight victories, including a satisfying 40-point thrashing of Manual in the regional final. It was an incredible way for Daniel Ruffin to go out as a senior. The terrific floor leader had an excellent career, but point guards are judged on winning and Ruffin hadn't won big in his first three high school years. Furthermore, becoming the *it* basketball school in town? That . . . that was pure satisfaction for Ruffin.

"When Manual had their run, I was in middle school at Roosevelt and when they had their four-peat, we had a four-peat in middle school," Ruffin said. "The majority of guys talked about going to Manual because that's where it was. Everyone wanted to be those guys. I was a ball boy for Peoria High and the only guy going to Peoria High. I wanted to be that guy to beat Manual, and we had the opportunity."

As a junior without Livingston and Lee, Ruffin averaged what he called "a hard 16–17 points."

"(Livingston) comes over and Brandon Lee comes over and they made life easy. I probably averaged 13 points I guess, and I'll take that any day."

Ruffin was the type of heady court general that opposing coaches admired.

"Never got emotional, he ran the team," former Richwoods coach Bobby Darling said of Ruffin. "Kinda like saying, 'Whose team is this?'—that would be Danny Ruffin on the floor. It's Danny's team. The rest of them followed. He could make big shots, too. He wasn't known for his shooting, but boom

2003 IHSA AA STATE CHAMPS

The first of back-to-back titles for Peoria Central. Led by Daniel Ruffin, front left, Shaun Livingston, front right, and Brandon Lee (22). It was the first title for highly successful coach, Chuck Buescher, back right. (Photo by John Grap)

all of a sudden he would make a big shot on you. Really good player, great competitor, winner. Just a winner."

"Coming to Central, it was his basketball team," Livingston said. "He was the unquestioned leader for sure. He was a helluva high school basketball player, helluva teammate. One of those guys that never got all the credit that he deserved."

In the 2003 Class AA state semifinals versus Evanston in a sold-out Peoria Carver Arena, Ruffin took center stage in his second-to-last high school game. He scored a game-high 23 points, and his 8 steals were the second most in state tournament history as the Lions advanced to the state final against Thornwood.

"Needless to say, Daniel Ruffin put on a show," Buescher told reporters after the game. "He made four or five plays that were out of this world."

Later that night, the Lions capped a 31–1 season and their first state title since 1977 when Livingston made a beautiful drive to the basket and laid the ball in with 4 seconds left to give Central a 45–43 win over Thornwood in front of its hometown fans.

"The atmosphere was ridiculous," said Ruffin, who in 2020 succeeded his father as Peoria Central head coach. "It was quite an experience, especially for guys that didn't go to the next level and play. It was their last game, just having that atmosphere as part of that. Not everyone can say they've been a part of something like that. I still tell people that's one of the greatest moments in my life."

All the offseason workouts. All the missed school activities because of basketball commitments. All the tough practices. It all feels worth it when you are the last team standing. For Ruffin, a coach's son who had grown up around Buescher since he was about six years old, it was a moment that validated all the rules and sprints and defensive drills. At the end, the former ball boy was a champion.

"When I was younger I felt like he was a high school version of a Bobby Knight," Ruffin said of Buescher. "Yelled a lot. Strict, had a lot of rules. And those rules a lot of people didn't like. But it's the sacrifices you make and that's what he was trying to get at: how important is it for you to be on this team? Can you go without wearing your earrings? Can you keep your shoes tied? Can you keep your pants pulled up? It was challenging, but at the end of the day it prepared us for life and made us who we are. I think a lot of people who played for him would say they disliked Coach Buescher as a high school player, but they respect what he did for them now."

At five-foot-10 and 137 pounds, Ruffin had scholarship offers from Bradley, Northern Illinois, Wisconsin-Green Bay, UTEP, and Pepperdine. He chose the hometown Braves and had to sit out his freshman season because of an eligibility problem with his ACT score. But a couple years later, Ruffin was starting for Bradley when the 14th-seeded Braves knocked off Kansas and Pittsburgh to reach the NCAA Sweet 16. Ruffin's father was in attendance in Detroit as the Braves became the highest seeded team in 2006 to reach the Sweet 16.

However, one family member was noticeably absent: Rhonda Ruffin. Daniel's mother was in Italy, where she was in the midst of a month-long trip visiting her older son A.J., who was playing professionally for an Italian team, Viola Reggio Calabria, at the time. The previous week, Rhonda had been in attendance when Bradley lost in the Missouri Valley Tournament in St. Louis. She figured that was the end of their NCAA Tournament chances, but the Braves received an at-large bid as one of four Missouri Valley teams to make the Big Dance.

"Ugh, I was sick," Rhonda says about missing the games. "A.J. figured it out (how to watch), and we watched at like four in the morning. It was on TV. I don't know how he did it. He made it happen. After the first game, A.J.

looked at me and said, 'Mom, I can fly you out there if you want.' I said oh no, I'm good (because of the back-and-forth time changes)."

"And she picked us to lose the first game, too, in her bracket," Daniel laughed. "She picked us to lose! My brother told on her."

Bradley's Cinderella run ended the following week when it lost to top-seeded Memphis in Oakland. But what a run it had been.

9

Shaun Livingston and the Burden of Expectations

The little boy with arms as skinny as a phone cord, and seemingly as long, dribbles a basketball in front of his house. Right hand, left hand, between his legs, he's got all the moves. The boy is only seven or eight, but he is already a basketball expert, and can intelligently hold his own in a hoops debate. "Pistol" Pete Maravich. That's his favorite. He grows up in the era of Jordan, Magic, and Bird, but Pistol Pete, that's his guy.

The boy dribbles and dribbles and dribbles. As he pounds the ball into the pavement on Peoria's south side, mimicking moves from "Pistol," a movie he's seen more times than he can count, he can start to see a figure in the distance. He keeps working on his craft, and the next time he looks up, the figure is closer, and now he sees who it is: Dad. The boy smiles. The only parent he knows is coming home for the day.

Reggie Livingston didn't own a car. He worked at McDonald's for a while, then Hardee's, to support himself and son, Shaun. He walked to and from work because, hell, there was no other option. Taking care of Shaun? No option there, either. It wasn't easy, but Reggie was committed to his boy. Whatever it took, he was determined to give the spindly runt a better life than he had.

Starting around age four, young Shaun took a basketball with him wherever he went. Church, school, didn't matter. That ball was coming along, too.

"That was his girlfriend, Spalding," Reggie says.

Reggie and Ann Baer met at Illinois Central College in Peoria in 1983. Baer, five-foot-ten and White, grew up in a tall basketball family and played ball at now-closed Peoria Woodruff High School. When Reggie, who is Black, and Ann met, he was a college sophomore and she was a freshman. By 1985, the couple had married and Shaun was born that September. The marriage lasted less than two years, and Reggie soon took custody of Shaun.

"She never came around," Reggie said. "She went with another guy, she said we'd never make it. So, I put all my time and energy into Shaun. We tried to call her and talk to her all the time, but she said she never had time, she had a new family. I prayed for her, wished her luck. I'm trying to raise a kid, I'm working two jobs to make sure he's OK. I don't regret one minute of it, it was a great time. If I can do it, anybody can do it."

In the early years, Reggie had help from his beloved grandmother, Marie Crooks, a woman who helped raise him. But she died when Shaun was three. Reggie also received assistance from his father, Frank, a former Marine and Korean War veteran. It was hard, no doubt, but Reggie and Shaun had each other. And as Reggie observed Shaun taking a liking to sports, he pushed down on the accelerator, doing research on drills, reading magazines and borrowing books on coaching from the library for tips to give the precocious boy.

"It started out definitely a passion of mine," Shaun said. "I loved the game, I really enjoyed it. I breathed it, I lived it."

Reggie would take Shaun to the Peoria Central parking lot, and while driving his rusty maroon Buick Century, he'd have the boy dribble a ball out the passenger window—an incredible test of hand-eye coordination made famous by Maravich and his father, Press. Reggie would start off driving slowly, then speed up a little as Shaun learned to push the ball ahead to keep his dribble alive. Other drills included Shaun riding his bike and dribbling, dribbling a tennis ball—thankfully with both feet on the ground—and dribbling two balls at once.

"Want to make your legs stronger?" Reggie asked Shaun. "Then take the seat off your bicycle and ride around with no seat to make your legs stronger."

From then on, Shaun rode his red Huffy without a seat.

The boy was a sponge and never asked for the lessons to stop. One night when Shaun was little, Reggie got out of bed at around 1 a.m. for a drink of water. He peeked into Shaun's room, but it was empty.

"I get all nervous, where's my kid at? And I hear boom, boom, boom (dribbling). Look outside and he's dribbling a basketball. I said, 'OK, go to bed.'"

Starting in kindergarten, Reggie enrolled Shaun at Concordia Lutheran, an excellent—and mostly White—academic school. After four years there, he transferred to Roosevelt Magnet School on the south end, where he won city basketball championships and played with future high school teammates Daniel Ruffin, Brandon Lee, and Jacob Motteler. At Roosevelt, a mostly Black neighborhood school, students were required to play an instrument, and Shaun played drums in the marching band and sang in the choir.

But the Roosevelt experience wasn't all positive. After two and a half years, Shaun transferred back to Concordia in the middle of his sixth grade school year.

"Roosevelt was a lot different from Concordia," Shaun told the Journal-Star *in 2004. "It was a lot more survival. On the good side, it makes you tougher, makes you appreciate the little things you have: family, home, love. A lot of the kids at Roosevelt didn't have that. Coming to the south end like I did, they look at you as the preppie kid, and they want to take that from you. You have to be strong. On the bad side, you can get caught up in that stuff, where you're not focusing on the right things."*

Reggie was doing all he could to normalize his phenom son, giving him non-basketball activities, encouraging other pursuits, and trying to foster diversity for a biracial kid. Easier said than done for a kid who was tabbed as Peoria's next basketball star by the third grade, and who was "ranked" as the nation's second-best seventh grader by Hoop Scoop talent evaluator Clark Francis.

"That helped keep me rounded and just exposed me to different things," Shaun said of Roosevelt. "Something I was grateful for as I got older, just being exposed to different things, different people, different experiences."

In middle school, Reggie was driving Shaun around to high school open gyms all around Peoria. The prodigy was holding his own with varsity players as River City basketball observers wondered openly which high school he would attend. Shaun was tall for his age, five-foot-six in sixth grade and six-feet by eighth grade, but it was never his physical stature that wowed the masses. Ball handling and passing—that is what set him apart and made him a known commodity in the hoops community.

"When he was in maybe fifth or sixth grade in our open gym, he was competing with our high school kids," said Wayne Hammerton, Richwoods head coach for 26 years before retiring in 1996. "Pretty obvious that he was going to be a superstar."

Asked when he realized he had a special talent on his hands, Reggie says, "Maybe third grade. There was just something about him. He was always tall. First time I put him on a bike, he just went. No training wheels. He started walking at six months old. I guess you can say he was a prodigy. There was something about his walk. He just had that mindset that he wanted to be better. He just loved ball. We got up at four or five in the morning . . . if that's overbearing I don't know. If he said he wanted to quit, we'd stop. But he never stopped. No dad, keep going."

It wasn't easy being young Shaun Livingston in Peoria, Illinois. Even now, after a fifteen-year NBA career that included three championships, you can hear the exasperation in Livingston's voice when he thinks back on those early years.

Everyone thinks being a star is the dream life, and no doubt it comes with perks, but there are downsides, too. Pressure to perform. Eyes always on you. Constant expectations. Oh, those expectations.

"You just want to be a kid sometimes," Livingston said. "You're always expected to kind of perform. And once your name starts to become really big and it travels, it becomes a myth. There was no social media, it wasn't like the tech phase. You might see some video and stuff, but people want to see what they heard. When they see you for the first time, they expect you to pull a rabbit out of your hat. That's kind of the expectation, but that's what comes with it. And I would be lying if I said that's the only thing I felt. There were times that I relished feeling that way, and there were times that I didn't."

Reggie says Shaun was always hungry to work and that his boy savored the process. Shaun agrees. Still, it was a lot. Early morning workouts, endless pickup games, drill work, literally driving around and looking for outdoor games, etc. He might only be in his mid-30s now, but Livingston has already lived what feels like a lifetime in basketball's public eye. And with the maturity and perspective that comes with age, he appreciates his father more than ever.

"It was overbearing but I'll tell you what, you look back on it 20 years later and you see kids that didn't have a father or families that just didn't have any guidance, didn't have any direction," Livingston says. "Kids that didn't have the direction but they had all the talent, they had God-given gifts. But that direction that they so badly needed (was missing). It can be life-altering. That's why fathers are so important. Looking back 20 years, you're winning a championship, standing on that court, confetti is coming down and you realize, 'Holy shit, I could be in jail, I could be dead.' So many situations and circumstances that have fallen on friends or counterparts of mine growing up back home. Then you do your research and realize the lack of direction or lack of acceptance or love that they didn't have."

"More than anything, it's just the expectations—that's where it gets exhausting. Expectations period. Over years, over years, over years, and then you're expected [to perform]. So, for me, I would have enjoyed more flexibility in being able to be anonymous. Being a little more organic. I was very fortunate to have a father who really was ahead of the game when it comes to a lot of his deals and teachings and stuff like that. A lot of kids aren't doing that stuff at 5, 6, 7, 8 years old. I had a leg up on a lot of kids growing up. Driving me around, going to lots of tournaments, constantly reading up on how I can get exposure. He was doing the work for me. I didn't know who had the best camps and where I could be seen. But obviously with that comes expectations, pressure to perform."

• • •

Date: March 2002
Location: Peoria Richwoods head basketball coach Bobby Darling's office
Cast: Darling; Richwoods assistant coach Mike Ellis; Reggie Livingston;
Shaun Livingston
Reason for meeting: Discussion of Shaun Livingston's future at
Richwoods

Days earlier, Peoria Richwoods' season ended with a disappointing 57–53 loss to Limestone in front of 4,500 fans in a Class AA Pekin sectional semifinal. Richwoods (24–5) was the top seed among 4 sectional participants but failed to reach the sectional final. It was the end of a trying year for the coaching staff, as well as Livingston, a sophomore who was hyped as a middle school phenom but had failed to make a significant impact in two years of varsity basketball at Richwoods.

Darling called the meeting, which took place in his office just off the Richwoods main gym floor. Wedged between the school's gymnasium and pool, the office featured a unique combination of smells—chlorine and sweat. Regardless of odor, the meeting, which lasted about 45 minutes to an hour, would have a permanent impact on Peoria basketball for years to come. Darling and Livingston had clashed for two years, and the coach finally drew a line in the sand.

"I never told him that he had to leave," Darling says. "I just suggested that he should leave. I said to Reggie and Shaun that I think he should probably transfer. Because if you come back like this, like the two years you've been here, you probably won't be able to finish the season. Because it just wasn't working. He wasn't doing well in the classroom. It just was a struggle. So, I said I'm not telling you that you have to transfer. I'm just saying if you ask my opinion, I'd probably say you have to transfer because I'm not sure how this is going to work out for you guys here at Richwoods."

Ellis, who has close relationships to this day with Darling and Reggie Livingston, remembers feeling a swirl of emotions as his head coach was essentially inviting a massively talented player to walk out the door. On one hand, Ellis respected the hell out of Darling standing up for principles and not caving to his win-loss record. On the other hand . . . when Livingston was good, he was *really good*.

"It felt right what Bob was saying, like maybe this isn't the best place for you," said Ellis, who later succeeded Darling as Richwoods head coach. "If you want somewhere where you can come into the gym and be the last one here and the first one to leave, if you don't want a person who demands more of you in the classroom to get A's and B's because you're intellectually gifted enough to do that, maybe I'm not the best coach for you. Maybe you need to find someone who will let you get away with that and you'll be more at peace. Reggie, I think was frustrated. Shaun, I don't think had an opinion either way. Reading Shaun, it was kind of like he didn't care if he stayed or left. It didn't matter to him. Reggie was hot because for the first time someone was telling his son he wasn't good enough. That's the first time he's ever heard that."

No one was denying the previous two years had been a slog. Livingston entered high school with expectations longer than the line at an Apple store during the holidays. Known around the city's basketball circles by the third grade, he was drawing crowds for his games at Roosevelt and Concordia Lutheran well before entering high school. At the beginning of Livingston's sophomore season at Richwoods, *Journal-Star* sports columnist Kirk Wessler wrote a column with the headline, "Already legendary? Don't be ridiculous."

> *"Everybody who has seen Livingston play seems to have an opinion on what's best for him, and they can't wait to tell him," Wessler wrote. "That's part of the problem. It's been that way since he was 7, maybe 8 years old, and he would stroll around the local high school gyms, gracefully dribbling the ball between his legs, back and forth with each step, joyously oblivious to the adult jaws dropping around him. That, too, became part of the problem."*

But back to that meeting. Darling was frustrated with what he refers to as Livingston's "camp." Mostly he is speaking of Verdell Jones II, Livingston's

Urbana-based AAU coach who was part of the Livingston family's inner circle. Verdell and Reggie grew up together in Peoria and stood up in each other's weddings. Darling and others contended Verdell was wielding too much influence over Shaun, egging him on to transfer and telling him that Darling and Richwoods was not a good fit for his future. Shaun, meanwhile, thought Darling was over-the-top hard on him and was essentially penalizing him for things out of his control—a big reputation that preceded him and the influence of adults hovering around the program.

When asked if he thinks Darling wanted him to transfer, Livingston says, "Yeah, definitely. No question about it. If you recommend it, that's something that's on your mind, something that you propose. That's how I took it and that's what it was." To his credit, Livingston also agrees with the contention that he wasn't working as hard as he should have at Richwoods.

Naturally, there's more to the story. This one has layers upon layers making it hard to untangle in determining what led to a meeting with four people in an office reeking of chlorine and sweaty athletes. For a few years before Shaun entered high school, Reggie was a volunteer coach for Darling at Richwoods. When Shaun was in eighth grade and schools around the area were clamoring for him to enroll for his high school years, Darling's team finished fourth in the Class AA state tournament. That same year, Darling and Reggie ended their working relationship.

"I wasn't happy with Reggie so I dismissed him during Shaun's eighth grade year," Darling said. "Reggie told me he was going to move into Richwoods' district even though we had a falling out. I said OK, as long as you move into the Richwoods district, that's fine. I knew people were going to be watching so you have to move into Richwoods district if you want your son to come to Richwoods. Too much attention on Shaun . . . there'll be someone taking pictures of him coming out of the apartment in the morning. You're going to have to move to the Richwoods (district) and he did that. I was surprised that Reggie still wanted Shaun to play at Richwoods even though we had a disagreement and falling out."

Reggie tells a different version of why he stopped coaching; he says Darling gave him an ultimatum that Shaun had to stop attending non-Richwoods open gyms or Reggie had to stop working at Richwoods. Either way, the bottom line is that Shaun enrolled at Richwoods and was elevated to varsity as a freshman despite sporting such a slender frame that his jersey barely stayed atop his bony shoulders.

"I think he wasn't ready for varsity," Reggie says.

Shaun's freshman year was fraught with injuries and frustration. Broken hand. Broken foot. Varsity opponents, who, at 17 or 18, were physically too much for a frail freshman to handle. It was a rude awakening for a kid who had always been the best player on the court. The city's hype was still present, but the production was not. Sports fans are always thirsting for the next big star, and the eyes of Peoria basketball were staring squarely at Livingston.

"They keep telling me I need to work harder, I don't even know what hard work is," Livingston said. "I thought I always worked hard. My reputation followed me in, and I think that hurt the relationship I had with (Darling). You got this little freshman coming in, and now you have reporters asking you about this kid and calling you, and it's like who the hell is this kid? I've been coaching basketball 20 years . . . I'm not saying that was his thought, but I know for a fact that my reputation coming in definitely hindered our working relationship."

Livingston showed flashes of that preternatural ability, seeing things on the floor no one else did, making passes from angles no one else knew existed. But at six-two or six-three and less than 150 pounds, he was physically overmatched versus varsity competition.

"Just his knowledge of the game was on the level of a varsity starter as a seventh grader," Ellis said. "There would be times as the coach his freshman and sophomore years in varsity games where you'd be sitting on the bench and he would hit somebody or change the angle of a play, and you'd be like, 'Why's he doing that?' as he's doing it. And you see the end result . . . 'Oh that's why he did that.' As a freshman. Shaun never put himself in a tough spot on the floor. So that tells you how much he knows about the game. He was always in a position to make a play."

Sophomore year was more of the same as Livingston's play was up and down, and Darling was constantly hearing rumors that a transfer was imminent. Livingston again couldn't stay healthy. This time it was more ankle injuries and walking pneumonia. The coach continued to push and push his young point guard, hoping something would click. But the two never seemed to be on the same page.

"He always had someone pulling on him, taking him places," Darling said. "If we lost a game or whatever, by Wednesday of the next week we'd hear Shaun is going to transfer someplace else. And that wasn't Shaun, that was other people. (His camp) thought our number one goal should be to get Shaun ready for the NBA, when our number one goal was to run a basketball program which has more than just Shaun Livingston on our team. Because he was such a young kid, he was 14, 15 years old, and he was skinny, I just think he was thrown into the lion's den."

Livingston says after a game against Champaign Centennial in December of his sophomore season, he cleared out his locker and was prepared to quit basketball. The walls were caving in, and the game was no longer fun for the kid once called the second-best seventh grader in America.

"I was just tired," said Livingston, who missed 22 games with injury and illness as a freshman and sophomore. "I felt like he was riding me, but I just didn't feel like it was warranted. Of course, any player or kid sometimes (thinks it) feels unfair. I just got to my breaking point, I'm not gonna let this guy break me, I'm not gonna let this guy break me, nope, nope, nope. Through that season I'm seeing players in the city are passing me up, they're playing on varsity and making an impact. I'm just kind of mediocre, luke-warm. Just very disappointed in myself, very disappointed in the circumstances, frustrated with the coach, I was done. I told Verdell, I told my dad. That's it."

Livingston returned to the team in December, but it was temporary.

After the meeting in Darling's office, the Livingstons knew a change was needed. The only question was where and when. Rumors circulated that he might go the prep school route or perhaps head to Champaign-Urbana to be near Jones and his AAU team, Ft. Sooy. In the end, Livingston decided to head less than five miles southwest. Reggie and Shaun moved out of an apartment they were renting in the Richwoods district, and headed back to live with Grandpa Frank on Orange Street, near Peoria Central, in a brick house where the three had lived together previously for parts of Shaun's childhood.

In May of his sophomore year, Livingston enrolled at Central, putting his faith and basketball future in the hands of veteran coach Chuck Buescher.

• • •

Livingston's first impression at Peoria Central was not a good one. It was mid-May, and the heavily hyped but disappointing player (thus far) was having a bad day. Buescher sat in the stands with assistant Chuck Westendorf, who had switched sides after many years sitting on Manual's bench. The two Chucks were simply observing an open gym, not coaching, when Westendorf turned to his head coach and said, "Do you think we want him?"

"I swear to God, Westy said that," Buescher remembers. "If Richwoods were honest with you, they weren't unhappy that he left. I don't think Richwoods was surprised that he left. And my answer to Westy was, and this was about May 15 or May 20 . . . he wasn't playing hard and was playing absolutely no defense . . . and I said, 'Well if he's going to play like this, no, we don't want him.' But he never played like that again. The story gets better."

Before making his mark at Central, Livingston first embarked on a truly incredible transformation in the late spring and summer of 2002. Livingston left Richwoods with a wounded reputation as a future star who wasn't living up to expectations. Whether it was the pressure, the coach, or injuries, his first two seasons in high school were basically a failure. He was determined to get his swagger back and it started with the AAU season that April.

Playing for Jones and Ft. Sooy, Livingston was gaining confidence. He also was growing. First six-five, then six-six, while retaining the incredible ball handling and court vision that had always been the hallmark of his advanced, mature game. Livingston was invited to the Adidas ABCD Camp in Teaneck, NJ, in July 2002, and that is when things exploded for him.

Livingston entered the nationally renowned camp as just a guy. After showing his stuff against the best high school competition in America, he left as a top 10 national recruit in the class of 2004. North Carolina-based Bob Gibbons, probably the premier recruiting expert of the era, ranked Livingston as the second-best point guard in the class and No. 5 player overall. Frank Burlison of foxsports.com ranked him as the second-best player in America, behind only Philadelphia's Mustafa Shakur.

To recap: in March, Livingston was essentially asked by his high school coach to transfer schools after two disappointing seasons. In July, he was tabbed as one of the five best juniors-to-be . . . in America. That simply does not happen.

"The stars just aligned, that's really all that happened," Shaun says. "That was the 10 years prior of playing basketball and all the skill-work and drill-work I did, and it was God stretching my body out. I grew a couple inches, my body catches up, all the injuries I had the first couple years were growing pains, ankles, knees and stuff. And finally, here I am, I'm six-six. I'm dunking, I'm a different player. I just kind of sprouted.

"Going back even in grade school, my dad is taking me to all the open gyms in high school. We've got five high schools in Peoria. I'm playing open gym in all five of them, all five think I'm coming to their school. I'm being recruited out of grade school for a high school. It feels like college already. So, I already had a reputation coming in that I was a prima donna, that my dad just wanted to shop me around and be in the best position to make it into college. Which partly was true. With how important basketball was, playing college ball was definitely realistic. Free college education, all that. It's amazing, from that February/March to August/September, I was a completely new player."

"I firmly believe it was that intrinsic motivation from Shaun," said Ellis, the Richwoods assistant. "No one goes from being not even All-State to a top 10 player in the nation in six weeks. Six weeks? He got to like six-five and a half, almost six-six. I think it was the finality of it and the ownership that Shaun placed on himself. It may have been Shaun saying, 'I can't let Coach Darling be right.' Shaun's a competitor. I have a feeling that inside of Shaun was, 'I'm going to prove him wrong and I can't let him be right.' And he started driving himself to be better."

Livingston had his swagger back and was locked and loaded to join a talented team at Central in the fall. Meanwhile, back at Richwoods, Darling confronted the uncomfortable scenario of facing his former player who was now reaching the potential which failed to materialize under his watch. Darling had been an assistant for nine years under Buescher at Central in the 1980s and early 1990s, and the two remained friends. Still, it was a weird situation as Darling tried to move his program forward in the shadow of forcing out a now-top 10 junior in America.

"It's almost like you're defeated," Darling said. "I had a pretty good relationship with my players, I think I had a decent rapport with my players and most of them liked to play for me. So yeah, it was frustrating as hell. I don't want to put this on Shaun, but it almost wasn't fair for the program. We were very successful his sophomore year, but it just didn't feel right. The shoe didn't fit, the glove didn't fit. It didn't feel good."

Richwoods' loss was Central's gain. The Lions lost their third game of the 2002–3 season to Limestone, and never fell again. With Livingston, Ruffin, Lee, Motteler, and DeAndre Miranda leading the way, Central won its first state championship since 1977, finishing 31–1 on the season. With the score tied 43-all in the closing seconds of the title game against Thornwood, a baby-faced Livingston made a terrific drive left to the basket and put in a contested layup for the game-winning basket in front of a sold-out Carver Arena. It was a full-circle moment for a teenager who had already been through so much athletically and personally.

"It was incredible, it felt like (being on the) Bulls," Livingston said. "We all went to school together at Roosevelt, that was *the* public school for basketball. It's a legendary school in Peoria. We all came from that umbrella.

Junior Shaun Livingston makes a move in the 2003 Class AA state tournament in Peoria. A six-foot-seven point guard, Livingston became the fourth pick in the NBA draft by the Los Angeles Clippers. (Photo courtesy of IHSA)

When we all linked back up at Central, it was just rolling the ball back out there on that court. We all knew how to play, we all came from that school of basketball, we all knew each other, we all competed against each other. Once we all linked back up, once we all came back together, it was basketball nirvana."

"It was like the band is back in town and a lot of people are going to be in trouble," said Motteler, a 3-point specialist who played with Livingston, Lee, and Ruffin at Roosevelt. "We knew what it was. Once we got together, we knew we were going to win."

A consensus five-star recruit, Livingston was coveted by every blue-blood school in the country. At an AAU tournament in Las Vegas heading into his senior year, Jon Baer and his two daughters, Taylor and Tori, drove more than 400 miles from Reno to watch their nephew and cousin play on the big stage of high school basketball. Baer, a younger brother of Livingston's mother, was six-foot-eight and had been a Division 1 player himself. A 1986 graduate of Peoria Spaulding (now Notre Dame), Baer went to ICC and then transferred and played two years at the University of Nevada-Reno before playing professionally overseas for five seasons.

Baer had maintained a relationship with his nephew over the years, even as Livingston was estranged from his mother, though it was difficult as the uncle was not living nearby. Baer says every time he visited family back in Peoria, he made sure to get in touch with Shaun and Reggie and spend time with Shaun. Uncle and nephew would go to ShowBiz Pizza Place, which later became Chuck E. Cheese, in Peoria's Westlake Shopping Center, play games, and eat pizza. Or sometimes they'd go shoot hoops.

"Shaun loved all sports," said Baer, who still lives in Reno. "It wasn't just shooting the basketball. It was 'toss me the Wiffle ball' or 'toss me the football.'"

Now, Baer sat in the gymnasium bleachers as his six-foot-six nephew was one of the nation's most sought-after basketball recruits along with the likes of Dwight Howard, Josh Smith, Rudy Gay, and Sebastian Telfair. It was a thrilling moment for the man who was an excellent player in his own right, but not on this level.

"I'm looking over and seeing Coach K and Jim Boeheim watching Shaun, and I'm just going no way," Baer said. "It was surreal. I knew he was good, but that's when I'm sitting in the gym going, 'Wow.'"

At the Nike Camp in Indianapolis that summer, Peoria television reporter Jim Mattson was on hand covering Livingston. College coaches are not permitted to discuss specific recruits in the media before they sign a letter of intent, but Mattson shot footage of Livingston and talked with the youngster as he competed against the best high school players in America and in front of all the top coaches. Knowing that Livingston was considering Arizona, Mattson approached legendary Wildcats coach Lute Olson and asked if he would be willing to do an on-camera interview. Olson quickly declined.

"As I walked away, I literally heard his assistant coach whisper, 'Hey he's from Peoria,'" Mattson said. "Olson immediately chased me down and was like, 'I'll do the interview.' He wanted his name on the Peoria TV."

This was an era when high school players were permitted to skip college and jump straight to the NBA, and it was a realistic possibility for players ranked top 10 or 20 nationally in their class. Livingston was a six-six, maybe six-seven point guard, and with his incredible court vision and feel for the game, he was on NBA teams' radars. After another excellent summer on the national camp AAU circuit leading into his senior year, his name became attached to lists of potential players going straight to the pros.

In August shortly before his senior year at Central was to begin, Livingston and Buescher had a talk in the school parking lot next to the coach's car.

"I just said what do you think of the NBA?" Buescher said. "He said, 'Coach, that's great, I really don't . . . I'm going to prepare to go to college. If something like that were to happen, sure.' The way I remember it is sure I would look at it, but I'm planning on going to college."

Livingston narrowed his college choices to Duke, Arizona, North Carolina, and Illinois. Pressure—that word is never far from his name—was intense to pick the home-state Illini. The Peoria-to-U of I pipeline was strong and many people, notably Verdell Jones II, his AAU coach and close family friend, were pushing for the orange and blue. All four collegiate head coaches made trips to Peoria to woo the transcendent point guard. UNC coach Roy Williams, who had left Kansas for Carolina a year before, came to the in-home visit with a small box. Inside the box were Michael Jordan's six championship rings from the Bulls, which was passed around the room for Shaun, Reggie, and Buescher to see in a "this is what happens if you come to Chapel Hill" pitch. Olson, the longtime Arizona coach, came to Central and had a cab wait outside for him for the two or three hours he spent at the school.

As things got close to the November signing day, Livingston made a much-anticipated official visit to Illinois. The Illini had hired Bruce Weber earlier that year when the domino effect of Roy Williams leaving Kansas sent

Coach Bill Self from Illinois to KU. Livingston had an affinity for Self so it definitely worked against Illinois when he left. Still, Livingston had built a close relationship with Illinois assistant and fellow Peorian Wayne McClain, and he was tight with Jerrance Howard, a Peoria Central grad and reserve player with the Illini. He knew how bad the local school wanted him. Illinois players even attended a Central game during Livingston's junior year, ironically the only game the Lions lost—the early-season contest against Limestone.

With pressures and anxieties building up, a rift developed between Reggie and Verdell Jones II. The biggest reason was Reggie thought Jones was pushing Shaun to Illinois, and the father was concerned about all the influences swirling around his 18-year-old. As Reggie and Shaun took in an Illinois practice on the official visit, the final blow to the Illini's chances to land the star may have occurred when Reggie saw Jones enter the gym.

"I said, 'Coach (McClain), why is he here? He shouldn't be here,'" Reggie recalls. "When he did that, I was like (Shaun) is not going here. If (Jones) is here now, what will he do when I'm in Peoria? Shaun didn't need no help from anyone."

For his part, Jones says he did not have any ulterior motives. Now the head coach at Urbana High School, Jones had been heavily involved in Shaun's life since he was very young. He took Shaun and other players to tournaments and camps around the country and saw the kids progress through their formative years.

The decision weighed heavily on Shaun, an 18-year-old who didn't want to tell people no or feel like he was disappointing them. With no one truly knowing what he was going to do, a press conference was set at Central where Shaun would announce his decision. Hopeful Illini fans thought he was tipping his hand when online message boards got word that he wore a Brian Cook No. 34 Illini jersey to school the day before the announcement.

"Bad timing, bad taste, bad look all around," Livingston says now. "It was an outfit for the day, I had these shoes that were gonna go with the jersey. One of those things. Then it comes out and it's like, 'Why the hell did I even do that? What was I thinking?' It is what it is. No ill will."

The next day with loads of print and television media packed into the Central library, Livingston said he would be signing with Mike Krzyzewski and Duke. It was not a huge surprise considering Duke's longstanding tradition of reeling in five-star recruits. But Livingston says it was a tough decision to go against the grain in turning down the Illini, something Peoria stars had not typically done.

"The deal breaker for me was Bruce Weber," said Livingston, who finished high school ranked No. 2 in the 2004 class behind Dwight Howard. "It just gave me flashbacks of Coach Darling. Once I came to that realization, it was a no. That was a very, very, very difficult no because of the relationships I had with those guys (Wayne McClain and the team). I really felt that I was disloyal in a way. It felt disloyal. As a kid, it feels disloyal. Not backstabbing, but that I'm letting those guys down in a way. Because the pipeline and the whole nine. But that was just part of me stepping into my own shoes. Living my own life and being my own man. A lot of that comes from my childhood of having to do things when sometimes you don't want to do them. Now when it's my turn to make decisions, I'm making a decision that I want to make. It really came down to I need to start doing what's best for me and not what's best for everybody else."

"I was always up front: I want him to go to Illinois," Jones said. "Not only because I was a fan, but I thought the fit would have been perfect. I made no bones about that. That was the worst-kept secret in America. It wasn't because I had any particular thing to gain from it other than he would have been here close, and I would have gotten a chance to see him and it would have been a great feather in the cap for Wayne McClain. Unfortunately, it evolved into a very ugly time. There was a lot of mistrust and things like that. It was unfortunate, but it showed me the underbelly of recruiting."

For those who thought he was destined for Duke from a young age, Livingston says that is not true.

"Duke was something where it was like I knew it was the best situation for me to succeed and get to where I was trying to go, which was the NBA," he said. "NBA is the goal, Duke is the best way for me to get there. I knew I was razor-thin, I knew I needed to put on so much muscle. I was a skinny, scrawny kid that really needed to get up and down and show my skillset and I felt Duke could maximize that. That was where that decision came from."

In the winter of 2003–4, Central games were an event. Thanks to boasting a bonafide superstar, the Lions were invited to showcase games all over the country and in high-profile matchups versus teams with other blue-chip recruits. In December, Central faced Dallas Seagoville High and its star center LaMarcus Aldridge in the Shop 'N Save/KMOX Shootout in St. Louis. Livingston put on a show in front of 41 NBA representatives as the Lions coasted to an easy victory. Afterward, Buescher walked out of the arena with Indiana Pacers scout George Felton and asked the NBA rep what he thought of his star.

"He will never see Duke," Felton responded.

Central was 11–0 and rolling by the time the calendar flipped to 2004. With Livingston, Lee, and Motteler leading the way, the Lions were a well-oiled machine and simply too talented for most high school competition (Ruffin graduated a year earlier.) Similar to their Manual rivals less than a decade earlier, Central and Livingston had become must-see basketball and everyone in central Illinois wanted a glimpse. Gyms were sold out nearly everywhere they went, and sometimes for road games the opposing school would call ahead and ask if they could set up a table after the game for Livingston to sign autographs. Chuck Westendorf, the former Manual assistant coach who was now Central's athletic director and assistant coach, tasked Kelvin Jordan to sit near the team's bench and essentially serve as a bodyguard. Twin, as Jordan was called because he had a twin brother named Kevin, was about 6–8 and in the neighborhood of 300 pounds. Twin was a former Central basketball player in the 1970s and a close friend of assistant coach Dan Ruffin.

"He was a rock star," Westendorf said of Livingston. "Everywhere we went, it was like a mob scene. I had to kind of protect him because (fans) were trying to get in the locker room, by the locker room. It was a mess."

Central was assigned to the Ottawa Regional and won its first two playoff games by a combined 85 points, destroying LaSalle-Peru, 78–43 and Streator, 93–43. First thing the next morning back at school, the phone rang in Westendorf's Central office. "Are you the AD?" a woman's voice at the other end asked. The woman proceeded to tell Westendorf that her 10-year-old daughter was next in line the previous night in Ottawa when Central's staff shut down Livingston's postgame autograph session, and the little girl cried all the way home. Westendorf took down the woman's information and had Livingston sign something for the young girl, which the AD then put in the mail.

"Shaun probably had 5 to 10 envelopes or pictures to sign every day," Westendorf said. "I'd put them in my office and he'd come there during third hour, he had study hall, he would come every day and sign that stuff. Most of them had self-addressed envelopes."

A typical high school experience, it was not.

In this Peoria *Journal-Star* file photo from 2004, Shaun Livingston poses for a photo in front of the Illinois River in his hometown. As something of a basketball prodigy, Livingston's name was well-known in Peoria basketball circles by the time he was in middle school. (Photo by Fred Zwicky—USA TODAY NETWORK)

Central took a 28–2 record into its second consecutive trip to the Class AA quarterfinals at Peoria's Carver Arena. With three more wins in front of large hometown crowds, Livingston could end his tumultuous high school career with back-to-back state championships. Wins over Chicago Farragut in the quarterfinals and Carbondale in the semifinals set up a state final matchup against a very talented Homewood-Flossmoor team.

Roy Condotti, H-F's coach, said his team was exhausted from its semi-final win over top-ranked West Aurora earlier in the day. (For many years, the IHSA's semifinals and state final were inexplicably played on the same Saturday.) After defeating West Aurora and two future high-major Division 1 players in Shaun Pruitt and Justin Cerasoli, Condotti and H-F retreated to their Peoria hotel.

"I could not find a guy on the (hotel) floor," Condotti said. "I looked down the floor and there was nobody around. I turned to my assistant Jim

McLaughlin and said, 'Where is everybody?' He said they're all asleep. They were absolutely spent after that game. Going into the state championship game, they just didn't have any juice. They eventually got to the locker room and when the time to play came, to their credit they gave everything they could. But we never had our legs that game. We never pressed up in the first half, and it was because I knew we did not have the legs to sustain that for the whole game."

Livingston capped his high school career with a game-high 27 points and nine rebounds as Central downed H-F, 53–47, as the sea of maroon in the stands rejoiced. In addition to expected praise for Livingston, Condotti said he thought two 3-pointers by Jacob Motteler off offensive rebounds were two of the biggest plays of the game. And the coach, who had a very successful nine-year run at Chicago Westinghouse before continuing his winning ways at H-F for 10 seasons, said one of Peoria's basketball hallmarks, defense, made a difference, too.

"I think what separated Peoria from some of the other teams we played is Chuck had them playing just great defense," Condotti said. "You really had to earn every basket. You couldn't cheat and steal one every once in a while. He had them playing at such a high level defensively that you had to be right there every single time."

Livingston, a young man who had been gawked at since grade school, felt a flood of emotions as he closed the book on his high school career. Immediately after the game, in a post-game television interview on the court, reporter Lee Hall introduced Livingston by saying, "You've faced expectations since fifth grade, and boy you stepped up bigger than ever here tonight . . ." The fresh-faced teenager, sporting an afro, replied, "Man, it's sweet. Just to end my high school career like this, you know what I mean. All the pressure I had to face . . ."

Expectations and pressure. For Livingston, those truisms traveled with him every time he left the house in the same way a cell phone and keys do for normal people.

"It was such a small place, it was a fish bowl," Livingston says now of Peoria. "And for how long I had to carry on it just felt like I had to work to maintain the love for the game. That's kind of the unfortunate part because it can't just be natural. Then you see other guys who have it natural, and you're almost kind of envious. Because you can't help your feelings. For me having to carry those expectations as a kid all the way into adulthood, championship years, end of your career, that's the exhausting part. Then it's like, 'What are you complaining about?' You got to carry that with it. But you gotta talk about it, too. That's real shit, that's real life."

In the end, the college choice was inconsequential. During the spring of his senior year, Livingston continued to raise his NBA stock with tremendous performances at national All-Star games and NBA workouts. He also began making trips to Chicago to workout with renowned trainer Tim Grover, who previously trained Michael Jordan and countless other pros. Livingston would either leave after school on Thursday or during the day on Friday, sometimes with Reggie and sometimes taking a charter bus by himself to Joliet, where someone from Grover's gym would pick him up for intense basketball weekends in Chicago.

As Livingston began to weigh his decision of Duke or the NBA, Grover, who had great contacts all over the league, told him that he received a guarantee from the Atlanta Hawks that they would draft the Peoria native if he was still available when they picked sixth overall. For a kid who remembered seeing his father working at McDonald's and Hardee's to make ends meet, it was too much money to pass up. Being selected in the top six of the draft meant in the neighborhood of $10 million guaranteed. All along, Reggie and Frank, Shaun's grandfather, were truly hoping Shaun would attend Duke. Frank, especially, was excited about his grandson playing for Coach K and going to a prestigious university.

Throughout his senior season, despite the fact that NBA scouts were regularly attending Central games, Livingston planned on attending college. Not until he exploded on the All-Star game circuit and began seeing his name prominently listed in mock drafts did he consider leaping to the NBA as a realistic option. But now, along with fellow high schoolers such as Dwight Howard, Josh Smith, JR Smith, Sebastian Telfair, and Robert Swift, the gangly teen from Peoria was ready to forego college. Unlike most of his peers, he was quite accustomed to being in the limelight.

"I already felt I was somewhat in the NBA in Peoria to be honest with you because of the celebrity thing," Livingston said. "It just wasn't that much of a concern for me like it was for the other guys."

On June 24, 2004, the Los Angeles Clippers selected 18-year-old Shaun Livingston with the fourth pick in the NBA Draft at The Theatre in New York City's Madison Square Garden. Three months earlier, Livingston was playing for Peoria Central. Six months earlier, he thought he was definitely going to Duke. And just a smidge more than two years prior, his former high school coach said it's probably best if he finds another high school to attend.

"Come out of Peoria a snot-nosed kid, everybody said he's not gonna make it," Reggie Livingston said. "Broken toes, fingers, ankles, get kicked off the team. Just knowing the struggles he went through to get there. It was amazing, I still get goosebumps thinking about it."

Livingston signed for eight million dollars guaranteed for three years, in addition to a multimillion-dollar deal with Reebok. He turned 19 in between the draft and the start of his rookie season, and when the *Journal-Star* caught up with him in November 2004, the Central grad was adjusting to his new world on the West Coast.

> *Livingston's most ridiculous expenditure to date?*
>
> *"My house. Seriously," the 19-year-old point guard says of the modest, three-bedroom place he purchased in Playa del Rey for a little more than $1 million. "The cost of living out (in LA) is so crazy. In Peoria, I'd be living in a 'Scarface' home, a mansion."*

By now, Livingston's NBA journey has been well-documented. Still, it is worth revisiting the horrific knee injury Livingston sustained in his third year with the Clippers. For many, the story would have ended there, but to his credit, that was not the case. From the *Los Angeles Daily News* in February 2007:

> *An MRI exam Tuesday on Clippers' point guard Shaun Livingston's dislocated left knee revealed tears to the anterior cruciate ligament, posterior cruciate ligament, medial collateral ligament and lateral meniscus.*
>
> *The only ligament he did not tear was the lateral collateral ligament.*
>
> *There had been doubt about whether Livingston had dislocated his knee or dislocated his knee cap. Clippers physician Dr. Tony Daly cleared that up—Livingston dislocated both.*
>
> *"It's probably the most serious injury you can have to a knee," Daly said. "It's the most serious injury I've seen in my 24 years with the Clippers."*
>
> *The time frame for a possible return to basketball was set at eight to 12 months, but even that may be in question because of all of the variables involved with surgery—or surgeries—and rehab.*
>
> *"He might miss all of next year," Daly said. "But he works hard. He's 21, and that's a big plus."*

The *Daily News* article went on to say the injury is not only a major blow to Livingston, but also the Clippers, who considered him their point guard of the future. It said, among other things, that Livingston's entire career was now in doubt. He was taken to the hospital where blood tests were administered to determine if an artery had burst, then he was at risk of having gangrene. Doctors worried that the left leg might require amputation. One can only imagine the grueling physical rehabilitation, not to mention the mental toll it took, for Livingston to return to the court and compete with the best basketball players in the world again. But if anyone was built for that grind, it was the Peoria kid who felt compelled to prove himself every day on the court since he was a kid.

Livingston missed the entire 2007–08 season. After 20 months, he returned to the court as a member of the Miami Heat. It's perhaps not surprising that when asked about it now, some old themes are revisited in Livingston's answer about dealing with the brutal knee injury.

"If I never played again, people would probably understand," Livingston said. "That's how dramatic my injury was. But it meant more to me than that. I was always in the overrated category because of all the expectations. There was never a time when you're gonna look back and say, 'Man this dude is underrated.' Because I was always *the* guy. So, I was always overrated. Having to constantly prove yourself that you're good enough, or that you're accepted or that you're worthy or all these things. For me to do that and prove to myself, that was an accomplishment that nobody could take away from me. No matter how many times I got cut or didn't make it back or didn't play. Whatever it was, that was a personal victory."

Livingston played just four games with the 2008–09 Heat, but that wasn't the point. He made it back to the league against incredible odds. This would also be the beginning of a six-year hopscotch around the league during which Livingston played for seven different teams, mostly on the East Coast. But his heart was never far from Peoria. He came back each summer to host camps for kids, and those who were there said the NBA player's focus was impressive. He was not there to be seen or for positive media publicity. He also was not bashful about bouncing around from team to team and playing limited minutes, failing to become the NBA star that many expected as the fourth pick overall.

The mother-in-law of Jim Mattson, the Peoria TV reporter, lives in Denver and is a huge Nuggets fan. One year when Livingston's NBA team was heading to Denver, Mattson sheepishly got in touch with him and asked if he might be able to leave tickets for her to attend the game. Livingston said no problem, and put her on the pass list.

"Then I ask the next year, and by the third, fourth, fifth year he'd say, 'Hey does your mother-in-law want tickets?'" Mattson said. "He'd be texting me. And he set her up. Who does that? He's a great guy."

Brian Randle, who played at Peoria Notre Dame and Illinois, was a year ahead of Livingston in school. The two were friends as kids and grew up playing against each other when Randle was at St. Mark's Catholic Grade School and Livingston was at Concordia. Randle says even back then Livingston was a sight to behold on the basketball court.

"He was fun to watch," Randle said. "Even as a friend back then and a competitor, I'd sit at the game and say, 'Hey Shaun, put it through this guy's legs. Now do the Shammgod.' He was just different. It was like a Broadway musical. You hear the music going up and up and up to a crescendo and he does something unbelievable, and you're like, 'That's why I'm sitting here.' Because I knew it was coming. It was almost a foregone conclusion of what was to come."

As the years went on with Livingston playing in the NBA and Randle playing professionally overseas, the two old friends inevitably didn't see each other much. Randle's parents had an annual Fourth of July party at their East Peoria home that could have between 80 and 100 people in attendance throughout the day. Friends and family congregated in the front yard, backyard, and in the house at different points in the day, but the tradition held that when it got dark outside and was time for fireworks, the remaining guests would head to the front yard for the optimal view of the sky. And every year, a familiar six-foot-seven friend would arrive around fireworks time.

"He'd kind of slink in there under the radar and we'd stand and talk off to the side," Randle said of Livingston. "His father would be up there and he'd get out before anybody saw him. That kind of worked out as our time to connect and check back in. He was very strategic about it. He's the pride of Peoria and people look to him for a lot of different things. I can only imagine trying to navigate that. It blessed myself and my family that he would take that time because there's a lot of people pulling at him."

In 2013–14, at the conclusion of Livingston's six-year, seven-teams period, he enjoyed an excellent season with the Brooklyn Nets. At 28 years old, he started 54 games for coach Jason Kidd's playoff team and averaged 8.3 points and 26 minutes played per game. It was enough to catch the eye of the Golden

Shaun and Reggie Livingston pose for a photo in recent years. Reggie raised Shaun as a single parent, and the two have always been close. (Photo courtesy of Reggie Livingston)

State Warriors, who signed the veteran to a 3-year, $16 million contract. In his first year with Golden State, Livingston was a key bench player as the Warriors won the 2015 NBA Championship. In his second year in the Bay Area, he scored a playoff career-high 20 points in Game 1 of the NBA Finals, helping the Warriors down the Cleveland Cavaliers. (The Warriors lost that series in seven games.)

Livingston finished his impressive career playing five seasons in Golden State, going to the NBA Finals five straight times and winning three titles alongside Steph Curry, Klay Thompson, Draymond Green, and Kevin Durant. In September 2019, he announced his retirement after 15 topsy-turvy seasons in the NBA. He was 34 years old.

"It was amazing," Livingston said. "Best times in the league, best times playing basketball. It brought me back to my junior and senior years (at Central) again. Really the joy in playing ball. Especially the first three years that I was here. The last two, it felt like work. First three years was basketball nirvana. A dream come true to wake up and have to go into the gym for work and call that a job. That's perspective for sure, personified."

Following Livingston's retirement, Warriors coach Steve Kerr shared his thoughts on Twitter on his former player. "It's hard to express how thankful I am to have coached this man the past 5 years," Kerr tweeted. "What an amazing combination of talent, grace & character. I will miss his calm leadership, his presence, his passing & his turnaround jumpers in the post. Nothing but great things ahead."

Throughout his time in the pros, Reggie Livingston encouraged his son to give back to the community. It didn't take much urging. Shaun greatly enjoys giving back to kids, particularly in Peoria. He can easily jog his memory and think back to his own childhood, when the NBA was only something on television and video games, and his basketball heroes were Peoria icons Howard Nathan and Frank Williams.

"They're asking me questions and picking my brain, and then you realize how much influence you can have just giving advice or sharing experience," Livingston said. "For a kid, giving them five minutes of your time . . . the most valuable resource we can give somebody is our time and attention. When we do that, even if it's five minutes you can change somebody's life."

"Honestly, that's where my heart really lies is in service. That's who I am. That's something that's important to me. That chapter is not finished. Until the day I'm lying in the casket, that's gonna be something that's gonna be near and dear to my heart. Being able to give back or help or serve, mentor, whatever it is. To whom much is given, much is received and much is asked for. I was the person that was in that position. I was the chosen one to make it out of our city, to have the resources and the platform to make a dent, so that's how I looked at it. It wasn't always perfect. But I'm still writing the book on that. Still trying to give back."

In 2016, Livingston donated one million dollars to his former school, Concordia Lutheran. The school had been fundraising since 1994, and the donation from its most famous alum enabled Concordia to reach its goal and build a 16,000-square foot expansion that holds a newly structured gymnasium with bleacher seating for 500, a new stage with a sound system for band and orchestra players, and an EF—5 rated storm shelter. Livingston, whose signature is featured on the new court, was present for the gym dedication, announced to the gathered crowd that his bronze-plated footprints will be on display in the school's hallway.

"It's amazing how this has come full circle," he told the *Journal-Star*.

Shaun Livingston has not lived in Peoria since he was 18. He has been gone for nearly two decades now, but Peoria is never far from his thoughts. How could it be? It is a complicated past, and they are not always positive thoughts. The expectations. The pressure. Growing up without knowing his mother. (Livingston says he is trying to repair that relationship, but he chose not to comment further on it.) Of course, there are happy thoughts, too. The support from his father and grandfather, his friends, and the satisfying back-to-back state titles at Peoria Central.

"It will always be my first home, and it will always be near and dear to my heart," he said. "I will never be able to fully separate myself and my life from Peoria because of the impact that I've had and the impact it's had on me. Traveling the world has broadened my perspective, of course, but that gave me the start. Peoria . . . we'll forever be connected. If you can mention Peoria without mentioning some of our names and vice versa, then I've been gone a long time. I wasn't always where I'm at now. These kids have a chance to be great, they have a chance to be better, they have a chance to hope. I'm just trying to provide inspiration and hope that kids will do more than what's around them in their environment."

A star, indeed.

Acknowledgments

It's an interesting thing, this book writing. With a nonfiction book, which is the only kind I've written, the hunt for sources and knowledge and information takes you in many different directions. And I love that. You learn a ton and are fascinated by people and facts you never knew existed. But there are so many gaps to fill in, so many details to unravel, even after exhaustive research and interviewing.

I relied on a plethora of Peorians for this project but none more than Derrick Booth, the former Manual player and coach and current Peoria school administrator. Derrick is a wealth of knowledge about all things Peoria, and his ability to track down phone numbers and answering my endless (and sometimes random) questions was absolutely invaluable. I keep telling him he should run for mayor because the man cannot go anywhere in town without being stopped for handshakes and hugs. Thus far he has declined said suggestion. I promise the days of receiving a question over text message at 11 p.m. about a player or coach from 25 years ago are officially over, DB!

Another person who should be glad this book is done is my close friend, Bob Warner. Bob was a newspaper editor for many years, and we worked together several years ago at the Battle Creek Enquirer in Michigan. A super talented editor and writer, Bob was my trusted reader and sounding board on Peoria hoops. The first thing I did after finishing a chapter was to send it Bob's way, and invariably he would return it promptly and give outstanding feedback. I can't thank you enough, good sir.

John Grap offered to take photos for the book as an excuse to return to Peoria, a town where he once lived and worked, and I'll forever be grateful. John used to be the photo editor in Battle Creek, and his images add so much depth and texture to these pages. I wish we could have used more, but the ones in the book give readers a keen sense of the people and places they are reading about. John's generosity is incredible and I owe him a ton.

Thanks also to my mother, Marilyn Karzen, who dutifully read each chapter along the way and provided excellent edits and big picture thoughts. I recommend all writers have an editor nearby who isn't afraid to shoot straight and say, "This doesn't need to be in here."

Thanks to my childhood friend Gabe Conroe, who helped me sift through legal documents and was exceedingly patient in explaining legalese to me. Having a friendly lawyer just a phone call away was a relief.

Barely four months after Peoria legend Howard Nathan tragically passed away, I sat in the Nathans' living room with his mother Sue and three of Howard's siblings. The anguish in their voices and mannerisms was heartbreaking. The kindness they showed in sharing stories and fighting through the grief to chat with a stranger about their beloved Howard is something I will never forget. Learning about his endlessly interesting life and big personality was one of my favorite aspects of this project.

Unfortunately, those weren't the only conversations about grief and sadness. Thanks as well to the Dunnigan family for opening up about the life and death of Marshall Jr. (Mud). Learning about his senseless death at age 18 tore me up, and I can't imagine the hurt you all went through when it happened, not to mention in the years since. Sadly, Mud's father, Marshall Sr., passed away prior to book publication, but I'll always remember his warm smile and man-sized handshake.

Thank you to the McClains—Robin, Deshe, and Sergio—for sharing your wonderful stories about Wayne. Hearing those come from a place of such genuine love and gratitude was a real treat. He touched so many lives in Peoria and beyond.

Thank you to Reggie and Shaun Livingston for willingly rehashing some unpleasant memories and being generous with your time. The bond between you two is amazing. Shaun's story is fascinating, and I loved learning about it.

I also want to thank my acquiring editor at the University of Illinois Press, Danny Nasset, and his team. Thanks for believing in this project from start to finish and seeing it through. It wasn't always easy but we did it.

Interviews

Jon Baer; December 17, 2020, by phone
David Booth; February 7, 2020, in Peoria
Derrick Booth; December 14, 2019, in Peoria; May 31, 2020, by phone
Dee Brown; April 14, 2020, by phone
Isaac Brown; March 23, 2020, by phone
Chuck Buescher; August 2, 2020, in Peoria; August 3, 2020, by phone
Willie Coleman; October 12, 2019, in Peoria
Roy Condotti; January 7, 2021, by phone
Dan Dakich; December 1, 2020, by phone
Bobby Darling; August 13, 2020, by phone
Danielle Davis; January 21, 2020, by phone
Marshall Dunnigan Sr.; February 7, 2020, in Peoria
Meechie Edwards; July 29, 2020, by phone
Hedy Elliott; May 30, 2020, by phone
Mike Ellis; September 28, 2020, in Evanston
Shelley Epstein; June 30, 2020, by phone
Sandy Farkash; May 30, 2020, by phone
Marcus Griffin; December 14, 2019, in Peoria
A.J. Guyton; July 31, 2020, in Peoria
Wayne Hammerton; November 18, 2020, by phone
Marsha Harris; September 15, 2020, by phone
Jerry Hester; October 13, 2020, by phone
Rocky Hill; January 4, 2021, by phone
Bobby Humbles; December 12, 2019, by phone
Nick Irvin; December 9, 2019, by phone
Teneal Johnson; June 4, 2020, by phone
Verdell Jones II; April 29, 2020, by phone
Verdell Jones III; July 20, 2020, by phone

Tim Kenny; January 15, 2020, by phone; May 21, 2020, by phone
Tom Kleinschmidt; November 4, 2019, in Chicago
Peter Kobak; June 30, 2020, by phone
Reggie Livingston; November 12, 2020, in Peoria
Shaun Livingston; December 15, 2020, by phone
Deondrae Mack; May 19, 2020, by phone
Oscar Mack; May 21, 2020, by phone; August 1, 2020, in Springfield
Beverly March; September 19, 2020, by phone
Jim Mattson; November 13, 2020, in Peoria
Deshe McClain; April 17, 2020, by phone
Robin McClain; November 1, 2019, by phone
Sergio McClain; October 20, 2019, in Champaign
BJ McCullum; July 20, 2020, by phone
Scott Meister; June 4, 2020, by phone
Joey Meyer; November 25, 2019, by phone
Vernon Morris; January 25, 2021, by phone
Jacob Motteler; September 1, 2020, by phone
Sue Nathan; December 13, 2019, in Peoria
Aerial Nathan; January 3, 2020, by phone
Angenette Nathan; November 15, 2019, by phone
Charles Nathan; October 28, 2019, by phone; December 13, 2019, in Peoria
Stacey Nathan; December 13, 2019, in Peoria
Jim Ralph; July 10, 2020, by phone
Brian Randle; November 27, 2020, by phone
Antwaan Randle El; December 18, 2020, by phone
Chris Reynolds; December 12, 2020, in Peoria
Mike Robinson; November 16, 2020, by phone
Dan Ruffin; November 13, 2020, in Peoria
Daniel Ruffin; July 31, 2020, in Peoria
Rhonda Ruffin; November 13, 2020, in Peoria
Rick Spencer; December 5, 2019, by phone
John Stenson; June 9, 2020, by phone
Alex Stephens; January 10, 2021, by phone
Greg Stewart; May 14, 2020, by phone
Tai Streets; December 7, 2019, in Chicago
Damon Stoudamire; January 7, 2020, by phone
Courtland Tubbs; October 12, 2019, in Peoria
Dick Van Scyoc; October 12, 2019, in Peoria
Mike Vining; March 25, 2020, by phone
James Watson; October 12, 2019, in Peoria

Bruce Weber; March 23, 2020, by phone
Charles White; December 21, 2020, by phone
Da'Monte Williams; October 20, 2020, on Zoom
Tom Wilson; May 28, 2020, by phone
Alexander Wolff; June 29, 2020, by phone
Jim Youngman; April 1, 2020, by phone

Bibliography

"ACLU Releases Crack Cocaine Report, Anti-Drug Abuse Act of 1986 Deepened Racial Inequality in Sentencing." *ACLU.org*, October 26, 2006, https://www.aclu.org/press-releases/aclu-releases-crack-cocaine-report-anti-drug-abuse-act-1986-deepened-racial-inequity.

Armour, Terry. "Peoria Manual No. 1 in the End." *Chicago Tribune*, March 20, 1994, https://www.chicagotribune.com/news/ct-xpm-1994–03–20–9403200467-story.html.

Brown, Dayna R. "Rams Get DC Date, but Manual Team Won't Meet Government's No. 1 Player." Peoria *Journal-Star*, April 12, 1997.

Brown, Dayna R. "You Are Going to Live in Our Hearts Forever — About 2,000 People Bid Emotional Farewell to Slain Manual Player." Peoria *Journal-Star*, April 30, 1996.

"Central's 6–7 Tom Wilson Transferring to Manual?" Peoria *Journal-Star*, January 1987.

Dawson, Brett. "McClain a Finalist for Top Bradley Job." Champaign *News-Gazette*, April 3, 2002, https://www.news-gazette.com/sports/illini-sports/mcclain-a-finalist-for-top-bradley-job/article_221b0514–3cfe-52df-893d-e85018ff6c83.html.

Hamilton, Brian. "An Accident Left Peoria Basketball Legend Howard Nathan Paralyzed, but He Says His Life Is Headed on the Right Path." *Chicago Tribune*, December 17, 2006, https://www.chicagotribune.com/news/ct-xpm-2006-12-17-0612170232-story.html.

Jan, Tracy. "Redlining Was Banned 50 Years Ago. It's Still Hurting Minorities Today." *Washington Post*, March 28, 2018, https://www.washingtonpost.com/news/wonk/wp/2018/03/28/redlining-was-banned-50-years-ago-its-still-hurting-minorities-today/.

Jauss, Bill. "DePaul's Epic Rally a Nathan Production." *Chicago Tribune*, February 21, 1992, https://www.chicagotribune.com/news/ct-xpm-1992-02-21-9201170218-story.html.

"Junior and Jackie Watkins: Paying It Forward." *Peoria Magazine*, July 2020, https://www.peoriamagazines.com/pm/2020/jul/junior-jackie-watkins.

Kravetz, Andy. "Shooting Clerk Nets 24-year Sentence; Mack, 19, Pleaded Guilty to Aggravated Battery in Grocery Store Robbery." Peoria *Journal-Star*, January 29, 2011.

Leavitt, Bob. "Longtime Journal-Star Prep Writer Bob Leavitt Shares His Thoughts on Wayne McClain." Peoria *Journal-Star*, October 15, 2014, https://www.pjstar.com/story/sports/2014/10/16/longtime-journal-star-prep-writer/36152013007/.

Meidroth, Tim. "Pair Testify They Saw Trio Fire Shots Outside Proctor Center." Peoria *Journal-Star*, January 13, 1993.

——. "Perry Pleads Guilty in Killing of Dunnigan, Gang Member Says He Was Told to Retaliate for Earlier Shooting." Peoria *Journal-Star*, August 6, 1996.

Meidroth, Tim and Mark Fitton. "Perry Given 60 years in Dunnigan Murder. State's Attorney: Killing Stranger on Gang's Order as Cold, Calculated as It Gets." Peoria *Journal-Star*, January 11, 1997.

Mertens, Megan. "NBA's Shaun Livingston Helps Dedicate New Concordia Lutheran's Gym." Peoria *Journal-Star*, November 20, 2016, https://www.pjstar.com/story/news/education/2016/11/21/nba-s-shaun-livingston-helps/24501857007/.

Reynolds, Dave, and Nick Vlahos. "Former Mr. Basketball Howard Nathan Hospitalized, but Showing Improvement." Peoria *Journal-Star*, July 11, 2019, https://www.pjstar.com/story/sports/high-school/2019/07/11/former-mr-basketball-howard-nathan/4703441007/.

Reynolds, Dave. "Iconic Peoria Basketball Coach Wayne McClain Dies at 60." Peoria *Journal-Star*, October 15, 2014, https://www.pjstar.com/story/sports/college/basketball/2014/10/15/iconic-peoria-basketball-coach-wayne/36123132007/.

Sakamoto, Bob. "Manual's Dynamic Duo Pulls Switch, Picks Illini." *Chicago Tribune*, November 21, 1996, https://www.chicagotribune.com/news/ct-xpm-1996-11-21-9611210022-story.html.

Sakamoto, Bob. "This Team Plays (Mostly) in Peoria: The 1995–96 Tribune All-State boys Basketball First Team." *Chicago Tribune*, March 24, 1996, https://www.chicagotribune.com/sports/ct-xpm-1996-03-24-ct-spt-1996-prep-bkb-all-state-story.html.

Stevens, Joe. "Livingston's Injury Serious, Wrecked Knee Will Keep Clips Guard Out 8–12 Months." *Los Angeles Daily News*, February 28, 2007.

Stewart, Greg. "Manual Boys Coach Suspended with Pay." Peoria *Journal-Star*, February 20, 2003.

Stewart, Greg. "Reinforced on Court — Frank Williams Lost His Love for Basketball When His Mother Passed Away." Peoria *Journal-Star*, February 14, 2007.

Sullivan, Paul. "Mr. Basketball? It's Manual's Howard Nathan." *Chicago Tribune*, March 31, 1991, https://www.chicagotribune.com/news/ct-xpm-1991-03-31-9101290048-story.html.

Van Scyoc, Dick. *Manual Labor*. Self-published, 2018.

Vlahos, Nick. "Peoria Listed among National News Network's Deadliest U.S. Cities." Peoria *Journal-Star*, December 18, 2019," https://www.pjstar.com/story/news/columns/nick-in-the-morning/2019/12/18/nick-in-am-peoria-listed/2059765007/.

Wessler, Kirk. "Already Legendary? Don't Be Ridiculous." Peoria *Journal-Star*, September 2, 2001.

Wessler, Kirk. "Shaun Livingston, A Docudrama, in Three Acts, with Contemporary Commentary from Principal Players." Peoria *Journal-Star*, March 1, 2004. https://www.pjstar.com/story/sports/high-school/basketball/2015/06/17/shaun-livingston-docudrama-in-three/34149322007/.

Wessler, Kirk. "So Far, So Fine as a Pro." Peoria *Journal-Star*, November 14, 2004.

Williamson, Terrion L. *Black in the Middle: An Anthology of the Black Midwest*. Belt Publishing, 2020.

"Wilson Could Play for Manual Tonight." Peoria *Journal-Star*, January 1987.

Wolff, Alexander. *Big Game, Small World*. Warner Books, 2002.

Index

JEFF KARZEN is a sportswriter who has covered basketball recruiting for twenty years. He is the author of *Homer: The Small-Town Baseball Odyssey.*

The University of Illinois Press
is a founding member of the
Association of University Presses.

University of Illinois Press
1325 South Oak Street
Champaign, IL 61820-6903
www.press.uillinois.edu